MARIVAUX

A STUDY IN SENSIBILITY

MARIVAUX

A STUDY IN SENSIBILITY

RUTH KIRBY JAMIESON

1969

OCTAGON BOOKS

New York

Reprinted 1969
by special arrangement with Ruth Kirby Jamieson

OCTAGON BOOKS
A DIVISION OF FARRAR, STRAUS & GIROUX, INC.
19 Union Square West
New York, N. Y. 10003

LIBRARY OF CONGRESS CATALOG CARD NUMBER: 75-86278

Printed in U.S.A. by
TAYLOR PUBLISHING COMPANY
DALLAS, TEXAS

To *PAUL FLETCHER JAMIESON*

ACKNOWLEDGEMENTS

I WISH to express my appreciation to Professor Norman L. Torrey, whose knowledge of eighteenth-century literature has been of invaluable assistance to me, for his unfailing encouragement and advice. I am also deeply indebted to Professor Horatio Smith for the discipline of his criticism and the stimulus of his teaching, without which this study would never have been undertaken. Other members of the Department of French at Columbia University, including Professors Paul Hazard, Jean-Albert Bédé, and Jeanne Vidon-Varney, have made valuable suggestions.

The librarians of Columbia, Harvard, and the Library of Congress have been most helpful. I am especially grateful to Miss Helen M. Dowd and Mr. Andrew K. Peters of the St. Lawrence University Library for their many courtesies.

To Paul Fletcher Jamieson, assistant professor of English at St. Lawrence University, whose scholarship and critical intelligence were always at my disposal, belongs the final and most deeply felt word of gratitude on the completion of this study.

CONTENTS

INTRODUCTION

INVITED to name the "ten best" French novels of modern times, André Gide, after protesting the restriction "French," struck off a list headed by *La Chartreuse de Parme* and including several acknowledged classics. Wishing to add a fillip to a fairly conventional selection, Gide closed with the remark: "Now for something different! This, for instance, which I blush to admit I have not read myself: the *Marianne* of Marivaux."[1] Gide was aware that Marivaux, known chiefly as the author of a group of delightful comedies, is seldom named with such novelists as Balzac, Zola, Flaubert, and Stendhal. Yet Marivaux's first considerable literary efforts were novels, and his two major works in this field, *La Vie de Marianne* and *Le Paysan parvenu,* were widely read in their day in France and in England, where Marivaux was favorably compared to Richardson and Fielding.[2]

Pierre Carlet de Chamblain de Marivaux (1688-1763), journalist, playwright, and novelist, has had one of the most puzzling of literary reputations. He is for some critics an acknowledged genius, for others only a second-rate talent. Edmond Jaloux in a recent article calls for a complete reappraisal of the writings of Marivaux: "The case of Marivaux is one of the most tragic misunderstandings ever to occur between an author and his public. Marivaux is at the same time famous and unknown, praised and unappreciated."[3] This difference of opinion as to his place on the ladder of fame has existed since Marivaux's day. His friend d'Alembert, in *Eloges des Académiciens,* acknowledged the difficulty of appraising Marivaux justly. Apologizing for the disproportionate length of his estimate of Marivaux, he explains:

> Les ouvrages de Marivaux sont en si grand nombre, les nuances qui les distinguent sont si délicates, son caractère même avoit des traits si variés et si fugitifs, qu'il paroît difficile de faire connoître en lui l'homme et l'auteur, sans avoir recours à une analyse subtile et détaillée, qui semble exiger plus de développemens, de détails, et par conséquent de paroles, que le portrait énergique et rapide d'un grand homme ou d'un grand écrivain.[4]

In 1763 Thieriot wrote to Voltaire: "Carlet de Marivaux has just died at the age of seventy-five. He leaves comedies, novels, and other forgotten works, in which some people maintain that there is genius."[5] The indifference of Thieriot illustrates the prevailing attitude toward Marivaux after mid-century. In spite of early successes in the theatre and the novel, Marivaux was never a popular author. Before his death he had outlived his fame and was viewed as an eccentric in both literary and social circles.

Sainte-Beuve was one of the first nineteenth-century critics to offer a word in praise of Marivaux. Deprecating the common view of Marivaux as superficial, Sainte-Beuve declares, "He is a theorist and a philosopher, much more penetrating than one would believe under his coquettish exterior."[6] He admired the theatre, setting it above the novels and concluding of the latter that their author deserves a place beside and perhaps a little above that of Crébillon *fils.*[7] Later writers continued to pay their respects to Marivaux, his plays in particular being the subject of several excellent studies.[8] With the exception, however, of a fairly comprehensive treatment by Brunetière,[9] the novels were passed over with brief mention by most nineteenth-century critics. Today four or five of his plays have survived in the repertory of the *Comédie Française* and continue to be admired. His journalistic writings, patterned on Addison, are viewed as literary curiosities and figure briefly in discussions of Anglo-French cross-currents in the eighteenth century.[10] Among his novels *La Vie de Marianne* has always had a few enthusiastic readers, and although *Le Paysan parvenu* has been out of print for many years, the importance of both is quite generally recognized, particularly in the development of the novel of manners.[11]

It is not the purpose of this study to trace the literary reputation of Marivaux. It is hoped rather that an examination of his novels, plays, and essays in relation to the social background of the early eighteenth century and to certain literary currents, will make possible a clearer understanding of these writings and especially of Marivaux's role in the movement of sensibility, that curious blending of affectation and genuine sentiment which flourished in the century of enlightenment and was one of the forces which swung French literature far from the well-worn paths laid out by the classic writers.

The eighteenth century, in the early years, is marked by a ferment of ideas and by relatively few literary masterpieces, as compared with the preceding classic age or with its own '50's and '60's. It is a period of preparation, a bridge between the seventeenth century, which had produced a literature correct in form and limited in range, and a new era, which submitted to few restrictions either in form or content. Sensibility as a literary and social phenomenon first manifested itself about

1700.[12] M. Trahard places its literary beginnings in 1720, with the presentation of Marivaux's first comedy.[13] The movement is characterized by a new freedom of emotional expression, in contrast with the intellectuality dominant in the seventeenth century. In this transitional period, however, much of the classic restraint still survives, and sensibility does not reach the extremes of a later time. Nor has conflict yet arisen between the man of reason and the man of sentiment, a conflict embodied in the enmity between Voltaire and Rousseau. In the beginning there is an attempt at a balance between heart and head. Feeling being granted the initial impulse, reason justifies the impulse and prevents excess. Of this early period Marivaux is the outstanding representative. In him, the primacy of the heart is undisputed, but the head, at once an accessory and an indulgent censor, imposes restraint where it is due and makes possible the fine discrimination and the tasting of emotion which characterize the Marivaudian hero and heroine. We shall attempt to show this balance of forces as it affects the various aspects of Marivaux's sensibility.

In his championship of the emotional life Marivaux usually applies two tests, one of inward satisfaction, the other of outward success. Marianne and Jacob, the great characters of his novels, support the author's hypothesis that the feelings are a safe guide to conduct and that reliance on them results in ultimate benefit both to the individual and to society. Marianne's career exemplifies the rewards attendant upon submission to the emotions of tenderness and gratitude, and Jacob's emphasizes more especially the humanitarian impulses, such as pity and generosity. In all Marivaux's characters, however, emotional impetus is followed so quickly by the application of reason and common sense to the situation that one sometimes loses sight of the fact that these people are fundamentally creatures of feeling, "sensitive souls" both by bent and creed.

Fine-spun analysis is applied to every aspect of the emotional life, no matter how trivial or esoteric, and distinguishes Marivaux from the seventeenth-century analysts of feeling, who examined only the stronger passions universal among men. Marivaux is not primarily concerned with portraying the broad and enduring characteristics of man's affective life, though these of course figure in his works. He prefers to spy out the peculiar and individual aspects of feeling, and so he anticipates a later age, for which particularities will become far more interesting than generalities.

The interpenetration of reason and emotion is the central problem in dealing with the sensibility of Marivaux. The question has been faced before by several critics and interpreted in various ways. For Lanson sensibility is merely a literary fashion which excludes the possibility of analysis. Lanson holds that in an age of sensibility anything may serve as an excuse for the display of feeling, but that with such abandonment to feeling, psychological observation disappears, leaving only a conventional description of emotional states, repeated so often as to become trite and insincere. In his study of Nivelle de La Chaussée, whose *comédies larmoyantes* mark for Lanson the beginning of the movement in literature, he says:

> L'avantage et l'inconvénient à la fois de la sensibilité, c'est de supprimer l'expérience personnelle, l'étude originale et précise, et de fournir à tous les écrivains la même psychologie sommaire et conventionnelle, toujours très superficielle, parfois tout à fait fausse.[14]

Marivaux's *La Vie de Marianne,* he believes, does not belong in the literature of sensibility. It is full of sentiment, but its sensibility is "too subtle, too discrete, too delicate, too simply touching,"[15] to represent exactly what is meant by the word in the eighteenth century. His definition of the method of the sensibility school is sufficient to exclude all of Marivaux's works.

> Le poète ne donne que des sensations fortes, aux coeurs vertueux. La violence des émotions sera une marque de bonté native, et l'honnête homme sera un frénétique. On bannira donc de la scène, on effacera de l'âme humaine les sentiments moyens, les mouvements doux, les demi-émotions, tout ce qui est germe, ébauche, commencement, ou bien prolongement, apaisement, refroidissement, tous les petits effets des petites causes, la sourde et lente préparation des grandes crises, enfin ce qu'il y a de plus profond dans la vie morale.[16]

Marivaux's treatment of the emotions is, as Lanson realizes, the antithesis of this conventionality and exaggeration.[17]

Saintsbury is in agreement with Lanson in making of sensibility an affected and extravagant emotional attitude. "The chief note of sensibility," he says, is "the taking of an emotion as a thing to be savoured and degusted deliberately—to be dealt with on scientific principles and strictly according to the rules of the game."[18] He finds that most of the great writers of the eighteenth century fall out of the current of sensibility, though all of them except Le Sage are influenced by it. Prévost is "hardly a novelist of sensibility," Diderot is too sincere and too great an individualist, Rousseau too serious, Voltaire not serious enough.[19] Genuine sensibility, "the odd quintessence of conventional feeling, played at steadily till it is half real if not wholly so," is to be found in Marivaux and the group of women novelists who precede and follow him. *La Vie de Marianne,* he says, represents "the acutest form of *sensibilité* in its palmy days."[20]

Pierre Trahard, in his recent work, *Les Maîtres de la sensibilité française au dix-huitième siècle,* considers Marivaux, Prévost, and Voltaire the initiators of a movement which reaches fruition in the works of Rousseau and Diderot.[21] Sensibility, for M. Trahard, is not feeling alone, but the combination of feeling and analysis.

> Etre sensible, pour Prévost, Diderot and Jean-Jacques, ce n'est pas se borner à sentir, c'est se rendre compte que l'on sent, étudier la sensation, réfléchir sur ses émotions lorsque la première flamme est tombée; c'est, au besoin, provoquer la sensation pour l'analyser avec un raffinement cruel; c'est, en un mot, prendre conscience du sentiment qu'on épreuve.[22]

He disputes Lanson's claim that sensibility excludes observation.

> Non seulement l'être sensible cherche la cause de ses émotions, mais il étudie celles des autres hommes avec une perspicacité accrue. Souvent même il pèche par excès d'analyse, s'égare dans son propre coeur, souffre de son impuissance à se bien saisir.[23]

M. Trahard's definition of sensibility is all-inclusive, embracing man's emotional life as a single and all-powerful unit as contrasted with his rational existence. For him it is not a passing literary fashion, but simply the freer revelation of the emotions as literary and social restraints are thrown off. I do not find it necessary to differ often with the conclusions of this discerning student of the movement of sensibility, whose sensitive literary perceptions make him a master of the impressionistic method of criticism. But in the case of Marivaux, at least, M. Trahard's neglect of the historical approach results in a half-truth. In Marivaux, sensibility appears to me to be the expression of a current social and literary fashion as well as of individual genius and hence to be explicable largely through the period in which he lived, early eighteenth-century France. With him too its nature becomes clearer when the

several aspects that compose it are distinguished and separately analyzed. This is particularly true of the novels of Marivaux, which M.
Trahard discusses far less satisfactorily than his theatre.

The writings of Marivaux which contribute to a study of his sensibility include the theatre, the two great novels, *La Vie de Marianne*
(1731-41) and *Le Paysan parvenu* (1734-36), and one early work, *Les
Effets surprenants de la sympathie* (1713-14). In addition I have considered the journalistic writings, including the early *Pièces détachées*,
originally published in 1717-18 in the *Mercure de France*, which contain
the theory and some of the first ventures of Marivaux in his study of
the *âme sensible*; *Le Spectateur français* (1722-23); *L'Indigent Philosophe* (1728), a novelette published in *feuilleton* form; *Le Cabinet du
philosophe* (1734), and a few later papers and essays.

The theatre of Marivaux has been treated throughout this study in
a subordinate and complementary way. Two aspects of Marivaux's
sensibility appear to special advantage in the plays: his delineation of
love as tender emotion and his stress on *amour-propre* as a controlling
motive. The emotional awakening of adolescence receives in his plays
full and sympathetic treatment. Perhaps even more significant are the
newness and the variety of Marivaux's handling of *amour-propre*. The
characters of his comedies show an even greater refinement of sensibility in self-love than in love. With the exception of humanitarianism,
touched on in the group of plays known as "social comedies," other
manifestations of Marivaux's sensibility are not conspicuous in his
theatre.

In the novel, Marivaux accepted the mantle of no predecessor. Here
the originality of his talent appears to best advantage and his role as
an innovator becomes clear. A new approach to the emotional life, of
which the theory appears in the essays and a partial representation in
the theatre, receives unhampered development in Marivaux's novels.
In examining the novel, moreover, the student of sensibility has an
advantage lacking to a critic of the theatre. Its broad scope and freedom
from formal restrictions make the novel a better medium for the analysis of emotional states than is the drama. M. Cazamian points out the
appropriateness of the novel, which "will beget a mood of reflectiveness
applied to conduct" and "will have recourse to feeling," as a vehicle
for "ethics and sentiment."[24] D'Alembert, Marivaux's contemporary,
makes a similar statement:

Les romans de Marivaux, supérieurs à ses comédies par l'intérêt, par les situations, par le but moral qu'il s'y propose, ont surtout le mérite . . . de ne pas tourner, comme ses pièces de théâtre, dans le cercle étroit d'un amour déguisé, mais d'offrir des peintures plus variées, plus générales, plus dignes du pinceau d'un philosophe.[25]

D'Alembert makes a distinction between the dramatist and the novelist in Marivaux and appreciates the greater advantage of the novel for his particular talent, the portrayal of the emotions and their influence on conduct.

Marivaux's plays were admired almost universally by dramatic critics of the nineteenth century. M. Trahard's analysis of them, dealing especially with the matter of sensibility, and the essay by F. C. Green, "The Survival of Comedy," in *Minuet,* are the best recent studies. The novels, however, have not received careful attention from modern critics. M. Trahard deals with them briefly and in general terms, and Green's "Wise Virgins," likewise in *Minuet,* is a comparative study of Marivaux and certain English novelists, rather than an attempt to examine in detail the phenomenon of sensibility. Because of this comparative neglect, and in recognition of their rich contribution to the subject of this thesis, I have given major emphasis to the novels.

In this study I shall make a three-fold approach. First, I propose to present Marivaux in the *milieu* of early eighteenth-century society, a background important to the understanding of the man and of a dawning literary movement. Second, I shall take up one by one the several ingredients of sensibility in his work, with the aim of determining their degree and quality, as well as Marivaux's place in the literature of the movement. To this end I shall present a study of Marivaux's conception of the "sensitive soul," as represented in the above-mentioned works; of *amour-propre* both as an accompaniment to and as an essential part of sensibility; of *amour-tendresse* as Marivaux observed it in the society of his day; and of the morality of sentiment, the new creed of the heart just emerging in his time. Third, I shall keep constantly in mind the balance of reason and emotion, interpreted so differently by Marivaux's critics in the evaluation of his sensibility. It is my belief that the role of reason in Marivaux—distinguishing, holding in check, and refining upon the emotions of his sensitive characters—gives to his sensibility its especial flavor. Furthermore, his analysis of feeling is by no means cold and mechanical, but reflects an unusual richness of emotional response. The interplay of reason and emotion is to be expected in an author who stands on the threshold of the age of sensibility and has not yet abandoned the habits and convictions of an earlier time.

One other point remains to be dealt with here, the question of the authenticity of Parts VI, VII, and VIII of *Le Paysan parvenu*. *Le Paysan parvenu*, a novel in five parts, was first published in 1734-36.[26] Twenty years later three additional parts appeared, at least two of which have been printed in every subsequent edition of the novel, without explanation or qualification. Authority for their spuriousness rests on two pieces of documentary evidence, an early biography of Marivaux by Lesbros de la Versane (1769), who states that Marivaux wrote only five parts of *Le Paysan parvenu*,[27] and *La Bibliothèque des Romans* (1775), which repeats this statement, probably on the basis of Lesbros. *La Bibliothèque des Romans* gives the date of publication of the last three parts as The Hague, 1772, after Marivaux's death, and Larroumet says, "All editions published after the death of the author contain eight parts."[28] As a matter of fact, the parts in question appeared much earlier. We find in the novel itself the statement that twenty years have passed between the publication of the sixth part and that of the five preceding,[29] which would place the date of its first appearance around 1755. Harvard University has a copy dated 1756, which contains the eight parts.[30] These disputed parts, which appeared some eight years before Marivaux's death, were, so far as we know, never publicly disowned by him.

The title page of the first five parts of the Harvard University copy reads: *Le Paysan parvenu ou les Mémoires de M.****, *par M. de Marivaux*. The title page for the last three parts lacks the *par M. de Marivaux*. There is no other indication in the set that the three parts might not be genuine. The type, contrary to a statement of Fleury, is the same size in all eight parts.[31] Eight parts appear in the Duchesne edition of Marivaux (1781), the earliest complete edition of his works, and in the Duviquet edition (1826-30). The Garnier publication of *Le Paysan parvenu* (1865), which uses the text and notes of Duviquet, drops the eighth part.

About 1880 Marivaux was the subject of several monographs, the most noteworthy being those of Fleury and Larroumet.[32] Fleury, harking back to Lesbros, denies the authenticity of the last three parts of *Le Paysan parvenu* and devotes several pages to a discussion of the question.[33] Larroumet supports the contention of Fleury, and identifies

Lesbros as an eccentric provincial who seems to have had some acquaintance with Marivaux. Both authors support their claims by vague references to the flatness and commonplaceness of the style, awkwardness in plot development, and deviation from the tone of the earlier parts.[34] Fleury adds, "We feel the influence of the time, which was turning to sentimentalism."[35] These do not seem to me convincing reasons for holding the three parts spurious. The reference to sentimentalism is a highly questionable point. Gossot, a more recent critic of Marivaux, says of him: "In growing older . . . Marivaux inclined more and more toward the sentimental *genre,* like the society of which he had been for so long the living expression."[36] In *Le Miroir* (1755) Marivaux revised his opinion of La Motte, whose writings he had admired earlier as creations of "pure intellect," and complained that they neglected the emotional side of man's nature, which is fully as important as the intellectual.[37] One late play of his, *La Femme fidèle* (1757), is in decidedly sentimental vein. Furthermore, as will be shown in this study, a predilection for the life of feeling appeared early in Marivaux's writings.

Fleury overemphasizes what he considers to have been the purpose in writing the novel, the wish to point a lesson to Crébillon *fils,* who had cleverly satirized Marivaux's style in *Tanzaï et Néadarné.*[38] He considers Marivaux to have attained this end in the first five parts, the "scolding" being confined to two pages in the fourth part. Consequently there was no need for continuing the work. Censure of Crébillon is only one of many excellent *raisons d'être* for *Le Paysan parvenu,* if an author is obliged ever to account for a masterpiece.

The dropping of Part VIII of *Le Paysan parvenu* by nineteenth-century publishers can perhaps be justified by the fact that Part VII offers a satisfactory conclusion to the story and that Part VIII, which deals with Jacob's mature years and with the careers of his sons and nephews, is a rapid chain of events apparently intended to appease the over-curious reader. Perfunctory and superficial as it is compared to the preceding parts, it is not inconceivable that Marivaux could have written it, though certainly it is not, as Fontenelle would say, "du bon Marivaux."

We know that Marivaux was a fluent and prolific writer who became easily bored with his work and often dropped it without bothering to write an ending. Outstanding examples of this practice are *L'Indigent Philosophe* and *La Vie de Marianne.* For the latter an ending was quickly provided by an anonymous writer (1745) and a continuation by Mme Riccoboni, written about 1751 and first published in a collection *Le Monde comme il est*, 1760-61. This *Suite* is a *tour de force* which Marivaux himself admired.[39] Although the *fin* and the *suite* have often been confused, there is no temptation to attribute either of them to Marivaux. His approval of the Riccoboni *Suite* constitutes his own denial of the authorship of the 1745 *fin*. Moreover, the tasteless exaggeration of emotional display clearly reveals the spuriousness of the latter. The work of Mme Riccoboni is a much more clever imitation.

In the case of *Le Paysan parvenu* no continuation is known to have been approved by Marivaux. All biographers relate that during the later years of his life, Marivaux's popularity had waned, and that his income, always a problem for him after the Law crash in 1720, had dwindled seriously. In 1736 and 1737 he consented, because of financial necessity, to the publication of his *Télémaque travesti* and *Don Quichotte moderne*, both early and inferior works. Possibly the same necessity prompted him to continue *Le Paysan parvenu*. He may even have devoted considerable time to the task, for Parts VI and VII show none of the glaring faults which are to be found in the anonymous conclusion to *Marianne*. If they are the work of another hand, they represent, in my judgment, an even more remarkable imitation of the spirit and style of Marivaux than does the Riccoboni *Suite*. As for Part VIII, it may have been written hastily, in keeping with the author's well-known aversion for conclusions. A parallel could be found in the abrupt and inartistic conclusion of Marivaux's first published novel, *Les Effets surprenants de la sympathie*.

One other fact may be significant. On his reception into the Academy in 1743, Marivaux was censured for his plays and novels, particularly for *Le Paysan parvenu*, which was described as making vice attractive.[40] Though this unusual procedure awakened resentment at the time, it seems to have had a chastening effect on Marivaux. He published little after that, and several times he resorted to anonymity in presenting his works. This may well have been the case in regard to *Le Paysan parvenu*. Moreover, his acknowledged writings after that date are for the most part in keeping with the approved Academy tradition—*Réflexions sur les Romains, sur Racine, sur Thucydide*. Lesbros says in regard to *Le Paysan parvenu*:

> Son héros allant vivre dans le grand monde, notre auteur craignit les applications qu'on pourroit faire de ce qu'il écriroit de bonne

foi, et ses principes lui firent préférer son repos à la gloire de finir un ouvrage si ingénieusement commencé.[41]

Marivaux's "principles" did not prevent him from attacking in earlier works the faults of society, but they might explain a desire for anonymity once he became *académicien*.

Whether through carelessness or deliberate deception, the editors and publishers of the novel are largely responsible for the numerous errors and perplexities among Marivaux's critics. Duviquet, who accepts all of *Le Paysan parvenu*, praises highly several scenes in the disputed parts; there is "nothing more touching, nothing more delightful," he says, than the scene in the eighth part in which Jacob is welcomed as lord of his native village.[42] Edouard Fournier, in his preface to *Le Théâtre complet* of Marivaux (1878), considers Parts VI and VII to be authentic but rejects Part VIII. Fleury and Larroumet, following the statement of Lesbros, maintain that all three parts are spurious. M. Trahard discusses only five parts, using the Prault edition of 1734, but F. C. Green, in *Minuet*, seems to accept at least Part VI, for he speaks of the women who "fall a prey to the charms" of Jacob, "from Geneviève the chambermaid [Part I] to Madame de Vambures, the *grande dame* [Part VI]."[43] Both Trahard and Green go astray on the spurious twelfth part of *La Vie de Marianne*. Green attributes it to Mme Riccoboni and describes it as "a marvellous imitation of his [Marivaux's] style."[44] M. Trahard includes the entire twelfth part in his summary of *Marianne* and accepts as typical of Marivaux the exaggerated weepings and faintings that characterize it.[45] Later, in the *Addenda* to Volume IV, he states: "I have ascertained that the twelfth part is by Mme Riccoboni," thus substituting one error for another.

The errors and differences of opinion of such eminent critics are a counsel of humility. Pending the discovery of some incontestable piece of documentary evidence, the question of the authenticity of Parts VI, VII, and VIII of *Le Paysan* will not be solved to the satisfaction of everyone. The inclusion or exclusion of Parts VI and VII (there is no reference to Part VIII), though they add to the weight of evidence at various points, in no way alters the general conclusions of this study. Every reference to the disputed parts is indicated by an asterisk preceding the title in the footnote. In several instances an effort has been made to compare these passages with the general trend of Marivaux's thought and style. Although I feel an arbitrary decision impossible, several careful readings of *Le Paysan parvenu* have only strengthened the impression of consistency between the doubtful parts and the prevailing plan and tenor of the first five.

All references to Marivaux are to the Duchesne edition in twelve volumes, Paris, 1781. In addition, *La Vie de Marianne* and *Le Paysan parvenu* have been doubly documented, references being given to the more readily accessible Garnier editions.

I

MARIVAUX AND THE SALONS

"Vous n'avez rien fait, si vous n'y faites reconnaître les gens de votre siècle."
Molière, *Critique de l'Ecole des Femmes*, Sc. VII.

THROUGHOUT HIS LIFE Marivaux was a frequenter of salon society. Soon after his arrival in Paris about 1714,[1] he made the acquaintance of Fontenelle and La Motte, who presented him in the gatherings of which they were leaders. While Versailles was darkened by the stern piety of a dying monarch, society found relaxation in town and country houses. With the Regency the salons came into even greater prominence, some of them aping the licence of the court of Philippe d'Orléans, some professing to abhor it. Marivaux, fresh from provincial circles where he had acquired something of a reputation as poet and playwright, was impressed by the display of wit and intelligence in Parisian society. In the salon of Mme de Lambert, where social and intellectual interests were combined and where a certain sobriety of conduct was felt to be in keeping with aristocratic refinement, he was particularly at home. Though Mme de Tencin prized him among the "bêtes" of her menagerie, his name is not so closely associated with hers as with Mme de Lambert's during the early years in Paris. Mme de Tencin, embroiled in political intrigue, fell into partial disgrace after the Law affair, and it was not until after the death of Mme de Lambert in 1733 that her salon became outstanding among literary circles.[2] It was Mme de Tencin who in 1743 manoeuvred Marivaux into the Academy, but it was with Mme de Lambert that he was associated during the impressionable years of late youth and early maturity. Late in life he appeared in the salon of Mme Geoffrin, a liberal group in which the ideas of the Encyclopedists circulated. In this world of change and unrest he seems to have been definitely unhappy.[3] The earlier salons, where the prevailing tone was one of politeness and delicate persiflage, where new ideas were welcomed without disturbing traditional loyalties, and where reason did not exclude sentiment, appealed to the reserved and sensitive nature of Marivaux. When this order had crumbled, he began to feel out of place in society. Hence at the time of his death Grimm could say of him: "He has had among us the destiny of a pretty woman, that and nothing more; that is to say, a brilliant springtime, an autumn and a winter the harshest and most sad."[4]

It is to the springtime of his life that his association with Mme de

Lambert belongs. He became the sensitive recorder of the pattern of life that he observed in her circle and in the other salons of the time. His natural bent for analyzing and subtilizing emotion, his tenuous language, his sensibility moderated by good sense are in accord with an idle, vain, and sophisticated society which amuses itself by making an art of social relationships and then stands off to appraise its own finesse, admiringly or with self-indulgent irony. This society, soon to vanish completely, found its most discerning expression in the paintings of Watteau and in the theatre of Marivaux.[5] The former portrays its charming surface; the latter its inner flux of thought and feeling.

The setting of Marivaux's plays, when indicated at all, is usually a country house or a Parisian apartment. A few of the plays have a romantic background—"a palace," "in Barcelona," "the garden of the fairy," "the isle of the slaves." Though his heroes and heroines are usually of the aristocracy, they are not of the *haute noblesse,* the Versailles group, represented particularly during this period by the Duchess of Maine and the Cour de Sceaux. His marquises and countesses are of the lesser, often even of the provincial nobility, far more numerous than the court circle and perhaps even more exacting in their observance of social conventions. But in spite of their wigs and mannered ways, they show a streak of common sense and also a capacity for sentiment which indicate the penetration of bourgeois traits into this exclusive *milieu.* It is especially important to understand that Marivaux's characters are not creatures of a world of fancy, created by him as an "escape" from the licentious society of the Regency. This is an idea common among the older critics of Marivaux, especially in dealing with his theatre.[6] Strachey says: "All Marivaux's dramas pass in a world of his own invention—a world curiously compounded of imagination and reality."[7] F. C. Green has pointed out the fallacy of this belief and has stressed the "actuality" of the society Marivaux depicts.[8] Whether they live in palaces or country estates, the people themselves are Marivaux's chief interest, and their thoughts and feelings reflect the society he saw about him in the usual social gatherings of the early eighteenth century. His portraits of his contemporaries, presented perhaps in a somewhat flattering light, reveal the feelings and interests of normal people of the upper classes. Decency and sobriety of manners were not unknown even during the Regency:

En ce temps-là il y avait à Paris, et même à la Cour, une foule de personnes foncièrement honnêtes, celles qui nous paraissent ennuyeuses, parce qu'elles n'ont pas d'histoire, la reine de France, le dauphin et les filles de Louis XV, la duchesse de Choiseul, la marquise de Lambert, chez laquelle Marivaux a pu observer de près des esprits éclairés et fins, des âmes délicates et charmantes. . . .[9]

These are the people of his theatre, the aristocrats of his novels, such as Mme de Miran and Mme Dorsin, and the type into which the orphan Marianne rapidly transforms herself.

Mme de Lambert opened her salon in 1710, and it was brought to an end only by her death in 1733. During these twenty-three years it numbered among its habitués or occasional visitors many of the best talents of France, including such names as Rameau and Couperin, Baron and Adrienne LeCouvreur, Watteau, Nattier, and Rigaud, La Motte, Le Sage, Fontenelle, Marivaux, and Montesquieu. Contemporaries are agreed that it was an honor to be admitted to her circle.[10] Its atmosphere was more sedate than that of the Cour de Sceaux, where frivolity predominated, or of Mme de Tencin, considered somewhat licentious and déclassé. Mme de Lambert recognized that the first duty her influence imposed upon her was to preserve the best in seventeenth-century culture.[11] Yet she maintained an open mind to new forces. In spite of her breeding in the strict tradition of the preceding century, she was quite democratic in her selection of guests. Together with artists and men of letters, she dared to welcome actors and actresses, though as a concession to prejudice she made a neat division among her guests, Tuesday being the day for the *literati,* Wednesday for the nobility, the latter having the privilege of both days.[12] According to Fontenelle, her salon was the only one which people frequented to talk together reasonably and even cleverly, as the occasion called for.[13] Adrienne LeCouvreur records that her identification with the Lambertians gave her the reputation of an intellectual snob.[14] But grace and wit were not lacking. The presence of Fontenelle assured the flavoring of even the weightiest questions with sufficient wit to appeal to an intelligent but pleasure-loving society. D'Alembert says:

> On avoit le bonheur de l'éprouver à chaque instant auprès de Mme de Lambert, qu'une femme honnête, délicate et sensible, pleine d'âme, d'esprit et d'agrémens, étoit le lien et le charme le plus doux d'une société si heureusement assortie, rare assemblage de savoir et de grâces, de finesse et de profondeur, de politesse et de lumières.[15]

Mme de Lambert and her circle portray in miniature the intellectual life of the early eighteenth century. They represent the late flowering of preciosity, a sturdy plant which refused to die in spite of Molière's and Boileau's attacks. They exemplify as well the lay morality, "la morale des honnêtes gens," based on Cartesian rationalism. Deistic thought flourished among them. And in Mme de Lambert and certain of her friends we find anticipations of the new morality of sentiment, of which the fundamental tenet is a belief in the beauty and goodness of feeling. Reason and sentimentalism, the two great forces of eighteenth-century philosophic thought, appear side by side in this society. They are not yet in conflict because the former is dominant. There is as yet no conscious revolt against the rule of reason; sentiment is accorded only a supplementary value to the individual and to society.

In Marivaux too these three aspects of a transitional society are depicted—preciosity in its brilliant final phase, lay morality as the accepted code of conduct in worldly circles, and sentimentalism in tentative but unmistakable form. That this age was in thought and manners a short-lived phenomenon is shown by the brevity of the vogue of Marivaux's theatre and by the fact that he had no successor. Very popular for a time, especially when interpreted by the gifted actress Mlle Silvia,[16] his plays fell into disfavor in the 'thirties and were replaced by the works of other dramatists, more frankly sentimental, such as Diderot and Nivelle de La Chaussée. After many decades of neglect, the comedies once more attained popularity in the nineteenth century through the talent of Mlle Mars.[17] She alone knew how to portray the manners of the *ancien régime,* its elegance, its ceremoniousness, its good taste, and its urbanity.[18] With her decision to leave the stage, Marivaux, the critics said, would again fall into obscurity. On her retirement Jules Janin wrote:

> Molière soutenait Mlle Mars d'une main ferme; c'était elle qui soutenait Marivaux. Le premier survivra même à cette perte, mais Marivaux se sentait mourir le soir même où il perdait sa comédienne bien-aimée [Mlle Sylvia], et . . . à cette heure, est mort sans retour! Elle a emporté ce bel esprit qui s'éteignait sans elle, et qu'elle avait ressuscité. Il faut écrire son oraison funèbre en même temps que celui de Mlle Mars.[19]

This obituary notice was premature. Although clever acting is still necessary to recapture the atmosphere of a bygone day, a few of Marivaux's plays continue to be produced. Among the reasons for their vitality is their charm as period pieces, their portrayal of a unique society. In the salon of Mme de Lambert we are able to observe at first hand the society in which they found their model and inspiration.

Like Mme de Rambouillet, Mme de Lambert was a *précieuse*, not in the exaggerated sense of the Scudéry salon but with the dignity and grace which disarm ridicule. In her salon preciosity was less an affectation of speech than a way of living. The elevation of language betokened the self-discipline of a selective, high-pitched society, bent on living nobly.[20] The circle disliked the bourgeois virtues lauded by Molière.[21] In place of prudence and industry, the aristocratic virtues of honor and generosity were admired. In Mme de Lambert herself the conception of *noblesse oblige* was developed to the point of rigor.

Mme de Lambert's support of the tradition of *galanterie* appears in her admiration for Scudéry, in her love of subtle analysis of feeling, and in her championship of woman's role as a refining influence on manners and morals. She is aware that the old manners are passing, that the frank sensuality of the new age will bring a laxer standard of conduct. In the past woman's task has been that of refining masculine crudity.

> Ils [les jeunes gens] ont beau faire, ils n'ôteront point aux femmes la gloire d'avoir formé ce que nous avons eu de plus honnêtes gens dans le tems passé. C'est à elles qu'on doit la douceur des moeurs, la délicatesse des sentimens, et cette fine galanterie de l'esprit et des manières.[22]

She is *précieuse* above all when she exclaims: "I am always surprised that people do not wish to refine upon the most delicious sentiment that we possess."[23] She delights in a delicate weighing of emotion, in inclination checked by fastidious reluctance. "It is through resistance that the sentiments are strengthened and acquire new degrees of delicacy."[24] Marivaux and Fontenelle were able to supply in full measure these refinements.

Mme de Lambert was also considered a neologist, a *précieuse* in language. Purists of the day criticized her for her tolerance of new expressions, her fondness for the *recherché* in word and phrase. Marais says of her writing: "It was indeed the epitome of whatever is most affected and most precious in our language."[25] *Lambertinage*, as well as *marivaudage*, came popularly to mean a complicated way of saying simple things. Le Sage's description, in *Le Bachelier de Salamanque,* of a *bureau d'esprit* which served as high court of arbitration in matters of language, is doubtless the salon of Mme de Lambert.[26]

In her emphasis on decorum, her pleasure in analysis of sentiment, and her favoring of the unusual in thought and expression, Mme de Lambert is frankly *précieuse*. It has been said that her death marks the end of an institution now considered peculiarly "seventeenth century."[27] In truth the times were no longer ripe for it. Marivaux was to suffer from the decline of the tradition she represents, though in the novel he yielded more fully to the new forces which were to dominate the century. "Le souffle vigoureux de la philosophie" would soon be felt. Society too was tiring of formality, and naturalness in feeling and action was about to replace patterned behavior. There are signs of bending even in this last *précieuse*. But in the main, Mme de Lambert carried on in the manner of her predecessors. Her salon remained the traditional school of politeness, where "the art of conversation, the leisure of high-born living, produce, under the guidance of women, an incomparably graceful way of life, in which the metaphysic of sentiment, the science of love and its infinite nuances, remain in the end the most important matter,"[28] and from which, as d'Alembert said, "people of society departed more enlightened, men of letters more agreeable."[29]

Mme de Lambert and her group also reflect the "lay morality" which since the Renaissance had existed side by side with Christian morality and was to gain ascendency in the early part of the eighteenth century. Her writings, for she was a blue stocking as well as a *précieuse*, contain, d'Argenson says, "a complete course in ethics ideal for the use of present-day society."[30] The two *Avis,* written for her son and daughter, are sober treatises which map out the proper formulas for success in court and salon circles. Her later writings, in particular the *Considérations sur les femmes* and the *Traité de la vieillesse,* show a softer tone in keeping with a less rigid age.[31] The moral code she advocates guides the characters of Marivaux's novels and plays. It is not antireligious; but religion is not allowed to interfere with the pleasures and ambitions of extremely worldly people.

Lay morality, as defined by M. Mornet, is a way of life "which seeks its guiding principle not in renunciation and asceticism but in the pursuit of delicate pleasures, in a wise and generous organization of personal happiness."[32] Opposed to the other-worldly ideals of Christianity, it bases conduct on the aim of real and immediate happiness. This opposition is old, Christian and worldly ideals having been in conflict since the religion of Christ was founded. It is the central idea of the seventeenth century *libertins*, who in word and act opposed the moral ideals of Christianity. Though sophisticated society throughout the reign of Louis XIV was orthodox in theory, its practice differed little from that of the *libertins*. As the century declined, the cleavage between religious belief and moral conduct became more and more apparent. Among the causes of the ever-widening breach were the prevalent classical education, with its strongly pagan tendencies, and the success of Cartesianism, which extended the domain of reason to previously untouched spheres. Cartesian rationalism, with its principle of accepting nothing that cannot be proved, weakened the foundations of Christian theology and also of Christian morality. Reason, *le bon sens,* is universal—"la chose du monde la mieux partagée." It came to be regarded as a natural law, a guide to conduct more dependable than the external and often conflicting authority of ecclesiastical law. Pierre Bayle declares that morality is as possible in a society of atheists as in Christian France.[33] Montesquieu speaks of a universal spirit of justice, anterior to the establishment of religions.[34] Once reason is postulated as the natural law of human conduct, it is a short step to the optimistic notion of the natural goodness of man. All human instincts and passions, even those expressly condemned by Christianity, such as ambition and pride, are good and a source of happiness, if restrained and directed by reason. The good life consists not in denying our natural inclinations, but in understanding and regulating them. Thus the passions are rehabilitated, the idea of original sin is set aside, and the way to earthly happiness is left open. The idea of happiness, rationally pursued, as moral guide, is extended to embrace the social group as well as the individual. Père Buffier, writing in 1726, defined morality as "the science of living with other people in every-day life, in such a way as to produce, so far as we are able, our own happiness together with the happiness of others."[35] Since this conception makes the individual responsible for safeguarding the welfare of others, it leads to the growth of humanitarian ideas. The writings of Mme de Lambert are permeated with this rational morality, decorous, temperate, sane, and experimentally humanitarian, a guide to happiness through control of natural endowments. Marivaux follows his friend in this respect, and though outwardly respectful of convention, goes much farther than she in support of humanitarian impulses.[36]

Mme de Lambert held with Descartes that the passions are the great motivators of human activity,[37] good if properly directed, dangerous if allowed to take their course unchecked. In her desire to prepare her children to take their place in the complex society of her day, Mme de Lambert did not disdain their natural inclinations. "It is not the object of morality to destroy nature, but to perfect it."[38] Going farther than Descartes and running counter to Christian morality, she adds that vices are potential virtues and need only to be regulated by reason. Men are almost irresistibly drawn toward goodness, and their very vices, if the mind is employed to regulate them, may be changed into virtues. *Amour-propre*, if given a worthy aim, may be valuable to the individual and to society.

> On distingue deux sortes d'amour-propre, l'un naturel, légitime et réglé par la justice et par la raison; l'autre, vicieux et corrompu. . . . Nous ne savons pas nous aimer; nous nous aimons trop, ou nous nous aimons mal. S'aimer comme il faut, c'est aimer la vertu; aimer le vice, c'est s'aimer d'un amour aveugle et mal-entendu.[39]

Love, "the first of all pleasures," and the most dangerous, can lead to happiness only if skillfully guided. "The passions are strings which require the hand of a great master to touch them."[40]

Nature then is good if firmly controlled, and this check must be maintained at every period of life. In youth especially the passions should be subjected to will and reason. Mme de Lambert counsels her daughter:

> Faites réflexion aux funestes suites des passions: vous ne trouverez que trop d'exemples pour vous instruire. . . . Rien ne vous avilit tant, et ne vous met tant au-dessous de vous-même, que les passions: elles vous dégradent. Il n'y a que la raison qui vous conserve votre place.[41]

The approach of old age, when a life of passion can be only ridiculous, makes reasonable conduct particularly necessary, seclusion and meditation offering a way of life in keeping with one's waning attractions. When youth is gone, she says, "ce n'est pas vivre comme l'on doit, que de vivre au gré de ses passions et de ses fantaisies; et nous ne vivons comme nous devons, que quand nous vivons selon la raison; car ce qui s'appelle NOUS, c'est notre raison."[42]

The happiness which Mme de Lambert desires for her children is far from that envisioned by the Scriptures or by the great preachers of the day. She would not have her children free thinkers, however. Among the duties of the *honnête homme* she includes the acceptance of one "prejudice," religion, which Descartes himself had tried to protect from the clear light of reason. She defines religion as "the cult you owe to a Supreme Being," an early use of a phrase dear to Rousseau. In matters of religion one must yield to the authorities; but in all other subjects one should accept only the authority of reason and evidence.[43] The conformity, which is purely external, seems to be dictated by a wish not to offend or to set oneself apart. The guide she leaves with her children is conscience, "that inner sense of a delicate honor, which assures you that you have nothing to reproach yourself with."[44] Conscience for her is not so bold and free as Rousseau's "divine conscience." It is nearer to the "natural law" of Voltaire, more rational than instinctive.

> Si la raison nous luit, qu'avons-nous à nous plaindre?
> Nous n'avons qu'un flambeau, gardons-nous de l'éteindre.[45]

When Marivaux speaks of "cet esprit de justice que je trouve en moi, que je trouve dans un autre, qui fait ma sûreté et la sienne,"[46] he is echoing the opinion of a tolerant and emancipated society, still respectful of traditional forms but finding its sanctions within rather than in external authority.

That Mme de Lambert is concerned more with the gratifications of this life than with preparation for the next is shown in her humanizing, or more accurately, feminizing of religion. She bends it pliantly to the needs of the ages of woman. It indulges the young and indemnifies the old. As one grows older, it becomes more and more a reasonable and necessary practice, lending consolation for the growing asperities of life.

> A quoi se prendre? le passé nous fournit des regrets; le présent, des chagrins; et l'avenir, des craintes. La religion seule calme tout, et console de tout; en vous unissant à Dieu, elle vous réconcilie avec le monde et avec vous-même.[47]

Grimm, in reviewing her *Traité de la vieillesse*, comments:

> Les femmes y sont le principal objet de son attention; en leur donnant une fort bonne recette contre les inconvénients de la vieillesse, elle a montré bien de l'indulgence pour leur printemps.[48]

It is not surprising that lay morality should have acquired so wide a vogue. In spite of its indulgence to natural inclinations, however, the principle of reason always guards against excess.

Committed to the rule of reason, lay morality seems, as indeed it is, the antithesis of the morality of sentiment, "which appeals for direction of the inner life less to deliberation and will than to the ardor and enthusiasm of the heart, to the impulse of generous passions."[49] Yet the two have much in common. Both regard happiness as the end of life. Both resist external authority. Lay morality affirms in a guarded way the goodness of natural instincts, and this belief, strengthened by the influence of primitivism, will result eventually in the capitulation of reason to feeling and in the flood tide of sensibility. Civilization will be condemned as a corrupting influence, and simple societies, together with spontaneous abandonment to feeling, will be admired. The circle of Mme de Lambert does not represent this advanced stage of sensibility. There were no primitivists among her aristocratic guests, and advocacy of the return to nature would have caused a rude shock in this rarefied atmosphere. But Mme de Lambert not only recognized the importance of the emotional life; she knew how to savor the sweetness of feeling and to moralize about it. Her sensibility, an apparent inconsistency in this goddess of reason, is more than a veneer; it is the most sincere and personal note in her writing.

Mme de Lambert had not the quick feelings of Ninon de Lenclos or the passionate heart of Julie de Lespinasse. Her worldly views are difficult to reconcile with the ideals of the *coeur sensible*. Yet many pages reveal that she prized the heart as well as the head, and not infrequently she is inclined to give it primacy. Her *Réflexions sur les femmes* is almost as glowing a defense of sensibility as the effusions of Jean-Jacques or of Diderot, and the counsel of reason seems little more than an after-thought. Sensibility, she believes, is a peculiarly feminine felicity, for which no apology is necessary. There is no ground for the accusation that the intelligence of women is inferior to that of men because women are dominated by feeling. "Nature," she says simply, "reasons for them and saves them the trouble.[50] These ready-made syllogisms are just as dependable as the laborious ones of the plodding male intelligence.

> Nous allons aussi sûrement à la vérité par la force et la chaleur des sentimens, que par l'étendue et la justesse des raisonnemens; et nous arrivons toujours par eux plus vite au but dont il s'agit que par les connoissances. La persuasion du coeur est au-dessus de celle de l'esprit. . . .[51]

Sensibility is a source of happiness as well as a guide to truth. Individual happiness through friendship and love springs naturally from it, and the social virtues which safe-guard the happiness of others are the inevitable outgrowth.

> Je vous exhorterai bien plus, mon fils, à travailler sur votre coeur, qu'à perfectionner votre esprit: ce doit être là l'étude de toute la vie. La vraye grandeur de l'homme est dans le coeur. . . . L'on n'est estimable que par le coeur, et l'on n'est heureux que par lui; puisque notre bonheur ne dépend que de la manière de sentir. . . . Gardez bien votre coeur; il est la source de l'innocence et du bonheur.[52]

This confidence in the goodness of the feelings and in their value as a source of happiness, a doctrine accepted hesitantly by the characters of Marivaux's theatre, is fully embraced by Marianne.

Love as tender passion (not *l'amour-passion* of Racine and Prévost or *l'amour galant* of the seventeenth-century novels) finds an eloquent champion in Mme de Lambert. It is the love of the "delicate soul," free from grossness or violence, and a special property of the sex blessed with a full measure of sensibility.

> La plupart des hommes n'aiment que d'une manière vulgaire: ils n'ont qu'un objet. Ils proposent un terme dans l'amour. . . . Pour un coeur tendre il y a une ambition plus élevée à avoir: c'est de porter nos sentimens, et ceux de la personne aimée, au dernier degré de délicatesse, et de les rendre tous les jours plus tendres, plus vifs et plus occupans.[53]

Through *amour-tendresse* is not without preciosity, it differs from the *amour galant* of the first half of the seventeenth century. Both shun the rawness of passion and seek to ornament the sexual relationship. But in *amour galant*, if passion exists, it is under the control of the will and is masked by a rigid code of etiquette; in *amour-tendresse* it is dispersed in innumerable refinements of feeling. *Amour galant*, a mingling of chivalric ideals and Cartesian rationalism, is marked by a rigorous decorum.[54] *Amour-tendresse*, on the other hand, evades this cold discipline and gives freer rein to the heart; if the proprieties are observed, it is because the heart is naturally timid and respectful toward the loved one. *Amour-tendresse* is a divertissement in which the lovers join hands to exploit their emotions. *Amour galant* is a game of conquest in which the lady, while displaying her charms to the best effect, resists so long the advances of her lover and exacts such trials of obedience, perseverance, and enterprise that "the trouble of winning" her heart "almost equals the prize of conquest."[55] The drama of *amour galant* is the external one of resistance and attack; that of *amour-tendresse*, the internal one of sentiment and feeling. Heroism on the part of the lover is no longer necessary, but sensibility is.[56] To be in love no longer imposes on him the duty of being unhappy;[57] he is allowed to share at all stages the sweetness of loving and being loved. The sadness of love is part of its sweetness.

> Les caractères sensibles et mélancoliques trouvent des charmes et des agrémens infinis dans l'amour et en font sentir. Il y a des plaisirs à part pour les âmes tendres et délicates. Ceux qui ont vécu de la vie de l'amour savent combien leur vie étoit animée; et quand il vient à leur manquer, ils ne vivent plus. . . . Les caractères mélancoliques y sont les plus propres. Qui dit amoureux, dit triste; mais il n'appartient qu'à l'amour de donner des tristesses agréables.[58]

But Mme de Lambert is still too much of the old school to emancipate the heart completely. There follows the familiar warning of the Cartesian rationalist: "But our love cannot be happy unless it is regulated."[59] Mme de Lambert is herself astonished at the boldness of her flight. She concludes:

> On me dira: Voilà un terrible écart. J'en conviens. . . . Les idées se sont offertes assez naturellement à moi, et de proche en proche elles m'ont menée plus loin que je ne devois, que ne voulois. . . . J'ai donc imaginé une métaphysique d'amour.[60]

It remained for Marivaux, as we shall see in a subsequent chapter, to develop the metaphysic of love in which decorum was not imposed from without but evolved from the promptings of the heart.

Thus Mme de Lambert herself answers the question discussed earlier in this chapter: Is Marivaux, especially in the theatre, completely at variance with the tendency of his time? He was too much the eager observer of life about him to seek escape to a dream world. Through his intimacy with Mme de Lambert he saw her attempts to combat the prevailing corruption of manners and perhaps shared her belief in the refining influence of salon society. *Amour-tendresse,* as well as being an expression of Marivaux's genius for psychological analysis, is also an outgrowth of salons like hers, in which an effort was made to preserve the outward forms of gallantry and at the same time to give freer expression to feeling.

Friendship, for Mme de Lambert, is very close to *amour-tendresse.* "We enjoy in friendship all that is sweetest in love: the pleasure of confidence, the charm of opening one's soul to one's friend, of reading in his heart. . . . How light, how flowing are the hours with the loved one!"[61] Her *Traité de l'amitié* bases friendship more on feeling than on intellectual attractions. "The mind pleases, but it is the heart that links."[62] Her discourse on the fine shades of friendship, on its pleasures and its perils, is in itself significant of the emergence of a new sentimentalism. Yet underneath her fine-spun analyses lies a genuine warmth of feeling, a wish for a communion of hearts rather than of minds. In this respect it is interesting to compare the portraits of her friends Fontenelle and de Sacy, made by the great lady herself according to the time-honored custom of the *précieuses.* Fontenelle, the brilliant pivot of her salon from its opening until the end, receives full praise for wit and wisdom, but is reproved for a certain coldness, the result of over-intellectuality.

Il a les agrémens du coeur, sans en avoir les besoins; nul sentiment ne lui est nécessaire. Les âmes tendres et sensibles sentent les besoins du coeur plus qu'on ne sent les autres nécessités de la vie: pour lui, il est libre et dégagé; aussi ne s'unit-on qu'à son esprit, et on échappe à son coeur.

Il est incapable de sentimens vifs et profonds. . . . Un pareil caractère n'est fait que pour être estimé. Vous pouvez donc badiner et vous amuser; mais ne lui en donnez, et ne lui en demandez pas davantage.[63]

M. de Sacy joins to intelligence the added charm of sensibility.

Il se saisit aussi de nos sentimens: il sait que l'homme est plus sensible que raisonnable; qu'avec de la sensibilité on réveille des idées dans l'esprit, et qu'on excite des mouvemens dans le coeur.[64]

That Mme de Lambert should feel an emptiness of heart in her brilliant and gifted friend is not without significance. We shall see that Marivaux, skillful too in the art of pen portraits, presents in *La Vie de Marianne* two women of the salon group, whose qualities of heart are lauded above all other accomplishments.

The humanitarian impulses of Mme de Lambert do not fall within any organized movement for social reform. They are a part of her sensibility, the natural response of a heart moved by the sight of human suffering. Appeals to sympathy for the unfortunate are heard more and more insistently in the late years of the seventeenth century, in conversation, in sermons, and in literature. This sentimental humanitarianism is as yet little mixed with egalitarian ideas. In Mme de Lambert's writings the word *humanité* appears often, but always as a part of her conception of *noblesse oblige*. For those whom fortune has favored, charity is a duty and a privilege. "The happiness of great place is that others find their good fortune in ours. . . . Liberality is one of the duties of noble birth."[65] She toys with the idea of an aristocracy of merit rather than of birth. She holds no illusions as to the real worth of great names: "Approach them, you will find only men."[66] And she adds: "I call *peuple* all those who think in a common and vulgar manner. The court is full of them."[67] Merit rather than pride or title should form the basis of class distinctions. "You should regard the advantages of birth and rank only as possessions which fortune has lent you, and not as distinctions attached to your being, which form a part of yourself."[68] On the whole, however, her humanitarianism springs from natural kindness rather than from advocacy of social reform. She is not interested in attacking social evils at their source, but rather in alleviating individual cases of suffering, a practice which refreshes the heart and gives it new delights to take the place of the out-worn pleasures of a super-refined society. She exclaims:

> Pourquoi, dans ce nombre infini de goûts inventés par la volupté et par la mollesse, ne s'en est-on jamais fait un de soulager les malheureux? L'humanité ne vous fait-elle point sentir le besoin de secourir vos semblables? Les bons coeurs sentent l'obligation de faire du bien, plus qu'on ne sent les autres besoins de la vie.[69]

The satisfaction which follows generous acts inspired by pity and sympathy is as real as that which results from any other emotional experience and is more praiseworthy. "The most touching pleasure for *honnêtes gens*," she says to her son, "is to do good and to aid the unfortunate."[70] This early humanitarianism becomes a part of the code of behavior of the *honnête homme* and is at the same time one of the pleasures of sensibility. The latter aspect will develop in depth and extension as the century advances until it embraces the ideas of liberty, equality, and fraternity, and such ambitious attempts at social reform as the French Revolution, the freeing of slaves, and the regulation of living and working conditions. The humanitarian sentiment in Marivaux's novels, however, remains in the transitional stage represented by Mme de Lambert.

The salon of Mme de Lambert faced both the past and the future and formed a link between the seventeenth and eighteenth centuries. The best in the older tradition of preciosity and gallantry had a late blossoming in this Regency salon. Yet in its brilliance one feels a certain autumnal quality, a premonition of change. Henceforth, as Desnoiresterres says,

> . . . ce sera un autre esprit, une autre galanterie, un autre courant d'idées. On avait patronné Descartes et ses tourbillons, on avait philosophé avec le berger Fontenelle; que demander de plus à ces grandes dames du grand règne, qui, sur le retour, se faisaient dévotes? L'heure de l'*Encyclopédie* a sonné, le commencement de la fin: tout va prendre, tout a déjà pris une teinte rembrunie, presque sombre.[71]

There is, it seems, a certain slackening of tension underneath these polished manners and disciplined minds. The heart will have its due as well as the head. Gallantry is giving way before something gentler and more spontaneous.[72] Mme de Lambert, a worshipper at the shrine of reason, is caught up now and then by the emotional current which is fundamentally a reaction to correctness in thought and living. Poised and discreet, she is sure enough of herself to toy with new ideas, to the appeal of which she is not insensitive. Paul Valéry, in his study of *Les Lettres persanes,* describes the delicious moment between epochs of order and chaos, when under stable external forms a ferment of ideas goes on, the implications of which are both pleasant and terrifying.[73] The social satire of Montesquieu, behind its screen of Orientalism, is more daring than the sensibility of Mme de Lambert in its cloak of propriety. But they are of the same transitional quality; they constitute an end and a beginning. And Marivaux, whose impressionable years were spent in this challenging atmosphere, is far more representative than is his gracious hostess of the yielding, half willing and half reluctant, before a new spirit.

II

LES EFFETS SURPRENANTS DE LA SYMPATHIE

> "Yet, for ten times the pain that such a sensibility is attended with, would I not part with the pleasure it brings with it."
>
> Richardson, *Clarissa Harlowe.*

A ROMAN in the first half of the seventeenth century meant generally a series of fantastic adventures which befell characters of more than human excellence and which they endured with admirable fortitude until the author was ready to deliver them from their difficulties. Toward midcentury there was a shift in taste, largely through the influence of the theatre, and a preference arose for shorter novels with a more concentrated plot, dealing with an inner conflict, a *crise de l'âme* rather than an adventure story. Yet strangely enough, it is in the older form that Marivaux makes his début as a novelist. Since this early work, showing the conventional beginnings of a strongly original genius, is so unlike Marivaux's later novels, it is dealt with separately here. It cannot be overlooked in a study of the quality of sensibility in Marivaux, for it adumbrates his mature manner of thought and feeling.

Though the place of publication was Paris and the date 1713-14,[1] it is impossible to determine where the novel was written. It seems probable that the work is the product of Marivaux's provincial youth and that he threw it on the market soon after his arrival in Paris, in the desire to establish himself as a man of letters. The striking change in his writings in the course of the next twenty years may be attributed to his natural responsiveness to literary tendencies, stimulated by contact and discussion in the salon of Mme de Lambert and in other literary gatherings of the day.

Les Aventures de ***, or *Les Effets surprenants de la sympathie,* Marivaux's first published novel,[2] is dismissed by most critics as the misguided effort of a young author who has not yet discovered his true sphere. This early work is a *roman galant et héroïque* of the type which was developed in the first half of the seventeenth century by D'Urfé, La Calprenède, and Scudéry, and which, though *démodé*, still found readers after a hundred years.[3] As is usual in the novel of adventure, love forms the central theme. Time and place are uncertain; descriptions of characters and surroundings are vague and colorless. The complicated plot, endlessly weaving tale within tale, contains all the familiar devices of the adventure novel: kidnappings, shipwrecks, disguises, soliloquies opportunely overheard, miraculous resurrections. The impetus of the story sweeps the writer along and involves him ever more deeply. Surfeited with marvels and disasters, one reads on only to find out how the author will extricate himself. Finally, as if sharing this weariness, Marivaux ends his tale summarily just where the tangle is thickest, by a few swift strokes of explanation more ingenious than plausible. The brusque ending is not the only violation of unity. The first third of the novel moves at a more leisurely pace than the rest and develops an interest which disappears almost entirely in the whirl of adventure and intrigue that follows—an interest in the psychology of feeling. The early pages, in spite of their imitativeness and occasional sentimentality, anticipate the later Marivaux. They present in vague outline his first picture of the *âme sensible*.

Among the pirates, marauders, noblemen, and ladies in distress who crowd the pages of the novel, three form the center of interest—Clorante, the hero, Caliste, the "object of his affections," and Clarice, the loving and unloved. Clorante, attacked by a band of robbers, is saved from death by the intervention of Clarice and her suite. Following the Scudéry pattern of *tendre sur reconnaissance*, he falls in love with his fair deliverer, only to fall out again at the sight of Caliste, *la belle inconnue*, to whom he surrenders himself unconditionally before ever exchanging a word with her. This is clearly an instance of *tendre sur inclination*. Clarice, abandoned by her lover, becomes the victim of her passion. Throughout these pages we find for the most part the formal presentation of love as noble sentiment which marks the seventeenth-century novel from the *honnête amitié* of d'Urfé to the correct gallantry of the Scudéry hero.[4]

In speech and action Marivaux's characters differ little from the stock types of the earlier novel. Clorante is an *honnête homme*, courteous, tender-hearted, modest, proud without arrogance, possessing "that happy disposition which nature imprints in noble and virtuous hearts."[5] In his devotion he is a match for the faithful Céladon or the heroic Polexandre. "Une sensibilité pour les maux d'autrui" makes him eager to serve Clarice, whose merit he recognizes though he cannot respond to her passion. His acceptance of love as a *don fatal* and his fondness for solitude in moods of melancholy faintly suggest the pre-romantic hero, but on the whole he is a shadowy figure beside the Cléveland, the Des Grieux, or the Comte de Comminges of a later age. Caliste is a passive character, "belle et languissante," showing little response to her lover's devotion except an occasional shower of tears. Clarice is rather more complicated; jealousy, hope, and despair struggle in her heart. Love, however, is the purifying agent which makes of her a *belle âme*[6] of the La Fayette type, devoted and self-effacing, touching in her gentle melancholy. Her jealousy is short-lived, for she is incapable of base feelings.

> Les coeurs véritablement généreux ont leurs sentiments à part; s'ils ressemblent aux autres dans un premier instant, dont ils ne sont pas les maîtres, bientôt un caractère de vertu qui domine les ramène à cette grandeur de sentiments dont un premier mouvement les avait tirés.[7]

Though she suffers deeply—"les coeurs tendres et délicats se font mille chagrins, la moindre chose les blesse et les afflige"[8]—she transforms her sorrow into noble tenderness through a vow of life-long fidelity to her love. Her hopeless passion becomes the center of her life. "In spite of the despair which crushes me, yes, I still wish to find some pleasure in life. I shall live to love Clorante."[9]

Easily moved to pity and affection, the characters not only abandon themselves freely to their feelings but indulge in a conscious admiration of emotion both in themselves and in others. This is true even of the minor characters of the book. Clorante's mother on her death-bed notices the beauty of the grief displayed about her.

> Clorante arrosa cette main de larmes; il la baisait mille fois. Sa mère, en lui serrant la sienne, lui témoignait, malgré son peu de force, combien elle était charmée de sa tendresse. Ce spectacle émut ceux qui étaient présents; on n'entendait dans la chambre que soupirs entrecoupés.[10]

In a farewell letter the father, about to be put to death for treason, takes gloomy pleasure in picturing to himself the sorrow of his wife at the news of his death.

> Je vous vois baignée de larmes, cette idée fait couler les miennes. L'état funeste où je vous vois m'arrache des soupirs: mais l'avou-erai-je, Madame? il est des moments où cette idée a des charmes pour moi; vos larmes me prouvent votre amour, je n'en puis à présent souhaiter d'autres preuves; je meurs, je me représente votre afflic-tion, je la vois avec douceur. Cette douceur est bien triste, mais c'est la seule que je puisse goûter.[11]

The lovers find most frequent opportunity to taste the sweetness or bitterness of their feelings. Marivaux declares that while love sometimes brings with it a succession of terrifying events such as he is describing, it is more often of a gentler type, "a conqueror whose chains are a tissue of pleasures."[12] This is the tender passion with which the readers of the later Marivaux are familiar.[13] In the intervals of calm allowed in the first part of the novel, the characters luxuriate in the softer feelings of love. Clorante writes to his beloved Caliste:

> Oui, désormais, Madame, vous aimer sans espoir est une situation où je vais trouver mille charmes. Je gémirai, qu'importe? mes soupirs seront un hommage éternel que vous méritez, ils vous seront connus, vous me plaindrez quelquefois; et je préfère ce sentiment de pitié aux faveurs que j'aurais d'une autre.[14]

Clorante has the privilege dear to heroes of the adventure novel, that of rescuing his love from a pirate who holds her imprisoned. When she has descended by a silken ladder to the garden where her lover is waiting, the two are overcome by their emotions. Clorante feels his strength slip away—"effet prodigieux de l'amour." He is unable to speak: "soft sighs interrupt his words." Falling on his knees, "he opens his soul to the flood of innocent pleasures which the ardor of delicate passion affords."[15] Caliste, remembering *les bienséances*, makes a heroic resolve to restrain the "movements of her heart," but alas, at the sound of Clorante's voice, "Caliste no longer recognized herself; her heart responded to the sighs of her lover. She considered her weakness, and the charm she found in it convinced her that it was useless to combat it."[16] This abandonment to feeling ruins their plan to escape, and the lovers are separated once more. But the disappointment is not without compensation, for they have the sweet sadness of reliving in imagination their brief moments together. "It was that kind of pleasure which is bitter to lose, which both saddens and consoles a loving heart."[17] Clarice reveals herself most fully a devotee of this pleasurable sorrow beloved of the *âme sensible*. Marivaux explains her case: "Tender love, though unhappy, has a thousand little pleasures provided by the delicacy of its feelings."[18] She invents for herself the exquisite torture of constant exposure to her passion, either through following Clorante in his search for Caliste or in listening patiently to Caliste's tale of her love. She pleads with Clorante:

Je vous suivrai, je vous verrai sans cesse, vous me confierez vos peines; la confiance que vous aurez pour moi me soulagera; vous serez charmé vous-même du peu de contrainte où vous vivrez avec moi, votre reconnaissance en augmentera, je me croirai heureuse ou toujours près de le devenir.[19]

And she is able to forget the ingratitude of her lover in the pleasure of judging through the sighs of her rival how charming he is.

This ability to find pleasure in painful emotions, in melancholy or even in genuine grief, is, according to Lanson and Waldberg, indicative of the new sensibility which appears in the late seventeenth century. The portrayal of melancholy is less generalized and more intimate, a revelation of the inner self which the late classic age no longer shuns. Waldberg quotes La Fontaine's line from the poem *Volupté*, "le sombre plaisir d'un coeur mélancolique,"[20] as perhaps the earliest example of this sentiment in modern literature. In the sentimentalizing of melancholy (*Wandlung der Melancholie in die Sentimentalität*) he sees the presage of a new *Weltanschauung*, that of the age of sensibility.[21] This transformation of sentiment appears in sharper form in the sorrows of the Portuguese nun: "Farewell! Love me always and make me suffer even more."[22] And again, "I am jealous of my transports, as of the greatest wealth I have ever possessed."[23] The enjoyment of one's capacity to feel finds frequent expression in Mme de Villedieu and the group of feminine novelists in the closing years of the seventeenth century. Clarice exemplifies it fully, the reward for her suffering being a "contentement de soi-même" which denotes the heroine of sensibility.[24]

Another evidence of sensibility in *Les Effets surprenants de la sympathie* is the tendency to associate feeling and virtue, particularly among simple folk unspoiled by the life of court and town. Clarice in her wanderings finds refuge in a peasant's cottage, where a mother and daughter shower her with kind attentions. Clarice is delighted with their artless kindness and generosity. She says of the daughter: "She lives in tranquil obscurity; her pleasures are innocent and sweet. . . . She moves among charming companions whose ways are virtuous and whose hearts are true."[25] Marivaux seems to be thinking of the society of his own day when he contrasts these models of natural goodness with others "whose generosity is almost always merely the result of politeness or of the education they have received."[26] The scene anticipates Rousseau's description of the hospitable peasants of the Haut-Valais, one among countless descriptions of the kind in eighteenth-century literature.[27]

The neglect into which this early novel of Marivaux has fallen is deserved. The style is diffuse; the cluttered plot is confusing and wearisome; the novel lacks unity of effect; and the characters, with the partial exception of Clarice, are scarcely distinguishable from one another and from hundreds of their kind even by their names. Yet the first third of the novel is interesting as a revelation of the author's sympathy for the *âme sensible,* later to play so prominent a role in his theatre and in his novels. The curious shift in midcourse from psychological interest to interest in mere physical adventure cannot be satisfactorily explained. It is possible that the common sense and the ironic turn of mind that temper the sensibility of his later novels already warned Marivaux against the unguarded sentimentality of *Les Effets* and persuaded him to fall back on the tested if uninspiring model of the adventure tale. This early novel is predominantly of the latter type. But though sensibility is overshadowed by intrigue, its presence is undeniable and its nature clear. Marivaux's knowledge of the feminine heart and his interest in the subtleties of tender passion already appear and give to the work its only distinction. In tone this sensibility is less restrained than that of the later novels. But occasionally a bit of *badinage* like the following, with its delicate mixture of sentiment and irony, foretells the author of *Marianne.*

> Après tout, Madame, condamnez Clorante, plaignez Clarice; mais que sa destinée ne soit pas une raison pour vous de fuir l'amour. S'il doit vous paraître redoutable, c'est bien plus par les maux que des yeux comme les vôtres peuvent faire de concert avec lui, que par les maux que vous risqueriez vous-même.[28]

When he abandons fantastic scenes and heroes for the society of his own day, Marivaux's gift for observing the inner drama of the feelings places him among the authors of the age of sensibility.

THE SENSITIVE HEART

"Les âmes sensibles ont plus d'existence que les autres: les biens et les maux se multiplient à leur égard." Duclos, *Considérations sur les moeurs de ce siècle*, I, 69.

THE TYPE OF CHARACTER sketched by Mme de Lambert in her *Réflexions sur les femmes* is searchingly portrayed in Marivaux's Marianne, a "sensitive soul" representative of this early phase of sensibility when the reasons of the head are not yet in full retreat before those of the heart, when decorum and temperament are not yet sworn enemies. Endowed with natural taste, precision of judgment, a lively imagination, and above all an exquisite sensibility quick to respond to impulses of generosity, pity, and love, she is one of those "destined to live a life of sentiment."[1] Marivaux surrounds her with other sensitive souls, her lover Valville, her foster mother Mme de Miran, her convent friend Mlle de Tervire. In Jacob, Marianne's masculine counterpart and the hero of *Le Paysan parvenu,* we watch the awakening of a sensitive heart as it is initiated into the society best calculated to develop its latent emotional capacities. These two novels are milestones in the history of eighteenth-century sensibility[2] because they show the movement in the setting from which it sprang and also because many of the characteristics later inseparably associated with it find in them either partial or complete expression. In both of these novels the author adopts the device of having an older person tell the story of his life, and so the thoughts and feelings of the characters are more closely identified with Marivaux himself than is the case with the ordinary novel form. They become in a way the fulfillment of his theories which appear in the earlier essays and sketches. The characters of his plays retain more of the older decorum, and while they point the way toward a new emotional freedom, they do not go so far toward exemplifying it as do the characters of the novels.

The sensitive heart (described in the clinical perfection more closely approximated in mid-century than in Marivaux) is a character easily moved, who tends to give way to his feelings, to cherish them, and to exalt them. His quivering sensibility to impulses from within and impressions from without makes it hard for him to disguise his feelings and distasteful to restrain them. He finds the sense of his human worth not in the will or the reason but in the emotions. His capacity to feel is his dearest possession, and spontaneity seems to him more praiseworthy than self-control. The head becomes a kind of adjunct to the temperament, its function being to discriminate the quality of feeling or to justify the promptings of the heart, rarely to censor or direct. The sensitive heart is inclined to say with Faust, "Feeling is all." It takes an esthetic pleasure in its delicate and fluid sensations. It exalts its ready sympathies into a moral guide. It prides itself on an intuition which may be a reliable guide to truth. In Marivaux the natural exuberance of this type of character is held in check by the censor common sense, as an analysis of his work will show; but his Marianne and to a lesser extent his Jacob are nevertheless sensitive hearts, the parents of the Julies and Saint-Preuxs of the next generation.

Cherishing the emotions as both good and beautiful, the sensitive heart makes little effort to check their outward manifestations. Blushes, sighs, tears, faintings, and transports of joy are the most obvious marks of the character in the fiction and drama of sensibility. External manifestations of feeling are not a new thing in literature. The spectacle of Charlemagne and his peers weeping and fainting at the news of Roland's death, Chimène's magnificent cry, "Pleurez, pleurez, mes yeux, et fondez-vous en eau," and the noble Racinian portrayals of passion and grief are familiar examples. In these cases, however, the eminent tragedy of the situation is full justification for emotional display. At the other extreme are the unchecked tears of the *grands pleureurs* of the adventure novels, scoffed at by Boileau in his *Dialogue sur les héros de romans*. With them the cause for grief seems so disproportionate to the effects that the result is only ridiculous.[3] Late in the seventeenth century, particularly among the feminine novelists, tears became an index of noble character, as well as adding the charm of melancholy to a lovely face.[4] With relaxing social discipline, emotions are given ever freer expression, and greater importance is accorded to sensations. This is the dawn of the era of sensibility.

Ovid distinguishes the disease of love from all other diseases by its peculiarity of being both pleasant and painful at the same time. Its symptoms are paleness, trembling, fear, loss of appetite, sighing, sleeplessness, weeping, crying out, fainting, mental absorption, insanity, and even death.[5] Marivaux's characters display only the milder effects named by the great doctor of love, for Marivaux never pictures love as a violent passion, and with him affairs of the heart usually end happily. His characters reveal their feelings freely, not only in matters of love but in countless other emotional situations. Tearfulness is not as yet the almost constant state among them that we find in the *comédie larmoyante*; their weeping, though facile, is distinguished by a vibrant awareness of the occasion. They analyze and rationalize their tears with genuine insight, a procedure which sets them apart from the tearful heroes of the seventeenth-century novels. Marianne describes in detail her thoughtful preparation for weeping, from which actual tears bring delicious relief:

> Je ne pleurais pourtant point alors, et je n'en étais pas mieux; je recueillais de quoi pleurer; mon âme s'instruisait de tout ce qui pouvait l'affliger, elle se mettait au fait de ses malheurs; et ce n'est pas là l'heure des larmes: on n'en verse qu'après que la tristesse est prise, et presque jamais pendant qu'on la prend; aussi pleurerai-je bientôt.[6]

Reasons for weeping are many and varied, and frequently indefinable, though the characters always make an effort to divine the cause of their outbursts. Sometimes it is a wound to pride, as after Marianne's argument with the good-hearted but tactless Mme Dutour.[7] Again it may be genuine grief, as when she renounces her lover in compliance with family objections to the match.[8] Valville, Marianne's lover, weeps unabashed as he pleads for his mother's consent to his marriage with the nameless orphan. Often the merest suggestion is enough to call forth tears.

> Nous autres filles, ou nous autres femmes, nous pleurons volontiers dès qu'on nous dit: vous venez de pleurer; c'est une enfance et comme une mignardise que nous avons, et dont nous ne pouvons presque pas nous défendre.[9]

The utility of tears is something these sensitive hearts never lose sight of.

> Je pleurais donc, et il n'y avait peut-être pas de meilleur expédient pour me tirer d'affaire, que de pleurer et de laisser tout là. Notre âme sait bien ce qu'elle fait, ou du moins son instinct le sait bien pour elle.[10]

Where others are assembled, the tears of the sensitive heart are always extremely contagious.[11] For Marianne herself the sweetest tears are the tears of sympathy that she sheds over the sorrows of others. Thus the "taste for tears," so conspicuous in mid-century, is already past the formative stage.[12] In life and literature weeping will soon be the favorite pastime of women. As de Goncourt says,

La femme veut être émue, émue jusqu'aux larmes. Elle est dans cette étrange situation morale qui a fait dire à Mme de Staël de sa mère: "Ce qui l'amusait était ce qui la faisait pleurer."[13]

In contrast to facile weeping, the sensitive heart may sometimes experience a kind of numbness, the result of conflicting emotions. Marianne describes this state as "une tristesse stupide"[14] to which the sensitive are especially prone because everything which happens to them touches them deeply. Marianne's feelings are often compounded of so many elements that it is impossible for her to give a name to all of them, in spite of her untiring efforts at self-analysis.[15]

The joy of the sensitive heart is as unrestrained as its sorrow. Transports and ecstasies form an essential part of its existence. Lovers especially are given to these sudden and uncontrollable impulses of joy. Marianne and Valville experience many of them during the shifting fortunes of their love.[16] In a brief moment Marianne runs a gamut of emotions.

> Je pleurai d'aise, je criai de joie, je tombai dans des transports de tendresse, de reconnaissance; en un mot, je ne me possédais plus, je ne savais plus ce que je disais: Ma chère mère, mon adorable mère! ah! mon Dieu, pourquoi n'ai-je qu'un coeur? Est-il possible qu'il y en ait un comme le vôtre? Ah! Seigneur, quelle âme! et mille autres discours que je tins et qui n'avaient point de suite.[17]

This exclamatory enthusiasm, never found in the plays, is rarer and less indiscriminate with Marianne than with the later heroines of sensibility. Faintings, from excess of either joy or grief, so frequent in Rousseau and other writers of the sensibility school, have little place in Marivaux. In the anonymous Part XII of *La Vie de Marianne* (not the Riccoboni *Suite*) the numerous and prolonged faintings, one lasting for five days, form a part of the continuator's tendency to exaggerate the manner of Marivaux. In the eleven authentic parts, Mlle Varthon, Marianne's rival, faints once, Marianne herself not at all.

Tears and transports are the superficial manifestations of the sensitive heart. A more constant state, at least in Marivaux, is a quiet but voluptuous enjoyment of one's feelings, whether of joy or sorrow. The emotions offer countless pleasures; a sensitive nature finds in itself the truest source of happiness. Rousseau speaks of a certain "contentement de soi-même,"[18] independent of fortune or of external events, the key

to which lies in one's sensibility. We have observed scattered instances
of this pleasure in Marivaux's early novel. Marianne and to a lesser
extent Jacob, no matter what the world has in store for them, always
manage to preserve this inner complacency. The possession of a deli-
cately responsive nature is a constant source of pleasure to them. As
Marianne enters Paris for the first time, she rejoices in the fullness of
her response to a new scene and in the harmony between her imagination and the objects that she sees. She savors in advance the experiences
that lie ahead. She is seized with an anticipatory joy at the sight of
a city as strange and new to her as "the empire of the moon."

> Je jouis de toute ma surprise: je sentis mes mouvements, je fus
> charmée de me trouver là, je respirai un air qui réjouit mes esprits;
> il y avait une douce sympathie entre mon imagination et les objets
> que je voyais, et je devinais qu'on pouvait tirer de cette multitude
> de choses différentes je ne sais combien d'agréments que je ne con-
> naissais pas encore; enfin il me semblait que les plaisirs habitaient
> au milieu de tout cela.[19]

Her sensibility insures for her the maximum degree of pleasure from
any agreeable situation. "Quelle agréable situation! D'un côté, Valville
m'idolâtrait; de l'autre, Mlle de Fare qui ne savait quelles caresses me
faire; et de ma part un coeur plein de sensibilité pour tout cela."[20]
For Marianne cultivation of the feelings is an aim as earnestly pursued as material success, and when fortune turns against her, she falls
back on the luxury of self-absorption. Deserted by her lover, deprived
of hopes of acquiring name and position, Marianne finds refuge in
admiring contemplation of "the movements of her soul." Another character of Marivaux's explains this experience as follows: "Je ne pleure
que parce que je m'attendris; mais mon attendrissement me fait plaisir,
et les larmes qu'il amène sont, en vérité, des larmes que je répands
avec goût."[21] In a case like this, sadness seems more nearly the result
than the cause of weeping.

When the experience is pleasant, simple enjoyment is not enough.
No element of the situation escapes examination and comment. It is
clear then that this early sensibility is something more than pure feeling. A generation just emerging from the domination of rationalism
does not at once shake off its habits of analysis. Marianne would say
with Epicurus that discrimination is necessary to the possession of
pleasure.

Sad emotions offer even greater opportunity for the dilations of the sensitive heart than happy ones. Ninon de Lenclos, a *coeur sensible* of an earlier time, exclaims: "C'est un cruel présent du ciel que l'excès de la sensibilité, et les choses de tendresse font plus souffrir qu'elles ne portent finalement de joie."[22] Mme de Lambert was aware of the extremes of sorrow as well as of happiness of which the sensitive heart is capable.[23] Marianne complains that suffering is the most unlimited of our powers.[24] It is this capacity for suffering which sends the older Marianne into melancholy retirement from the world.

> Mon Dieu! combien de douleur peut entrer dans notre âme! Jusqu'à quel degré peut-on être sensible! Je vous avouerai que l'épreuve que j'ai faite de cette douleur dont nous sommes capables est une des choses qui m'a le plus épouvantée dans ma vie, quand j'y ai songé; je lui dois même le goût de retraite où je suis à présent.[25]

But deep or superficial, the sorrows of the sensitive heart afford the victim a melancholy pleasure. Outward catastrophe there may be for the heroine of sensibility, but not the suffering that destroys the ego. Her plight may be pathetic, but never tragic. She can never be deprived of the satisfaction of suffering.[26] The Marquise of *La Deuxième Surprise de l'amour* is a young widow who has retired to the country to mourn in solitude. When Lisette tells her that solitude only increases sorrow, she replies, "My sadness pleases me."[27] She meets the Chevalier, likewise sad over a lost love. He tries to hide his grief, but she protests, saying that it does him honor, that she considers it a virtue in him.[28] The Chevalier will understand the callousness of her friends, who reproach her for mourning so deeply.

> Il n'y a plus de moeurs, plus de sentiment dans le monde. Moi, qui vous parle, on trouve étonnant que je pleure depuis six mois. . . . Vous êtes le seul qui rendrez justice à mes pleurs. Vous me ressemblez: vous êtes né sensible, je le vois bien.[29]

The companionship in sorrow of another sensitive heart gives her pleasure, providing a sympathetic witness to the beauty of her feelings.

> Tenez, depuis six mois je n'ai eu de moment supportable que celui-ci; et la raison de cela, c'est qu'on aime à soupirer avec ceux qui vous entendent.[30]

When fortune is unkind to Marianne, her first concern is not to remedy the situation but to savor her own sadness, bringing to light its every nuance. Like Clarice in the earlier novel, she is both tortured and fascinated by her rival's story; she takes a perverse pleasure in the completeness of her undoing.[31] The triumph of her rival is not a real humiliation; her suffering gives her a kind of dignity in her own eyes. The pride of sensibility is a protection against mischance almost as effective in the end as the calm of the stoic. Suffering loses its sting. It becomes something to be cherished, displayed. The sensitive heart indulges at times in a rhetorical grief which seems exaggerated to the modern‍ reader.[32] A wound to vanity may call forth the following pseudo-Racinian transport:

> Ah! je ne sçais où je suis; respirons. D'où vient que je soupire? Les larmes me coulent des yeux; je me sens saisie de la tristesse la plus profonde, et je ne sçais pourquoi.[33]

Sometimes the character threatens to die of sorrow and bring everlasting regret to those whom it fancies to be the cause of its grief.[34] Its self-sacrifice is grandiloquent:

> Non, madame, non, ma généreuse mère; non, M. de Valville, vous m'êtes trop chers tous les deux; je ne serai jamais la cause des reproches que vous souffririez si je restais, ni de la honte qu'on dit que je vous attirerais. Le monde me dédaigne, il me rejette; nous ne changerons pas le monde, et il faut s'accorder à ce qu'il veut.[35]

For the most part the sorrows of the sensitive heart are distinguished more by their multiplicity and variety than by their depth. They provide the play of shadow that makes for richness of the emotional life. "Que de douleurs!" cries Marianne. "Il m'en venait toujours de nouvelles."[36] Tranquillity is a rare mood among these responsive creatures, nor do they really wish it.

> Dans une situation comme la mienne, avec quelque industrie qu'on se secoure, on est sujette à de fréquentes rechutes, et tous ces petits repos qu'on se procure sont bien fragiles. L'âme n'en jouit qu'en passant, et sait bien qu'elle n'est tranquille que par un tour d'imagination qu'il faudrait qu'elle conservât, mais qui la gêne trop; de façon qu'elle en revient toujours à l'état qui lui est plus commode, qui est d'être agitée.[37]

There is even a friendly rivalry between Marianne and Mlle Tervire as to whose sorrows are the greater, Marianne remaining unconvinced until the nun has finished her lengthy tale.[38]

As M. Trahard has pointed out,[39] Marivaux anticipates the talent of Greuze and Diderot in constructing *tableaux* of sensibility, scenes of filial devotion, death-bed scenes, scenes of forgiveness and of farewell. Such scenes, rare in the plays,[40] are calculated to touch the reader and to allow him to indulge in one of the chief pleasures of the sensitive heart, a generous enjoyment of the·sorrows of others. When a character is virtuous as well as unfortunate, its plight is all the more affecting. Tales of virtue in distress, "wept over with great pleasure," had appeared in the *Tatler* and its successors in England and in Marivaux's *Le Spectateur français*. Like Richardson's *Pamela, La Vie de Marianne* is the expansion into a full length psychological novel of the basic plot situation of such tales as John Hughes' *Amanda*[41] and the story of the poor young girl in the fourth paper of *Le Spectateur français*.[42] Marianne, a penniless orphan of unknown parentage, presents a touching picture of virtue in distress, a fact of which she is well aware.

> Premièrement j'avais mon infortune, qui était unique; avec cette infortune, j'avais de la vertu, et elles allaient si bien ensemble! et puis j'étais jeune, et puis j'étais belle; que voulez-vous de plus? Quand je me serais faite exprès pour être attendrissante, pour faire soupirer un amant . . . je n'aurais pu y mieux réussir.[43]

The admiration that her sorrows and her virtues win her smooths her path wherever she goes. Her worldly fortune depends entirely on the appeal she makes to the sensitive hearts of others. The sisters in her convent fall in love with this afflicted beauty.

> Je leur dis ce peu de mots d'un air si plaintif et si attendrissant, on a quelquefois des tons si touchants dans la douleur, avec cela, j'étais si jeune, et par là si intéressante, que je fis, je pense, pleurer ces bonnes filles.[44]

The knowledge of the admiration she awakens softens her sorrows and makes them amenable to the uses of sensibility. In a moment when all happiness seems lost to her, she confesses that she is more touched than grief-stricken. Through her generosity, courage, and tears she has aroused the sensibilities of three other hearts, those most dear to her, whose distress she finds consoling.[45] She admits that she is weeping "moins par chagrin que par mignardise." Delighted with the pathetic picture she presents, she is at times inclined to dramatize it, not, she protests, to the detriment of truth, but only through the effectiveness of well-arranged details.

> Elle me confiait son affliction; et, dans l'attendrissement où nous étions toutes deux, dans cette effusion de sentiments tendres et généreux à laquelle nos coeurs s'abandonnaient, comme elle m'entretenait des malheurs de sa famille, je lui racontai aussi les miens, et les lui racontai à mon avantage. . . . Mon récit devint intéressant; je le fis de la meilleure foi du monde, dans un goût tragique; je parlai en déplorable victime du sort, en héroïne de roman, qui ne disait pourtant rien que de vrai, mais qui ornait la vérité de tout ce qui pouvait la rendre touchante, et me rendre moi-même une infortunée respectable.[46]

Virtue in distress is capable of moving all but the stoniest hearts. The touching picture that Marianne presents before the family of Valville, formidable men and women of the world, wins all save one crusty old lady, who admits that she is not particularly susceptible to "vertus romanesques."[47] In *Le Paysan parvenu* a young wife appears with her mother to plead that the position of her sick husband be retained for him. Her appeal seems to be in vain, but as she is moving tearfully away, one rude financier is touched by her distress and offers to befriend her. He says to the mother:

> Elle est gentille, votre fille, fort gentille. . . . J'aimerais assez sa figure; mais ce n'est pas à cause de cela que j'ai eu envie de la voir; au contraire, puisqu'elle est sage, je veux l'aider et lui faire du bien. Je fais grand cas d'une jeune femme qui a de la conduite, quand elle est jolie et mal à son aise; je n'en ai guère vu de pareilles; on ne fuit pas les autres, mais on ne les estime pas.[48]

Whether sorrowing or joyful, the sensitive heart finds pleasure in its feelings. In the pursuit of happiness it puts more trust in its own spontaneous movements than in rational control of the feelings. The plays of Marivaux present more cautiously than do the novels this creed of the heart, which makes its center of interest the passive life of sensations and not the active one of will and judgment. It is clear, especially from his mature writings, that reason and decorum play for him a secondary role in right living. They are correctives rather than guides. In those "born naturally good," that is, in the protagonists of his novels, the feelings can be trusted in almost all circumstances. The moral sense of the sensitive heart is the subject of another chapter. Here it remains to deal with the feelings as a guide to beauty and truth.

Among the graces of her sex which spring from sensibility, Mme de Lambert mentions taste, "un goût fin pour juger des choses de l'agrément."[49] Taste is more a matter of sentiment than of intelligence, she feels; hence to account for it rationally or to persuade others of its rightness is often difficult. Taste for her is concerned largely with social relationships ("agrément" she makes synonymous with "sentiment, bienséance, délicatesse, ou fleur d'esprit"), matters so delicate and imperceptible as to escape fixed rules. Taste is a natural gift which enables one to perceive unhesitatingly, without any effort of reason, the essential quality of everything.[50] Natural taste gives rise to delicate sentiments; in society it assures an alert politeness which respects the *amour-propre* of others.

In Marivaux's writings the sensitive soul possesses a natural feeling for the delicate, the refined, and the beautiful. Silvia, Lucile, and Hortense prize this gift in themselves and look for it in others. Marianne is richly endowed with it. She is instinctively repulsed by grossness in manners and language. Introduced to the *lingère* Mme Dutour, she cringes before the tactless remarks of this woman and suffers inwardly from the crudities of the *petite bourgeoisie* among whom she is temporarily placed. She feels instinctively that she was made for something better.[51] On her first introduction to Parisian society, she feels immediately at home. She perceives at once and is able to respond to all the refinements of this sophisticated group. "Si je n'avais pas eu un peu de goût naturel," she says, "un peu de sentiment, j'aurais pu m'y méprendre, et je ne me serais aperçue de rien."[52] From her earliest days in Paris, her "delicate soul" was well aware of its vocation, "le monde," and ready to unfold naturally in a group which would appreciate the taste and refinement of feeling that were hers.

> Je ne connaissais personne à Paris, je n'en avais vu que les rues, mais dans ces rues il y avait des personnes de toute espèce; il y avait des carrosses, et dans ces carrosses, un monde qui m'était très nouveau, mais point étranger. Et sans doute, il y avait en moi un goût naturel, qui n'attendait que ces objets-là pour s'y prendre; de sorte que, quand je les voyais, c'était comme si j'avais rencontré ce que je cherchais.[53]

This natural taste serves the sensitive heart not only in social relationships but also in the appreciation of beauty. Though his place among eighteenth-century estheticians is not a conspicuous one, Marivaux's ideas are significant because they show how far-reaching is his conception of the uses of sensibility, and also because they set him apart to some extent from his friends Fontenelle and La Motte, with whom he has been mistakenly classed as a "geometrician" in matters of taste.[54] In the early eighteenth century the classic ideals of order and regularity were still adhered to in the larger literary forms. At the same time painting and the minor types of literature showed a tendency to greater suppleness; lightness and grace took the place of a more formal beauty. The period of the Baroque gave way to the Rococo; Watteau replaced Poussin. This was a part of the general reaction against the tradition of the *grand siècle*, already observed in the manners of the time. In the field of art appreciation, reaction from classical formalism shifted the emphasis from intellectual to intuitive and emotional response. A work of art is to be judged not according to an arbitrary standard of excellence but according to its appeal to the sensibilities of the individual. Beauty is manifold and can best be perceived by a fresh and lively sensibility. In the place of the *beau idéal* we have the *je ne sais quoi*.[55]

Marivaux's explanation of the *je ne sais quoi* is set forth in a graceful allegory found in the second *feuille* of *Le Cabinet du philosophe*.[56] For him it is "that charm of face and figure which makes a person attractive without one's knowing exactly why."[57] Classic beauty is always the same; its appeal is to the mind, which it satisfies through its orderliness. The *je ne sais quoi* is less uniform and more touching. Its appeal is to the heart.

> Dans tout ce que vous apercevez ici de simple, de négligé, et d'irrégulier même, d'orné ou de non orné, j'y suis, je m'y montre, j'en fais tout le charme. . . . Je suis le *Je ne sais quoi* qui touche dans les deux sexes: ici le *Je ne sais quoi* qui plaît en peinture; là le *Je ne sais quoi* qui plaît en architecture, en ameublements, en jardins, en tout ce qui peut faire objet de goût. Ne me cherchez point sous une forme, j'en ai mille, et pas une de fixe. . . .[58]

The *je ne sais quoi* then is grace or charm, rather than absolute beauty. Its essence is whatever is most individual and almost incommunicable in the impressions we receive from certain objects. Unattainable through the intelligence, it is another possession of the sensitive heart. The Abbé

Du Bos, in his *Réflexions sur la poésie, la peinture et la musique* (1719), defines taste as a sixth sense, commonly called "sentiment," localized in the heart.[59] To appreciate the beautiful, one must yield to sentiment, to the promptings of this sixth sense. Reason comes afterward and serves only to confirm and refine the judgments of the heart. Marivaux follows Du Bos in upholding the heart as esthetic guide. In *Le Spectateur français* he describes a certain dinner followed by the presentation of a tragedy. A gentleman beside him found fault with the play, though his eyes were wet with tears, "in such a way that his heart opposed the verdict of his mind." Two ladies hastened to agree with him, their tears also belying their words. Marivaux says:

> Moi-même, je l'avoue, j'avais quelquefois envie de désapprouver des choses qui me faisaient beaucoup de plaisir. Si c'est un défaut que de plaire ainsi, je vous le laisse à juger. Mais pour moi, je crois que notre esprit n'est qu'un mauvais rêveur, toutes les fois qu'en pareil cas il n'est pas de l'avis du coeur.[60]

Jacob's first concert, like Marianne's first dinner party, shows the intuitive response of the sensitive heart in matters of taste. This is an important event in Jacob's career because it reveals to him his *âme sensible*, which becomes the source of the happiness of his life.

> Un coup d'archet me rendit à moi-même, ou, pour mieux dire, saisit tous mes sens, et vint s'emparer de mon âme. Je m'aperçus alors, pour la première fois, que mon coeur était sensible. Oui, la musique me fit éprouver ces doux saisissements que la véritable sensibilité fait naître.[61]

This revelation of beauty transcends all experiences of the heart which he has previously known.

> Rien n'avait donc encore découvert en moi cette facilité à se laisser aller aux impressions que doit naturellement causer le vrai beau, quand la musique, en frappant mes oreilles, s'empara de mon âme et la réveilla; car c'était la première fois que je pouvais à loisir entendre, sentir et goûter son harmonie.[62]

The impressions he receives are so rapid and so varied that he is unable to retrace them. He knows only that this experience is one of pure felicity. It is entirely emotional. He has the natural esthetic sense of the sensitive heart.[63]

The heart is also a reliable guide to truth, truth as to ourselves, as to others, perhaps also as to the mysteries of the universe. This "substitution of feeling for logic," of which Rousseau is the most striking exponent, has always been the practice of the sensitive soul.[64] Duclos says: "Elles [les âmes sensibles] ont encore un avantage pour la société, c'est d'être persuadées des vérités dont l'esprit n'est que convaincu."[65] Marivaux is too much the product of the age of reason to accept without reserve an affective theory of knowledge, but to Marianne at least—perhaps because she is a woman—he does give non-rational powers of discernment. She often has a kind of mystic experience, an effortless revelation of truth, so complete and yet so delicate as to be almost inexpressible. After describing Mme de Miran and Mme Dorsin, for whom her admiration knows no bounds, Marianne declares that her analysis of character can give only a limited idea of her esteem for these two women who have befriended her. Her deepest insight into character is incommunicable.

> On ne saurait rendre en entier ce que sont les personnes; du moins cela ne me serait pas possible. . . . Il y a des choses en elles que je ne saisis point assez pour les dire, et que je n'aperçois que pour moi, et non pas pour les autres. . . . Ce sont des objets de sentiment si compliqués et d'une netteté si délicate qu'ils se brouillent dès que ma réflexion s'en mêle. . . . Il me semble que mon âme, en mille occasions, en sait plus qu'elle n'en peut dire, et qu'elle a un esprit à part, qui est bien supérieur à celui que j'ai d'ordinaire.[66]

This superior wisdom of the heart serves also in understanding oneself. Though she disclaims all pretense to philosophy, Marianne adopts the tone of Mme de Lambert when she says:

> Je pense, pour moi, qu'il n'y a que le sentiment qui nous puisse donner des nouvelles un peu sûres de nous, et qu'il ne faut pas trop se fier à celles que notre esprit veut faire à sa guise, car je le crois un grand visionnaire.[67]

The characters of the plays, as we shall see, are more reluctant to accept this intuitive knowledge, pride and reason having to be overcome before they admit what the heart has long indicated to be true. This lay mysticism is the creed of the sensitive heart. Julie, a *coeur sensible* of a later day, less prudent and reserved than Marianne, is more persuaded of the infallibility of intuitive knowledge.

Je me suis souvent trouvée en faute sur mes raisonnements, jamais sur les mouvements secrets qui me les inspirent, et cela fait que j'ai plus de confiance à mon instinct qu'à ma raison.[68]

Marivaux's sensitive hearts show surprisingly little religious feeling. He appears to share the distaste of the average man of the Enlightenment for religious "enthusiasm." Such zealotry in his minor characters is almost invariably exposed as hypocrisy.[69] The chief concern of Marianne and Jacob, as for the characters of the plays, is worldly happiness. It is the goal envisioned by Mme de Lambert for her children, a plan for success so ambitious as to shock the gentle Fénelon, her spiritual adviser.[70] The convent in which Marianne is placed has the aristocratic atmosphere of the fashionable eighteenth-century cloister. Marianne, like Mme de Lambert, is inclined to accept religion as one of the conventions of the society in which she moves. During the one church service described in the novel she is occupied exclusively in winning the admiration of the men and the envy of the women. In this she reflects faithfully the milieu with which Marivaux was familiar.

Marivaux himself, in *Le Cabinet du philosophe*, advocates a religion of the heart.

> En fait de religion, ne cherchez point à convaincre les hommes; ne raisonnez que pour leur coeur: quand il est pris, tout est fait. Sa persuasion jette dans l'esprit des lumières intérieures, auxquelles il ne résiste point.[71]

The passage which follows clarifies Marivaux's attitude toward the relationship of the reason and the feelings as guides to truth. Reason is not scorned as "that false secondary power by which we multiply distinctions." Marivaux simply divides the field of knowledge between the heart and the head. There are some truths, particularly religious truths, which offend the "little logic" of the head. If they are to be comprehended, they must first be impressed upon the heart.

> Il y a des vérités qui ne sont pas faites pour être directement présentées à l'esprit. Elles le révoltent, quand elles vont à lui en droite ligne; elles blessent sa petite logique; il n'y comprend rien; elles sont des absurdités pour lui.
>
> Mais faites-les, pour ainsi dire, passer par le coeur, rendez-les intéressantes à ce coeur; faites qu'il les aime. Parce qu'il faut qu'il les digère, qu'il les dispose, il faut que le goût qu'il prend pour elles

les développe. Imaginez-vous un fruit qui se mûrit, ou bien une fleur qui s'épanouit à l'ardeur du soleil; c'est là l'image de ce que ces vérités deviennent dans le coeur qui s'en échauffe, et qui peut-être alors communique à l'esprit même une chaleur qui l'ouvre, qui l'étend, qui le déploie, et lui ôte une certaine roideur qui lui bornait sa capacité, et empêchait que ces vérités ne le pénétrassent. . . .

Il faut bien qu'il passe alors entre l'esprit et le coeur un mouvement dont il n'y a que Dieu qui sache le mystère. Est-ce que la persuasion de l'un serait la source des lumières de l'autre? . . . C'est en aimant que notre âme rentre dans le droit qu'elle a de connaître.[72]

Those who have this knowledge of God acquired through love cannot communicate it by language to the human reason of others.

Cet esprit humain est à terre, et il faut voler pour aller là.

Ceux qui aiment Dieu communiquent pourtant ce qu'ils en savent à ceux qui leur ressemblent; ce sont des oiseaux qui se rencontrent dans les airs.[73]

In his personal religious beliefs Marivaux seems to follow the path leading to Rousseau, but his characters are too much absorbed in the affairs of this world to be concerned with religion except, perhaps, as Mme de Lambert suggests, as a consolation *sur le retour*.

We have noted several general characteristics of the sensitive heart as portrayed by Marivaux: the inclination to give free expression to the emotions, the love of feeling for its own sake, the reliance on feeling as a guide to truth and beauty. It remains to study the characters of the plays and novels in respect of attitude toward self, behavior in love, and moral theory and practice.

IV

AMOUR-PROPRE

"L'amour-propre, à parler exactement, n'est point une qualité qu'on puisse aug-
menter ou diminuer. On ne peut cesser de s'aimer, mais on peut cesser de se mal
aimer." *L'Encyclopédie*, "Amour-propre," l'Abbé Yvon, II, 419.

ONCE THE BEAUTY of the feelings and their efficacy in the pursuit of
happiness have been acknowledged, once the ideal of the sensitive heart
has been accepted, it becomes a point of pride to maintain the integrity
of this character. The man of reason and the man of feeling share a
sense of innate worth, but whereas the pride of the former is based
on conformity to objective standards, the pride of the latter is based
on singularity. The man of feeling has a lively sense of his own uniqueness.[1] His pride, or as Marivaux more frequently terms it, his *amour-
propre*, is hence in the foreground of his sentiments, each of which
gives him a thrill of self-satisfaction. In this way arises a sensibility
of self-love, which in Marivaux's writings is as delicate and various in
its turns as the sentiments with which his young lovers regard each
other.

The influence of *amour-propre* upon conduct, long recognized by
preachers and moralists, likewise formed the theme of *bels esprits* and
précieuses, who made a society game of revealing each other's weaknesses in this respect. Marivaux, far from seconding the warnings of
Bossuet and Fénelon, holds with other advocates of lay morality that
amour-propre may be a force for good and that its lighter aspects add
much to the charm of social relationships. An examination of the
various manifestations of *amour-propre* in Marivaux will aid in an
appraisal of the quality of his sensibility. This chapter deals primarily
with *amour-propre* in the novels, Marivaux's treatment of it in his
theatre being the subject of a later chapter.

Mme de Lambert cautions her son against the "violent desire to
please" which she declares is inborn in women and lays its snare in
unpredictable places.[2] The older Marianne, who regards frankness as
a privilege of advancing years, confirms Mme de Lambert's judgment
on her sex. "There is no pretty woman," she says, "who has not a rather
too great desire to please."[3] In other contexts, where she is not warning her son, Mme de Lambert tends to adopt a reminiscent and indulgent attitude toward the vanity of pleasing.

Pour celles qui ont de la beauté et des agrémens, elles jouissent

des avantages de leur propre figure et de l'impression qu'elles font
sur les autres . . . il n'y a guère de femme aimable qui n'ait joui
de ces triomphes secrets. De plus, quelle source d'amusemens ne four-
nit pas l'envie de plaire![4]

When it fails a woman, she is in desperate straits, as Lisette points
out to the Marquise, a widow of one month, who refuses to look at
her mirror: "Quoi! votre amour-propre ne dit plus mot, et vous n'êtes
pas à l'extrémité! Cela n'est pas naturel, et vous trichez. . . ."[5] Mali-
cious or ingenuous, vanity is an instinctive motive, to which all issues are
finally referred. Marianne is deeply convinced of the innate coquetry
of her sex. She says again, "This pride of ours, we do not learn it, we
are born with it. Nature is ahead of education."[6] But though it is instinctive, it is followed quickly, as in the case of sympathy, love, pity,
and gratitude, by the analysis characteristic of Marianne. Marivaux
does not confine *amour-propre* to one sex (Jacob's career is proof of
that), but he is an authority on its nature in women.

No incident in Marivaux's rather colorless life is better known than
the mirror episode, an experience of his seventeenth year, which he
recounts himself in the first paper of *Le Spectateur français*.[7] Attracted
to a young girl whose wisdom and apparent artlessness delight him, he
leaves her momentarily, only to find her, on his return, practicing her
arts before a mirror. "How simple I was in those days!" he exclaims.
From this revelation of feminine artifice he dates his "misanthropy,"
a word which certainly cannot be taken in its literal sense. In the eighteenth essay of *Le Spectateur* he enlarges upon this early experience,
describing once more a coquette before her mirror, where she expends
great resources of taste and attention on details of her toilet. "Observe
how petty is this soul," he comments, "who is never so judicious and
who never examines anything so closely, as on an occasion of so little
importance."[8] Marivaux's misanthropy probably represents a determination not to be duped twice by such behavior. Hence from this early
experience may date his absorbing interest in the motives of women.

In 1722, the year of this *Spectateur* paper, Marivaux produced *La
Surprise de l'amour*, which is perhaps one of the most personal of his
plays. Its leading character holds views similar to those expressed by
him in the "mirror" episode, combining, as does Marivaux, a distrust
of women with an absorbing interest in them. The important role in
this play is a masculine one, the hero being even more carefully studied

than the heroine, a situation not common in Marivaux. Lélio is an
embittered lover who, after his mistress deserts him, retires to the country to nurse his broken heart. The fact that even in seclusion thoughts
of women often disturb him only strengthens his resolve to avoid his
tormentors. Woman, he says, is like a poisonous snake, with the difference that the viper kills its victim, whereas woman leaves hers to suffer
a thousand tortures, from which death would bring welcome relief.[9]
With his bitterness is mingled a reluctant admiration of woman's natural coquetry, beside which man's love-making seems clumsy and
inept.[10] But Lélio's long discourses on the winning arts of women always end with the warning note:

> Le moyen de se voir adoré sans que la tête vous tourne! Pour moi,
> j'étais tout aussi sot que les autres amants; je me croyais un petit
> prodige, mon mérite m'étonnait: ah! qu'il est mortifiant d'en ra-
> battre. C'est aujourd'hui ma bétise qui m'étonne: l'homme prodi-
> gieux a disparu, et je n'ai trouvé qu'une dupe à sa place.[11]

Arlequin echoes his master's sentiments in blunter terms. To the maid
Columbine he says that he and his master have come to the country
"pour ne pas tomber dans vos pattes, race de chattes que vous êtes."[12]
He adds, "Et malgré tout cela, il ne s'en faut de rien que je ne t'aime.
La sotte chose que le coeur de l'homme."[13] In the ambivalent attitude
toward women of Lélio and Arlequin one is tempted to see a reflection
of Marivaux himself after the "mirror" experience. Like Lélio, he
was wary of but at the same time fascinated by the arts of women. "Il
faut avouer," Lélio sighs, "que les bizarreries de l'esprit d'une femme
sont des pièges finement dressés contre nous."[14]

In spite of his early distrust of the sex, Marivaux is not a woman-
hater. Writing at a later date (1734), he is sympathetic even toward
coquetry, justifying it on the ground that woman's position in society
renders it necessary. She has nothing else to occupy her, no other way
of succeeding in a competitive marriage market and of assuring her
future. If she is a coquette, it is men who have made her so.

> Notre coquetterie fait tout notre bien. Nous n'avons point d'autre
> fortune que de trouver grâce devant vos yeux. Nos propres parents
> ne se défont de nous qu'à ce prix-là; il faut vous plaire, ou vieillir
> ignorées dans leurs maisons. . . . Nous ne sortons du néant, nous
> ne saurions vous tenir en respect, faire figure, être quelque chose,
> qu'en nous faisant l'affront de substituer une industrie humiliante,

et quelquefois des vices, à la place des qualités, des vertus que nous
avons. . . .[15]

To understand all is to forgive all. Yet Marivaux never desists from
exposing the vanity of women. One of his characters says: "My dear!
if I have four lovers, I have for myself a love equal to all that which
they have for me."[16] Marianne observes that most women have a dual
mind, one which serves to reason and which learns only through time
and experience, and another present in all women, no matter how
stupid they are in other ways. "This," she says, "is the intelligence be-
stowed upon us by the vanity of pleasing, in other words, coquetry."
It is dependent neither on years nor on instruction, for it is "a child
of pride, born full grown." "I think it may be taught grace and ease,"
she continues, "but it learns only the form and never the fundamentals.
That is my opinion."[17]

The vanity of pleasing is an unremitting instinct, present even in
unhappy situations. When Marianne faces the hostile group of Valville's relatives, and again when she learns of Mlle Varthon's treachery
and of her lover's unfaithfulness, *amour-propre* is her solace.

> Dans quelle affliction que nous soyons plongées, notre vanité fait
> toujours ses fonctions; elle n'est jamais en défaut, et la gloire de
> nos charmes est une affaire à part dont rien ne nous distrait.[18]

Even when a woman has renounced love, as Marivaux's women sometimes do, they do not renounce being lovable. One of his Marquises
remarks: "Je ne veux point me marier; mais je ne veux pas qu'on me
refuse."[19]

Coquetry, or vanity in action, is an aspect of *amour-propre* which
Marivaux never tires of studying. One of his youthful coquettes defines
it as "the preference I give to the pleasure of being loved, over that of
loving."[20] The pleasure of provoking admiration brings some of the
keenest satisfactions of feminine existence. "Men talk of science and
philosophy," says Marianne. "What are they in comparison with the
science of placing a ribbon properly or of deciding as to its color!"[21]
The opportunities of coquetry are endless and absorbing. "My heart
throbbed at the thought of how pretty I was going to be!"[22] It may
continue to afford delight even when one is genuinely in love.

> Je te jure enfin que mon amant ne m'est jamais plus cher, que
> quand je me suis prouvée qu'il ne tient qu'à moi de lui donner des

rivaux. A leur égard, je ne les aime point, ce me semble: cependant ils me plaisent; mon amour-propre a de l'inclination pour eux; mais je sens bien confusément qu'eux et mon coeur n'ont rien à démêler ensemble.[23]

Coquetry can be ruthless too, as when Marianne exults in her triumph over the other women in church. "I enter, I am seen, and all those other faces become nothing at all; not the memory of a single one remains."[24] Valville, on an unexpected visit to the convent, sees Marianne *en négligé*, wearing a plain dress and crumpled linen. Coquetry quickly turns the situation to advantage, for Marianne reflects that her natural graces have full chance to display themselves, that her charms are entirely her own, unaided by an elaborate toilet.[25] But when Mme de Miran requests her to dress for a party, this opportunity gives her satisfaction, for it enables her to "practice her coquetry through obedience."[26] The skillful coquette should have no difficulty in holding her lover's affections. Marianne boasts about this, prematurely. Capricious, serious, tender, or retiring, she can hold captive the most inconstant male, for she knows how to be "several women in one." She continues: "I duped his inconstancy, because every day I renewed for him his mistress; and it was as if he had another."[27] Here indeed are the "secret pleasures" praised by Mme de Lambert. Knowing how deeply they are ingrained in woman's nature, she opposed the stand of Fénelon, who would have women renounce coquetry and cultivate modesty and domestic virtues.[28]

The mode of sensibility, reflected in the works of Marivaux, brought changes in the manners of coquetry. To be acknowledged a "sensitive soul" became the highest form of flattery.

> Sensible,—c'est cela seul que la femme veut être; c'est la seule louange qu'elle envie. Sentir et paraître sentir, voilà l'intérêt et l'occupation de sa vie; et elle ne s'extasie plus sur rien que sur le sentiment dont elle a, dit-elle, "plus besoin que de l'air qu'elle respire."[29]

A woman's tears, her pity, her generous impulses, all added to the picture she wished to present to the world. Passages quoted earlier[30] show that Marianne not only is but wishes to be regarded as a *coeur sensible*. The sincerity of her feelings does not exclude awareness of their attractiveness and efficacy. Her sensibility is tempered by the irony of the self-acknowledged coquette. In this respect she differs from other heroines of sensibility, from the Pamelas and the Julies, to whom any suspicion that their display of feelings is encouraged by the vanity of pleasing would be odious. Marianne has not yet discarded the social graces, the perspicacity, the irony, of the older generation in favor of the *bourgeois* innocence of the new. With Rousseau, a show of emotion is a proclamation of natural goodness. The creator of Marianne, not yet wholly committed to this view, allows his heroine to admit the influence on her conduct of *amour-propre*, of a desire to attain her ends by tastefully dramatic means.[31] While insisting on the sincerity of her sentiments, she recognizes their usefulness in a crisis. Her coquetry, designed to draw attention to her beautiful soul, is frankly motivated by the eternally feminine desire to please and attract a lover, benefactor, or friend.

The vanity of pleasing and coquetry are timeless; they are not the exclusive privilege of the heroine of sensibility. Only in the direction they take, in maintaining before the world an illusion of oneself as a *coeur sensible,* are they determined by the character. Another aspect of *amour-propre* in Marivaux, which I have called the "sensitive ego," does, however, belong to the character; only in the *coeur sensible* would one expect to find a self-love so intricate in design and so sensitive to stimuli as Marianne's. The sensitive ego reveals itself in several ways: in pique or "touchiness" resulting from an exaggerated sense of inviolable personal dignity, in susceptibility to flattery, and in elaborate measures to restore self-esteem after an affront.

The sensitive ego is prone to take offense at some real or fancied unkindness or disrespect. Slights, the exposure of one's personal affairs, slander, even indelicacy in extending aid—all these, whether real or imagined, are forms of torture to the sensitive ego. Marivaux himself suffered keenly from this type of sensibility and was quick to discern it in others. D'Alembert says of him: "Sensitive and even touchy in company . . . he forgot too often for his own happiness one of his favorite maxims: One must possess enough *amour-propre* not to reveal that one has much."[32] Marmontel describes him in the salon of Mme de Tencin as visibly anxious for his subtleties and *bons mots* to have a telling effect on the group.[33] Marmontel also recounts a life-long grudge which Marivaux held against him, the origin of which was Marivaux's delusion, on seeing several people smiling and whispering together, that he was the subject of their conversation.[34] Fontenelle, his most intimate friend, was obliged to ward off Marivaux's quick sensibilities with the remark, "M. de Marivaux, don't be in a hurry to get angry when I talk about you."[35] Collé and Grimm add their testimony as to his quickness to take offense and the difficulty, especially in his old age, of easy social intercourse with him.[36] At the same time several of his acquaintances speak of his solicitude for the feelings of others.[37]

Marivaux was aware of his sensitiveness to criticism, particularly in regard to his writings. He explains a long interruption between issues of *Le Spectateur français* as due to his mortification over the indifference of the public.

> Soupçonnerait-on un contemplateur des choses humaines, un homme âgé, qui doit être raisonnable: tranchons le mot, un philosophe, le soupçonnerait-on de s'être dégoûté d'écrire, seulement parce qu'il y a des gens dans le public qui méprisent ce qu'il fait? Voilà pourtant l'origine de mon dégoût: n'est-ce pas là un louable motif de silence? Quelle misère que l'esprit de l'homme![38]

His description of a *bel esprit*, absurdly apprehensive as to the impression he is making, is an instance of his ability to recognize the trait in others.

> Un bel esprit en pareil cas est si ombrageux; sa vanité lui donne des méfiances si subtiles; il est si sensible au moindre soupçon qu'il a qu'on ne l'estime point assez; et ce soupçon, il le prend sur si peu de chose, qu'il ne faut qu'un geste pour irriter sa superbe délicatesse.[39]

It is not surprising that Marivaux's leading characters possess a highly developed self-esteem and in many cases the touchiness that often goes with it. Marianne suffers keenly from what she calls her "miserable vanity." "There was such a gap," she sighs, "between my appearance and my humble condition."[40] We understand on these grounds her determination not to reveal to Valville the humiliating fact of her residence with Mme Dutour.[41] But she suffers from loss of dignity even in the eyes of an inferior (Valville's valet has followed her to learn where she lives):

> Il est vrai que ce n'était qu'un laquais; mais quand on est glorieuse on n'aime à perdre dans l'esprit de personne; il n'y a point de petit mal pour l'orgueil, point de minutie, rien ne lui est indifférent.[42]

She fears, moreover, the possible consequences of a slighting remark about her to Valville, since his pride too will have received a blow through the belief that he is in love with an unworthy person. Knowing the male ego, she says: "Adieu le plaisir d'avoir de l'amour, quand la vanité d'en inspirer nous quitte."[43] She would rather lose Valville forever, she declares, than suffer the loss of his respect.[44]

Marianne's touchiness over her humble origin is felt in other circumstances than in her love affair with Valville. It shows itself in connection with the benefactions of M. de Climal and leads to her discourse on the true nature of charity.[45] It appears in her convent life, where all the nuns and all the young girls admire her with the exception of one haughty young person, whose "catty" reference to her obscurity moves Marianne to tears of protest and self-justification.[46] Even with the servant Toinon she can bear no mention of her past.[47] Another example of her intolerance to such references is found in her speech to the abbess of the convent, who before Mme de Miran's intervention is inclined to turn Marianne away. The abbess offers her a purse, which she refuses with dignity, explaining that she is not yet a beggar.

> Non, ma mère, non, répondis-je d'un ton sec et ferme, je n'ai encore rien dépensé de la petite somme d'argent que m'a laissée mon amie, et je ne venais pas demander l'aumône. Je crois que, lorsqu'on a du coeur, il n'en faut venir à cela que pour s'empêcher de mourir, et j'attendrai jusqu'à cette extrémité; je vous remercie.[48]

This reluctance to accept aid, ungraciously offered, and thus admit dependence or obligation, is considered by Marianne an index of genuine elevation of soul. She ponders it with her usual acumen.

> D'où vient que les hommes ont cette injuste délicatesse dont nous parlions tout à l'heure? N'aurait-elle pas sa source dans la grandeur réelle de notre âme? Est-ce que l'âme, si on peut le dire ainsi, serait d'une trop haute condition pour devoir quelque chose à une autre âme? Le titre de bienfaiteur ne sied-il bien qu'à Dieu seul? Est-il déplacé partout ailleurs?[49]

Broadly speaking then, the justification for "touchiness" lies in the failure of most people to recognize worth as the true basis of rank, the snobbery which causes unmerited suffering among less privileged members of society. Marivaux's emphasis on this aspect of *amour-propre* becomes a part of his quiet but insistent protest against the social injustices of his day.

The sensitive ego is as responsive to flattery as it is open to offense. It is capable of an almost voluptuous gratification when respect is shown to it. Tervire, commenting on the indignities she received as a child, remarks: "A tout âge . . . on aime à se voir de la dignité avec ceux avec qui l'on vit. C'est de si bonne heure qu'on est sensible au plaisir d'être honoré."[50] Marianne, after being wounded by the crude and hypocritical charity of M. de Climal, responds warmly to Mme de Miran's kindness and appreciation. She repays this consideration for her *amour-propre* with transports of gratitude, which she explains as follows:

> C'est que notre âme est haute, et que tout ce qui a l'air de respect pour sa dignité la pénètre et l'enchante; aussi notre orgueil ne fut-il jamais ingrat.[51]

Fragile and exacting as the sensitive ego of a Marianne may appear in an indifferent world, it is not without protection. It cannot ward off injuries, but it is skillful in healing them. No matter how small or how great the wound, the appropriate remedy is always found. Sometimes chance aids the naturally strong convalescent powers of *amour-propre*. In one of the early sketches, for instance, Marivaux describes a young girl who learns that her lover's affections are turning elsewhere. For a whole hour, she says, she suffered intensely. The world seemed abandoned for her, a desert. Then guests arrive, the attentions of two young men repeople her world, and she experiences a gratifying resurgence of self-esteem.

> Je me sentis réconfortée, et je pris tant de courage dans cette soirée, que lorsque la compagnie sortit, je me félicitai de mes nouvelles conquêtes, sans me ressouvenir que trois heures avant, je regrettais la perte d'une. . . .[52]

The same technique of consolation is urged on Marianne by Mlle de Tervire after Valville's defection. Marianne's charms, which the nun enumerates, are indisputable. What is one lover more or less, especially one like Valville, who dishonors only himself by his inconstancy? "The least little sentiment of pride," pleads the nun, "joined to all I have just told you, is more than enough to console you."[53] And Marianne grasps at these arguments, to which she finds an echo in herself. "Others besides him shall love me, and they will teach him to esteem my heart."[54] Indeed, even when her sorrow is deepest, she offers an excellent example of the unremitting quality of feminine vanity and of its efficacy as a curative agent. A visitor arrives, sent by Mme de Miran, and Marianne congratulates herself that she has dressed with more than ordinary attention.

> Il est vrai que j'étais affligée; mais qu'importe? Notre vanité n'entre point là-dedans, et n'en continue pas moins ses fonctions: elle est faite pour réparer d'un côté ce que nos afflictions détruisent de l'autre, et enfin on ne veut pas tout perdre.[55]

Nor does Marianne by any means "lose everything." Even if other admirers were wanting—which is not the case—there would remain at the service of *amour-propre* the imagination, with all its subtlety and resourcefulness. Marianne takes the long view. In time, she feels, her grief will !end added charm and make her "more piquant than ever" in the eyes of her lover. Already her self-esteem is finding itself on firmer ground.

> Il me reverra . . . sous une figure qu'il ne connaît pas encore; ma douleur et les dispositions d'esprit où il me trouvera me changeront, me donneront d'autres grâces; ce ne sera plus la même Marianne.[56]

Thus far will *amour-propre* go in turning misfortune into profit. An interesting analogue can be found in Arnold's poem "A Modern Sappho," portraying a young woman who, when her lover abandons her, refuses to follow the example of her classic model and give way to despair, but counts on the enhancement of her attractions through suffering, together with time and his disillusionment with her rival, to bring him back to her arms.

> But deeper their voice grows, and nobler their bearing,
> Whose youth in the fires of anguish hath died.[57]

Marianne is spared the fires of anguish, but she makes the most of her pathetic situation. The sensitive ego, easily wounded, has remarkable powers of recuperation.[58]

Marivaux's preoccupation with *amour-propre* in its various aspects reflects his belief that it is the strongest of human motives, that its influence, whether for good or bad, is never negligible. He saw that the hurts inflicted upon *amour-propre* are the deepest of all. When through an unfortunate accident the fact of her former connection with Mme Dutour is made known to Valville's relatives, the disgrace is crushing to Marianne's sensibilities. She is powerless to control her emotions. "My tears and my sighs continued; I dared not raise my eyes, and I was like a person overwhelmed with grief."[59] The deepest hurt of all comes when Mlle Varthon tells Marianne of Valville's affection for her. Marianne cries out, "He never said anything so tender to me!" Mlle Varthon produces a letter from Valville. "He writes, but it is no longer to me!" Her heart, she says, is so crushed that she is for a long time stifled by her sighs.[60] Her recovery is due to the fact that the need of restoring her self-esteem is in the end stronger than the despair that might paralyze one less proud when deserted by a lover.

The compelling power of *amour-propre* is the theme adopted by Mme Riccoboni in her continuation of Marivaux's story of Marianne. The interplay between two *amour-propres*, Marianne's and Valville's, constitutes the entire scheme of her clever *Suite de Marianne* and gives it, in spite of occasional exaggerations, a genuine Marivaudian quality. There is no reason to suppose that the *Suite* is in any way a collaboration; yet Marivaux himself might well have written:

> Quoique l'amour-propre semble quelquefois négliger ses intérêts, il n'en est pas moins ardent à les soutenir. Il est l'âme de tous nos mouvements, il agit en secret; nous ne l'apercevons seulement pas, et souvent nous lui sacrifions intérieurement dans l'instant même où nous croyons l'immoler ou l'anéantir.[61]

As a power for good, *amour-propre* functions by creating a thirst for praise. Marivaux gives a number of instances of this social aspect of *amour-propre*, cynically recognized in La Rochefoucauld's statement: "La vertu n'irait pas si loin si la vanité ne lui tenait compagnie."[62] Through the power of flattery a grasping merchant can be made honest, at least for the moment. "On fait de l'homme tout ce qu'on veut par le moyen de son orgueil; il n'y a que la manière de s'en servir."[63] Again he describes the visit of a wife to her husband's mistress in an effort to win back his affection. The wife begins her appeal with a frank admission that her rival's charms are greater than her own and a plea that she be more merciful in her use of them. The ruse is entirely successful. The mistress finds the wife adorable, "a hundred times more beautiful than I am." She recognizes, however, that she has been taken in and remarks, "*Amour-propre*, when given its due, is so tender, so grateful, so modest. It repays whatever it receives."[64] Jacob says that his *amour-propre* is "gay and sociable," that he is never more charming and tender to his wife than when he has been flattered by some woman of rank.[65] After refusing a position offered him at the expense of Mme Dorville's sick husband, he is delighted to lunch in her company, partly because of her charm, but even more because of the opportunity to bask in the warmth of her gratitude. "It is pleasant," he says, "to be with people whose good will one so fully deserves."[66]

In an idle and effeminate society with no great issues to occupy its energies, *amour-propre* may afford a motive for the cultivation of sensibility. The history of salon society in seventeenth and eighteenth-century France might be written from the point of view of successive fictions of the ideal man, more or less consciously formulated, more or less successfully practiced. We have seen in Mme de Lambert, with whose salon Marivaux was associated, the growing emphasis on the cultivation of the feelings. "The true greatness of man is in the heart," she says.[67] Once such an ideal has been accepted, it becomes a matter of pride to realize it, at least in appearance. This deliberate pursuit of the refinements of feeling has led some critics to bring the charge of factitiousness against the sensibility movement in life and literature.[68] Even Marianne does not deny, with reference at least to others, that vanity may prompt a display of feeling. In accounting for the waning affection of Valville, she says that it is the fault of tender and delicate souls to relax their tenderness when an impression has been made. "The desire to please you provides them with infinite charms, forces them to exert themselves in ways which they find delightful; but as soon as they have pleased, they become indifferent."[69] There can be little doubt that in the social life of the eighteenth century the appearance of being an *âme sensible* often passed for the reality, and that the vanity of pleasing played a part in establishing the mode.

What begins in artifice and imitation, however, may become the thing itself. In his autobiography H. G. Wells points out, with acknowledgements to Jung,[70] that a *persona*, "the private conception a man has of himself, his idea of what he wants to be and of how he wants other people to take him," though it may start as a delusion of vanity, may eventually mold the personality to its likeness. "The mask, the *persona*, of the *Happy Hypocrite* became at last his true face."[71] Marianne's *persona*, her conception of herself as a sensitive heart, is firmly woven into the texture of her character. Her tenderness, unlike Valville's, does not relax once she has made an impression. Her touching expressions of gratitude and her generous acts are marked by a spontaneity that convinces the reader of their essential honesty.

In this very integrity of character of the sensitive heart lies the major source of gratification to *amour-propre*. In retrospect Marianne savors her sensibility with a thrill of pride. To look back on any lovely expression of her *persona* is her most constant source of pleasure, overcoming misfortune. Even self-sacrifice loses its sting in the recognition of its beauty. The exquisite adjustment of the flow of feeling to good fortune and to bad gives Marianne something akin to esthetic pleasure, though it lacks the detachment of the pure esthetic experience. She admires this beauty of emotional expression in others, but her richest satisfaction is admiring it in herself. This narcissism, or, as Rousseau called it, "contentement de soi-même," is perhaps the most distinctive characteristic of the *amour-propre* of the sensitive heart.

Marianne never tires of admiring the delicacy of her responses and her consideration for others, in small matters or great. When Climal brings her to the shop of Mme Dutour, she remarks fastidiously, "I felt in the frankness of that woman something gross which repelled me."[72] Repressing her pleasure over a new dress in order to avoid humiliating the servant girl Toinon, she reflects, "All my life my heart has been full of these little considerations for the feelings of others."[73] She prizes the warmth and beauty of her feelings above her physical attractiveness. "I was pleasing to the heart," she says, "and my least advantage was to be beautiful."[74] Her frequent gestures of renunciation in order to avoid embarrassment to others satisfy her ego. When Mme de Miran learns that Marianne is the one with whom her son is in love, Marianne offers to renounce him and enter a convent for life.

> D'ailleurs, je venais de m'engager à quelque chose de si généreux; je venais de montrer tant de raison, tant de franchise, tant de reconnaissance, de donner une si grande idée de mon coeur, que ces deux dames en avaient pleuré d'admiration pour moi. Oh! voyez avec quelle complaisance je devais regarder ma belle âme et combien de petites vanités intérieures devaient m'amuser et me distraire du souci que j'aurais pu prendre.[75]

Valville's infidelity gives her another opportunity for sacrifice. Loving him, she releases him from his obligations to her. This "generous vengeance," as she terms it, is highly gratifying to her, for never have her qualities of soul shown to greater advantage. Consciousness of the beauty of her conduct goes far to console her for the loss of a lover.

In adequate expressions of her "beautiful soul," Marianne finds the
greatest satisfaction to her *amour-propre*. All the qualities of heart she
rejoices in are inherent or develop very quickly and with no effort. It is
different with the hero of *Le Paysan parvenu*. The evolution of his
persona is perhaps the central interest in the novel. When he arrives in
Paris, his character is all to educate. He has no such unified and clearly
defined *persona* as Marianne's. He brings with him from the country
good looks, vivacity, good sense, honesty, and ingenuousness ("bon
coeur naïf"). Of these sound but rudimentary qualities he is sufficiently
proud. His appearance is especially pleasing to him.

> On se sent bien fort et bien à son aise, quand c'est par la figure
> qu'on plaît; car c'est un mérite qu'on n'a point de peine à soutenir
> ni à faire durer; cette figure ne change point, elle est toujours là;
> vos agréments y tiennent; et comme c'est à eux qu'on en veut, vous
> ne craignez point que les gens se trompent sur votre chapitre, et cela
> vous donne de la confiance.[76]

His good looks, his youth, and his amiability bring him many opportunities to better his station in life and to progress rapidly in his social
education, particularly through his associations with women. Gradually
we see the outlines of certain *personae* taking form. In his adventures
with the mistress under whom he first has employment in Paris and
with the servant girl Geneviève he is the "esprit gaillard,"[77] gay and
reckless, but already capable of generous impulses and with a primitive
sense of honor. His master tries to bribe him to marry a mistress.

> Allez, mon enfant, l'honneur de vos pareils, c'est d'avoir de quoi
> vivre, et de quoi se retirer de la bassesse de leur condition, entendez-
> vous?[78]

But Jacob rejects hotly this low estimate of his honor.

> Dans notre village, c'est notre coutume de n'épouser que des filles;
> et s'il y en avait une qui eût été femme de chambre d'un monsieur,
> il faudrait qu'elle se contentât d'avoir un amant; mais pour de mari,
> néant; il en pleuvrait, qu'il n'en tomberait pas un pour elle; c'est
> notre régime, et surtout dans notre famille. Ma mère se maria fille,
> sa grand'mère en avait fait autant; et de grand'mère en grand'mère,
> je suis venu droit comme vous voyez, avec l'obligation de ne rien
> changer à cela.[79]

Jacob's good luck in being elevated from a penniless street walker to a well-to-do bourgeois through his marriage of convenience to Mlle Habert disposes him to a demonstrativeness toward that lady which passes for love and in which he begins to discover his *bon coeur*. His gratitude and his natural vivacity make it easy for him to simulate tenderness.

> Rien ne rend si aimable que de se croire aimé; et comme j'étais naturellement vif, que d'ailleurs, ma vivacité m'emportait, et que j'ignorais l'art des détours, qu'enfin je ne mettais d'autre frein à mes pensées qu'un peu de retenue maladroite que l'impunité diminuait à tout moment, je laissais échapper des tendresses étonnantes; et cela avec un courage, avec une ardeur qui persuadaient du moins que je disais vrai; et ce vrai-là plaît toujours, même de la part de ceux qu'on n'aime point.[80]

Mlle Habert's reasonable doubts about the sincerity of this love prompt him to a touching eloquence which astonishes even himself.

> Hélas! de gaillard que j'étais, me voilà bien triste.
> Je me ressouviens bien qu'en lui parlant ainsi, je ne sentais rien en moi que démentît mon discours. J'avoue pourtant que je tâchai d'avoir l'air et le ton touchants, le ton d'un homme qui pleure, et que je voulais orner un peu la vérité; et ce qu'il y a de singulier, c'est que mon intention me gagna tout le premier. Je fis si bien que j'en fus la dupe moi-même, et je n'eus plus qu'à me laisser aller sans m'embarrasser de rien ajouter à ce que je sentais; c'était alors l'affaire du sentiment qui m'avait pris, et qui en sait plus que tout l'art du monde.[81]

His assurances are satisfactory to Mlle Habert, who estimates his character at this stage in his development as "open and gay," with a "coeur bon et sensible."[82] Thus we see emerging, partly through artifice and self-deception, another attitude, that of the *homme sensible,* adapted to social demands somewhat different from those to which the *esprit gaillard* responded. Strengthened in the process of his sentimental education, this *persona* loses its self-delusive character and its peasant rusticity, though not its *naïveté*. Commenting on his rush of sympathy for the unfortunate Mme Dorville, he remarks:

> Ce discours, quoique fort simple, n'était plus d'un paysan, comme

vous voyez; on n'y sentait plus le jeune homme de village, mais seulement le jeune homme naïf et bon.[83]

Still another conception of himself emerges, and an increment of
self-esteem, from the attentions he receives from aristocratic women.
His conquest of Mme de Ferval is especially flattering to his ego.

Une femme enfin qui nous tirait, mon orgueil et moi, du néant
où nous étions encore; car avant ce temps-là m'étais-je estimé quelque chose? Avais-je senti ce que c'était qu'amour-propre?[84]

From this amorous success he marks a new phase of his development.

Aussi étais-je dans un tourbillon de vanité si flatteuse; je me trouvais quelque chose de si rare! Je n'avais point encore goûté si délicatement le plaisir de vivre, et depuis ce jour-là je devins mécon-
naissable, tant j'acquis d'éducation et d'expérience.[85]

He begins to fancy himself as a cavalier; his sensuality has acquired a
varnish of refinement. And he sees open before him a career of gallantry.

The final accession to Jacob's personality is his notion of himself
as *honnête homme*, well-established in life, honored, generous, coura-
geous. This phase begins with his delight over the image of himself in
comfortable lodgings, garbed in handsome new slippers and dressing
gown, and reading a book.

Sur les trois heures après midi, vêpres sonnèrent; ma femme y alla
pendant que je lisais je ne sais quel livre sérieux que je n'entendais
pas trop, que je ne me souciais pas trop d'entendre, et auquel je ne
m'amusais que pour imiter la contenance d'un honnête homme chez
soi.[86]

This picture is completed when Jacob's courage is tested in the duel
in which he rescues the nobleman Dursan.

Oh! C'est ici que je me sentis un peu glorieux, un peu superbe;
mon coeur s'enfla du courage que je venais de montrer et de la
noble posture où je me trouvais. Tout distrait que je devais être
par ce qui se passait encore, je ne laissai pas d'avoir quelques moments de recueillement où je me considérais avec cette épée à la
main, et avec mon chapeau enfoncé en mauvais garçon; car je de-
vinais l'air que j'avais, cela se sent; on se voit dans son amour-propre,
pour ainsi dire; et je vous avoue qu'en l'état où je me supposais, je

m'estimais digne de quelques égards, et que je me regardais moi-même moins familièrement et avec plus de distinction qu'à l'ordinaire. Je n'étais plus ce petit polisson surpris de son bonheur, et qui trouvait tant de disproportion entre son aventure et lui. Ma foi! J'étais un homme de mérite, à qui la fortune commençait à rendre justice.[87]

The aftermath of this affair is no less gratifying. "Nouvelle fête pour mon coeur! On parlait de moi dans Paris comme d'un brave!"[88]

These elements of Jacob's character are never completely harmonized. He remains what Jung would call a "collective personality." The boisterousness of the *parvenu* frequently shatters the reserve of the man of honor. The cavalier sometimes renders the man of feeling suspect. His character lacks the fine consistency of Marianne's. Now one, now another *persona* is summoned to the fore by his quick perception of the demands of a situation. His several selves are dominated by his will to make an impression, to get ahead. His "gay and sociable vanity" is directed outward. He does not indulge in the introspective searchings that absorb Marianne. He experiences little or none of that brooding contentment which for her follows, as an end in itself, some manifestation of her "beautiful soul." Jacob regards his *personae* as instrumentalities. He is pleased with the discovery of some new resource in himself, but chiefly in respect to its usefulness in attaining something that he wants.

Though capable of many lively pleasures, avowed with an engaging frankness, the *amour-propre* of Jacob does not procure for him the rich satisfactions Marianne knows. She discovers within herself a new world, the world of the feelings, complex and various and yet with a self-contained artistic unity. Each fugitive pattern of her feelings is an end in itself, to be contemplated with a glow of pride, often conscious of but not dependent on spectators. Although it may be disturbed from without, this contentment with self quickly recovers through some new synthesis of self-admiration. Along with the pleasures of *amour-tendresse* and of benevolence—in which *amour-propre* likewise plays a part—the enjoyment of self, of one's own sensibility, is Marivaux's answer to the question of the moralists of his day: the sources of personal happiness.

AMOUR-TENDRESSE

"Il n'était pas amoureux, il était tendre. . . ."
La Vie de Marianne, G. 61; D.VI, 356.

Marivaux's treatment of love, which he held to be the absorbing interest of women, is one of his most original contributions to the literature of sensibility. Both shy and curious in feminine society, he was fascinated by the ways of women, pursuing openly and by subterfuge his observation of them. His preoccupation with the psychology of women in love prompted the charge of Voltaire: "Je lui reprocherais . . . de trop détailler les passions, et de manquer quelquefois le chemin du coeur, en prenant des routes un peu détournées."[1] Others, less keen to distinctions than Marivaux, have found in his analyses of love, particularly in the comedies, repetitiousness and monotony of theme. To this charge the author has replied:

> Dans mes pièces . . . c'est tantôt un amour ignoré des deux amants, tantôt un amour qu'ils sentent et qu'ils veulent se cacher l'un à l'autre, tantôt enfin un amour incertain et comme indécis, un amour à demi-né, pour ainsi dire, dont ils se doutent sans être bien sûrs, et qu'ils épient au-dedans d'eux-mêmes avant de lui laisser prendre l'essor. Où est en cela cette ressemblance qu'on ne cesse de m'objecter?[2]

Within their narrow frame there is no dearth of variety in the love comedies of Marivaux. The essays and novels present more fully his observations and his reflections, and contain, together with numerous sketches, one full-length portrait of a devotee of that peculiarly Marivaudian phase of sensibility known as *amour-tendresse*.

Various and finely nuanced as is its expression in Marivaux, *amour-tendresse* has a number of well-defined general characteristics which differentiate it from earlier portrayals of love in the French novel and theatre, as well as from later handlings of the theme in the eighteenth century. First of all, it is a prerogative of youth, an experience less possible when years have impaired the freshness and resilience of the feelings. *Amour-tendresse,* in its purest form, is adolescent love, a first experience, with its accompaniment of delight and confusion, of timidity and *élan*. Neither its self-awareness nor its eloquence can entirely hide its naïveté. Its piquancy, in fact, lies in a mingling of adolescent impulsiveness and boudoir sophistication. From a complex society Marianne has taken sophistication to embellish her love, not to corrupt or disillusion it. In youth, she says, the heart is "more advanced than the mind."[3] The grace of tender passion in the young is apparent to older persons, who view it with admiration. Mme de Ferval, long past her springtime, inquires of the youthful Jacob: "A propos de coeur, êtes-vous né un peu tendre? c'est la marque d'un bon caractère."[4] Marivaux depicts with evident sympathy the awakening of love in an unspoiled nature.[5] He dwells on the first moment of awareness in adolescent love, with its confusion of feelings impossible to the experienced.

> Son embarras me frappa, le mien l'intimida, parce qu'il le comprit; une intelligence mutuelle nous donna la clef de nos coeurs; nous nous dîmes que nous nous aimions, avant que d'avoir parlé; et nous en fûmes tous deux si étonnés, que nous nous hâtâmes de nous quitter, pour nous remettre.[6]

Again Marivaux shows us two young women, one already an accomplished coquette, the other a "sensitive soul," whose heart is "plus sage et plus neuf." The latter has always feared love as a peril; "but the peril has apparently pursued her, and as one flees slowly that which one flees reluctantly, it has overtaken her; she is in love."[7]

Another distinctive feature of *amour-tendresse* is its limitation to the softer feelings of tenderness, of sympathy and generosity, of pathos. It is not an elemental and destructive passion as with Racine's heroines or Manon's lover Des Grieux.[8] I have pointed out in discussing Clarice the rareness of tender heroines in the novels of an older period.[9] Protagonists of *amour-tendresse* are not torn by passion, nor are they ready for heroic exertion or extreme sacrifice. They prefer graceful and delicate sentiment to the fury of Venus. For the "coeur bien né" is ingenuous only within the limits of good taste. Marivaux's youthful lovers, though their hearts are fresh, are wise in the ways of the world, with a *savoir-vivre* in part instinctive and in part quickly learned from the society in which they move. A proud modesty marks their conduct, so that it is both eager and reticent, remaining within the conventions and always commanding respect.

A third characteristic of *amour-tendresse* is that, lacking the strength of passion, it also lacks its blindness. For in *amour-tendresse* mutual respect is essential to the progress of love. Considerations of dignity and worth receive due attention. One never falls in love with an unworthy person, though the object of love may be a person of lower rank. Valville is not concerned that Marianne's origin is obscure, but his love turns to disgust when he wrongly suspects that she is the mistress of M. de Climal. Throughout the course of Marianne's affair with Valville, her admirable character serves in lieu of noble birth and smooths the way for her against stubborn family prejudice. This recognition of the respect due to merit is in keeping with the tone of Mme de Lambert's salon. The same respect for goodness influences Jacob's friend M. de Dorsan in his suit of the poor but virtuous widow, Mme Dorville. Mme de Vambures, a duchess by birth, comments approvingly on this attachment which has sprung up in spite of differences in social position.

> La naissance est accidentelle à l'homme; mais une naissance qu'accompagne la vertu est digne des plus sincères hommages. . . . De pareils sentiments tiennent lieu de naissance, de beauté et de fortune. . . . Il n'y a rien de si précieux qu'on ne puisse, qu'on ne doive même sacrifier à une si noble façon d'aimer.[10]

And Mme de Vambures follows precept with example in marrying Jacob, thus making her conduct consistent with her earlier declaration.

> Ce ne sera point la disproportion des rangs qui gênera jamais mon inclination; si je me mariais un jour, je ne consulterais que mon coeur et celui de la personne pour laquelle le mien déciderait.[11]

In the matter of marriage between persons of unequal social rank, Marivaux seems to be much more democratic than his contemporary Richardson, who holds that while a man may ennoble by marriage a woman of humbler birth, a woman of the nobility only degrades herself by marrying below her station in life. After Pamela's marriage with Mr. B., his sister Lady Davers reproaches him:

> "Where can the difference be," she says, "between a beggar's son married by a lady, or a beggar's daughter made a gentleman's wife?"
> "Then I'll tell you," replied he; "the difference is, a man ennobles the woman he takes, be she who she will; and adopts her into his own rank, be it what it will; but a woman, though ever so nobly born, debases herself by a mean marriage, and descends from her own rank to his she stoops to."[12]

Richardson retains a romantic admiration for the upper classes, whereas Marivaux, like Mme de Lambert, considers the only real ground for esteem to be intrinsic worth. *Amour-tendresse* cannot exist without such esteem. The wealth and good birth and dubious reformation of Mr. B., which satisfied Pamela, would not have won Marianne.

Notwithstanding its moral and esthetic restraints, *amour-tendresse* is distinguished from *amour galant,* the rigidly patterned fashion of love of the seventeenth century, by its spontaneity. Marivaux's lovers are not the polite automatons of d'Urfé or of Mlle de Scudéry. One of his characters, formerly a devout reader of La Calprenède, has come to find those pompous lovers a bit boring.

> Mon coeur a déjà critiqué dans les amants de *Pharamond* des lenteurs, des timidités, des fiertés qui, autrefois, étaient tout à fait à mon goût. J'ai trouvé que ces gens-là s'amusaient trop à se respecter, à se fâcher ou à se plaindre; et que les meilleures occasions périssaient entre leurs mains. . . .[13]

The emotion of Marivaux's young lovers, however they seek to conceal it, is spontaneous, a *laisser-aller* of the heart, and they are under its spell as definitely, though not as tragically, as are the lovers of Racine. Mme de Lambert, bred to the seventeenth-century conventions, hinted nonetheless that the sensitive soul, in love, is at the mercy of the heart's impulses.[14] *Amour-tendresse* is a natural emotion, its trappings of artifice and propriety being, as we shall see with Marianne and with the heroines of the plays, in part a resort of youthful timidity, in part a device to enhance and preserve a fragile and valued possession. As it becomes a literary fashion in mid-century, it develops a ritual, the plan of which is contained in Stendhal's definition of *amour-goût.*

> C'est un tableau où, jusqu'aux ombres, tout doit être couleur de rose, où il ne doit entrer rien de désagréable prétexte, et sous peine de manquer d'usage, de bon ton, de délicatesse, etc. Un homme bien né sait d'avance tous les procédés qu'il doit avoir et rencontrer dans les diverses phases de cet amour; rien n'y étant passion et imprévu, il y a souvent plus de délicatesse que l'amour véritable, car il y a toujours beaucoup d'esprit. . . . Et, tandis que l'amour-passion nous emporte au travers de tous nos intérêts, l'amour-goût sait toujours s'y conformer. Il est vrai que, si l'on ôte la vanité à ce pauvre amour, il en reste bien peu de chose; une fois privé de vanité, c'est un convalescent affaibli qui peut à peine se traîner.[15]

Here love has become a society game, retaining the form of *amour-*

tendresse but not its essence. Stendhal finds this portrayal of love in the novels and memoirs of Crébillon, Lauzun, Duclos, Marmontel, Chamfort, and Mme d'Epinay, and places it a little past mid-century, about 1760.[16] For Marivaux the awakening of love and the course it will take are both unpredictable; there remains much of "passion et imprévu" in *amour-tendresse*. This is Marivaux's reply to the charge of monotony in his theatre. In the novels, Jacob goes through many adventures before experiencing this kind of love; Marianne recognizes it at once, only to lose it temporarily. Valville, through his susceptibility to beauty in distress, is able to repeat the experience, and Tervire's one meeting with it causes the sorrow of her life and likewise her only happiness. Each of these characters is a distinct personality, and Marivaux's careful examination brings out the variety in their response to the tender passion, as it does in the case of the lovers sketched more lightly in the plays and essays. Saintsbury, in his study of the novel of sensibility in France,[17] is unjust to Marivaux's heroine when he makes her the high priestess of a ritual of love copied by many lesser novelists of the sensibility school, particularly the women. He distorts the model in attempting to fit it to the contour of the copies, and the richness of Marianne's character, a compound of wisdom and caprice, of tenderness and perspicacity, is lost in the portrait of an accomplished coquette. To regard Marianne as the model of coquetry is a false simplification. Calculation has a part in her acts, but it is so closely allied to impulse that the two are inseparable. This alliance is resourceful, and the result of it cannot often be predicted. The Marianne of Marivaux is inimitable.

Living in an age in which love was made subservient to the pursuit of happiness,[18] Marivaux offers a specific for happiness in *amour-tendresse*. Although *amour-tendresse* offers no heights of feeling, it promises a diversity of agreeable sensations with a minimum risk of pain and disillusionment. The role of *amour-propre* is an important one in this gentle love-making. The desire to please is a powerful motive in all women.

> C'est le feu sacré qui ne s'éteint jamais: de sorte qu'une femme veut toujours plaire, sans le vouloir par une réflexion expresse. La nature a mis ce sentiment chez elle à l'abri de la réflexion et de l'oubli: une femme qui n'est plus coquette, c'est une femme qui a cessé d'être.[19]

But Marivaux distinguishes between the conduct of the indiscriminate coquette and the coquetry of the sensitive soul, of the "femme tendre." Of the latter he says:

Ce sont celles dont le coeur embrasse la profession du bel amour; leur esprit fourmille d'idées délicates; elles aiment en un mot plus par métier que par passion.[20]

In *amour-tendresse* whatever brings pleasure to the loved one brings pleasure to oneself, and so everything, from the display of a well-rounded arm or the clever arrangement of bows and ribbons to a gesture of modesty or self-sacrifice, serves to heighten the pleasure of an attachment. The ever-present desire to please calls upon all the resources of taste and sensibility; unlike the lust of the sensualist, it is insatiable.

Free from the violence of passion, *amour-tendresse* allows sufficient composure to taste every sensation. An early sketch published in the *Mercure* in 1717 describes the pleasure of a young girl in watching "the progress of her sentiments," in tasting and prolonging them, with an occasional glance at her mirror to assure herself of her charms. Her accustomed gayety has given way to revery. "I enjoyed a secret pleasure which occupied me so completely that it halted my frivolity; and to indulge in my day dreams, I forgot everything else."[21] Even the absence of the lover is not unpleasant. Sadness itself becomes a pleasure, for it serves as preparation for future happiness. "It offers an ever-ready supply of sweet reflections, which make me all the more disposed to happiness when I find it."[22] And finally, if all does not run smoothly, the heart can make a career of unrequited as well as of reciprocated love. Clarice, in *Les Effets,* and Marianne find a kind of gratification in the pathos of being unloved. Marivaux sums up the resources of these tender hearts: "An unfaithful lover brings their talents to light; without him one would never know that they have a thousand touching charms in every tender sorrow."[23]

The place of reason in *amour-tendresse,* though supplemental, is an important one. Indeed, his observation of the interaction of reason and emotion in love constitutes one of Marivaux's most original contributions to the literature of sensibility. The head is employed not to resist the heart's desire, as with the characters of Corneille, but rather to refine on it and draw out its full measure of sweetness. Occasionally it sounds a note of caution or restraint, so that the final yielding may give greater pleasure. In one of the early sketches a young girl exclaims:

Tu ne le croirais peut-être pas: mais rien ne nuit tant à l'amour que de s'y rendre sans façon. Bien souvent il vit de la résistance qu'on lui fait, et ne devient plus qu'une bagatelle, quand on le laisse en repos. . . . J'ai trouvé que la raison rend nos plaisirs plus chers en les condamnant.[24]

Sometimes the head plans an innocent ruse, designed to raise the lover's esteem or sharpen his desire. So Marianne chooses not to receive Valville when he calls at her convent, though she is impatiently waiting the decision as to their marriage. "This display of calculated prudence cost me dearly," she says,[25] but she knows too that Mme de Miran will be pleased by her discretion and Valville all the more ardent for the delay. In *Le Cabinet du philosophe* (1734) the mature Marivaux comments: "I have always been distrustful of passions which are extreme in the beginning; it is a bad omen for their permanence."[26] He continues:

> Les coeurs ardents et sensibles ne cessent bientôt d'aimer que parce qu'ils se hâtent trop et d'aimer et de sentir qu'ils aiment. Ils ne se donnent pas le temps de faire un fond.[27]

Most often in Marivaux the function of the head is to give a certain stability to emotion and by discrimination to assure the maximum of delight from an affair of the heart. Through his emphasis on the need of balance between reason and emotion, Marivaux's interpretation of love is psychological rather than lyrical. With his lovers, intense intellectual activity accompanies the awakening of the heart. We do not find in Marivaux Rousseau's capacity for lyric expression. Marianne, touched with seventeenth-century intellectuality, shows us the workings of her heart; Julie and Saint-Preux give us its song.

Toward the understanding of a further characteristic of *amour-tendresse,* it is necessary to look again briefly at the social life of Marivaux's day. We have seen that Marivaux's portrayal of love as tender emotion contrasts sharply with the prevalent conception of the sensuality of Regency society. The decline of the seventeenth-century ideal of decorum in the last years of the Grand Monarch continued during the interregnum and by no means halted with the accession of Louis XV. The frank voluptuousness of the eighteenth century ("its atmosphere and its breath, its element and its inspiration, its life and its genius," says de Goncourt[28]) lived in the persons of the Duc d'Orleans and his sister, found foothold in the notorious Société du Temple, and was reflected in both public and private life. But in full Regency appeared the first comedies of Marivaux and the twenty-five issues of *Le Spectateur français*, both of which treat love as tender emotion, an interpretation finding its ultimate expression ten years later in *La Vie de Marianne*. Marivaux's description of tender passion, essentially feminine in its charm and variety, its satisfaction to *amour-propre*, its delicacy and restraint, its urge to become more worthy in the eyes of the loved one, accords perfectly with Mme de Lambert's idea of the role of feminine sensibility in love. It is her belief that woman's duty is to hold in check the desires of men and so to add grace and nobility to what would otherwise be pure sensuality.[29]

But Marivaux, though he inclines toward this feminine conception of love and distinguishes sharply between sensuality and *amour-tendresse*,[30] portrays both in his novels. While *La Vie de Marianne* contains his fullest and most detailed analysis of *amour-tendresse*, *Le Paysan parvenu*, particularly in the early parts, is concerned almost entirely with sensual love. It is supposed that one of Marivaux's objects in writing it was to prove to Crébillon *fils* that licentiousness in literature could be presented more effectively under a cloak of decency than through a boldly frank narration. The experiences of the peasant Jacob leave no doubt in his mind as to the predominance of sensual love, though he acknowledges the existence of another sort, which he is eventually to experience.[31] His first affair is an *amour de tête*, culminating in his marriage with the elderly and pious Mlle Habert. As he becomes acquainted in the world of society and finance, he meets a number of women, most of them considerably older than he, whose physical charms he finds fairly irresistible. Jacob's shrewd appraisal of these women (his peasant *bon sens* makes him perfectly aware of the nature of their attraction) constitutes an amusing and truthful picture of the relaxed atmosphere resultant from the breaking down of class barriers and the passing of the older ideals of decorum. Mme de Fécour was endowed with "senses only and no sentiment and . . . passed nonetheless for the best woman in the world, because her senses on a thousand different occasions took the place of sentiments and served her equally well."[32] The fair skin, beautiful hands, negligent pose, and amorous glances of Mme de Ferval enthrall Jacob and cause him to exclaim: "At my age, when one has in mind these little considerations, one has no need to be in love to view with chagrin the interruption of a *rendez-vous*."[33]

Fresh from these adventures, Jacob is prompted to expand on the
nature of the tender passion, so far as his observation thus far has taught
him to know it:

> Il y a bien des amours où le coeur n'a point de part; il y en a plus
> de ceux-là que d'autres même, et dans le fond, c'est sur eux que
> roule la nature, et non pas sur nos délicatesses de sentiment qui ne
> lui servent de rien. C'est nous le plus souvent qui nous rendons
> tendres, pour orner nos passions; mais c'est la nature qui nous rend
> amoureux; nous tenons d'elle l'utile que nous enjolivons de l'hon-
> nête; j'appelle ainsi le sentiment; on n'enjolive pourtant plus guère;
> la mode en est aussi passée dans ce temps où j'écris.[34]

This blunt appraisal of "delicacies of feeling" is a surprising declaration from the pen of the Marquise de Lambert's friend. It is the pre-
ponderant attitude, however, in the first five parts of *Le Paysan parvenu,*
where tenderness is considered only an adornment to sensuality. The
tribute in *Le Paysan parvenu* to sensibility—"Plus on a de sensibilité,
plus on a l'âme généreuse, et par conséquent estimable"[35]—sometimes
quoted apart from its context,[36] is in reality the ironic comment of a
gentleman who has disturbed a lovers' tryst. Jacob adds: "Petite morale
bonne à débiter chez Mme Rémy, mais il fallait bien dorer la pilule."[37]
He has explained in an earlier passage, perhaps for the benefit of Crébillon *fils,* that considerations of delicacy and good taste are necessary in
the literary presentation of physical love. A reader will accept and enjoy licentiousness if it is offered in a manner not so brusque as to be
shocking to him in the quiet surroundings of his library.

> Il est vrai que ce lecteur est homme aussi; mais c'est alors un
> homme en repos, qui a du goût, qui est délicat, qui s'attend qu'on
> fera rire son esprit, qui veut pourtant bien qu'on le débauche, mais
> honnêtement, avec des façons et avec de la décence.[38]

The calculated love-making of the characters of Crébillon *fils* contrasts strikingly with the tender passion of Marivaux. Marivaux's
lovers explore all the paths of sentiment. The lovers of Crébillon *fils*
move toward their goal with tenacity and single-mindedness. They are
possessed by one passion—the lust for conquest. The whole game is
one of overpowering aggression on the part of the lover and skittish
defense on the part of the mistress, a game embellished by wit but
not by sentiment. Deferring the surrender enables the mistress to put

a factitious value upon it, but once she has yielded she can have no reasonable hope of holding her lover. She accommodates herself to this fact as best she can; if the satisfaction of being desired by many is not equivalent to that of being loved by one, it is at least a workable substitute. And the game is promptly resumed, with a change of *dramatis personae*. The lover has gained a new "experience," by recounting which in a deprecating manner he can entertain his next mistress, and the woman has gained a fond memory—a memory which is likely to outlast his.

> Comment voulez-vous qu'avec ce qu'on a à faire dans le monde, des gens que le hasard, le caprice, des circonstances ont unis quelques moments, se souviennent de ce qui les a intéressés si peu? Ce que je vous dis, au reste, est si vrai, que soupant il y a quelque temps avec une femme, je ne me la rappelais en aucune façon, que je l'aurais quittée comme m'étant inconnue, si elle ne m'eût pas fait souvenir que nous nous étions autrement fort tendrement aimés.[39]

Both Crébillon *fils* and Marivaux recognize the prevalent sensuality of the times. But Marivaux, representing an older generation, prefers to present either a more idealized love, as in the theatre and *La Vie de Marianne,* or a sensuality glossed with refinement, as in *Le Paysan parvenu.* The distinction between the two authors in this respect is neatly summed up in the speech of the Duke in *Le Hasard du Coin du feu* by Crébillon *fils*:

> L'embarras, la modestie, la pudeur, ont pour les uns des charmes inexprimables; les autres, moins délicats, ne s'émeuvent qu'autant qu'une femme leur montre moins d'envie d'être aimée que d'être séduite, et qu'enfin le coeur est ce qu'elle paraît le moins vouloir toucher.[40]

The "inexpressible charms" of sentiment were the natural medium of Marivaux's talent.

Although the mass of evidence in the plays, essays, and novels shows Marivaux largely in accord with Mme de Lambert in esteeming "delicacies of feeling," it remains nonetheless true that he was acquainted with many types of love, and that even in amour-tendresse there exists a measure of sensuality, disguised and refined. His ideal would seem to be a happy medium between sentimentalism and sensuality. In a short allegorical play, *La Réunion des Amours* (1731), Amour and

Cupidon dispute as to who is the true god of love. Minerva makes the decision:

> Cupidon, la Vertu décidait contre vous. . . . Avec votre con-
> frère l'âme est trop tendre, il est vrai; mais avec vous, elle est trop
> libertine. Il fait souvent des erreurs ridicules; vous n'en faites que
> de méprisables. Il égare l'esprit; mais vous ruinez les moeurs. Il n'a
> que des défauts; vous n'avez que des vices. Unissez-vous tous deux:
> rendez-le plus vif et plus passionné, et qu'il vous rende plus tendre
> et plus raisonnable.[41]

Marivaux gives support to the assertion of Taine and other social historians that social corruption led to the refinements of sensibility.[42] The veneer of refinement cast over his interviews with Mme de Ferval causes Jacob to admire his progress in the art of love.

> Voyez que de choses capables de débrouiller mon esprit et mon
> coeur! voyez quelle école de mollesse, de volupté, de corruption, et
> par conséquent de sentiment! car l'âme se raffine à mesure qu'elle
> se gâte.[43]

This reflection shows clear insight into the probable origins of such manifestations of sensibility as there were in the salons of Marivaux's day. It is not, however, applicable to Marianne and the adolescent lovers of the comedies. Marianne is too young to be *gâtée*; she comes by her sensibility naturally. Jacob, on the other hand, is not by nature a *belle âme*. His sentimental education is slow and uncertain, taking place under the dubious auspices of corrupt society women much older than he. Even in the delicate portrayals of *amour-tendresse* there are slight but piquant traces of sensuality. Marianne is aware that physical charms count considerably in the progress of the tender passion. Her pretty face and figure arouse a gratifying flutter wherever she goes, though she professes to disdain them in comparison with the qualities of her heart. She dwells on the sensuous appeal of a bare hand[44] and rejoices in the opportunity to display, without immodesty, "the pret- tiest little foot in the world."[45] Such artful behavior is only a part of woman's innate desire to please, but it shows that this precocious child of fifteen understands well the combination of refinement and sensuous- ness to be found in *amour-tendresse,* though her delicate nature leads her to dwell on the adornments of passion.

C'est un vilain amant qu'un homme qui vous désire plus qu'il ne vous aime: non pas que l'amant le plus délicat ne désire à sa manière, mais du moins c'est que chez lui les sentiments du coeur se mêlent avec les sens; tout cela se fond ensemble: ce qui fait un amour tendre, et non pas vicieux, quoique à la vérité capable du vice; car tous les jours, en fait d'amour, on fait très délicatement des choses fort grossières: mais il ne s'agit point de cela.[46]

In summary, Mme de Lambert's ideal of the tender passion is more purely Platonic than is Marivaux's, for she represents a more conventional society and was still strongly under the influence of the *précieuses*. But Marianne, though she belongs to an age of freer social standards, conforms quite well to the model set forth by Mme de Lambert, for she is a young girl whose heart and head are equally alert to aid in the perfecting of the tender passion and in the attainment of real and immediate happiness. Mme de Lambert sketches in broad outline the portrait which Marivaux fills out in minute detail.

Si vous voulez trouver une imagination ardente, une âme profondément occupée, un coeur sensible et bien touché, cherchez-le chez les femmes d'un caractère raisonnable. Si vous ne trouvez de bonheur et de repos que dans l'union des coeurs: si vous êtes sensible au plaisir d'être ardemment aimé, et que vous vouliez jouir de toutes les délicatesses de l'amour, de ses impatiences, et de ses mouvemens si purs et si doux, soyez bien persuadé qu'ils ne se trouvent que chez les personnes retenues, et qui se respectent.[47]

This, in essence, is Marianne, and her ardent but coyly judicious love affair, set against the more lusty adventures of Jacob, may serve to explain more clearly the nature and the course of *amour-tendresse*.

The tender passion, fleetingly portrayed in the Silvias and the Angéliques of Marivaux's "surprises de l'amour," receives a lengthy analysis in *La Vie de Marianne*, in which Marianne, her youth long past, tells the story of an early love, revealing every nuance of *amour naissant*. It is possible to find in Marianne's experience all the characteristics previously mentioned as belonging to the tender passion, but the variety and unpredictability of her love are even more apparent. I have said that the tender passion in Marivaux does not partake of the nature of a ritual. It is not yet the social pastime described by Stendhal and de Goncourt as *amour-goût*. The emphasis on detail, which disturbed

Voltaire, is designed to bring out the peculiar quality of each case, a method more interesting to Marivaux than the representation of universal truths.

It is the beginning of *amour-tendresse* that Marivaux studies most in detail. Forty pages of *La Vie de Marianne*[48] are devoted to the first chance encounter of Marianne and Valville. The surprises, the delights, the fears, the sentiments of tenderness and respect, which determine the character of *amour-tendresse* from its beginning and set its future course, are described in all their turns. Nascent love is love at first sight—there is always an initial surprise, a shock of discovery. It is an elective affinity, with which the heart has more to do than physical attraction. Superficially it resembles the *coup de foudre* of the seventeenth-century romantic hero, but only superficially, for the lover is left in possession of his faculties, and his devotion manifests itself in a discriminating consciousness of feeling rather than in marvelous exploits offered as proof of his submission. Love does not begin with passion but with tenderness; it continues through the complicated interaction of impulse and hazard and is enhanced by a kind of sentimental dialectic—advance and recoil, admission and denial—all of which characterizes Marivaudian love-making.

Marianne experiences the shock of first love on a morning when she appears in church, clad in the finery given her by Climal. Having chosen an advantageous place, she is soon the center of attention, a position which she exploits with the instinct of a coquette.[49] Suddenly among the group of young men casting admiring glances at her, one in particular attracts her attention. The attraction declares itself by an interruption, brief but significant, of the vanity of pleasing. Marianne, a coquette for all others, momentarily forgets to practice her arts for Valville.[50] This brief interval of self-forgetfulness, she reflects, is the first sign of love.

> Apparemment que l'amour, la première fois qu'on en prend, commence avec cette bonne foi-là, et peut-être que la douceur d'aimer interrompt le soin d'être aimable.[51]

Even for the novice, it is almost impossible to mistake the experience of nascent love. Marianne, in the midst of the confusion occasioned by a flood of "mouvements inconnus," realizes the significance of her feelings.

On se demanderait volontiers dans ces instants-là: Que vais-je devenir? Car, en vérité, l'amour ne nous trompe point; dès qu'il se montre, il vous dit ce qu'il est, et de quoi il sera question: l'âme, avec lui, sent la présence d'un maître qui la flatte, mais une autorité déclarée qui ne la consulte pas, et qui lui laisse hardiment les soupçons de son esclavage futur.

Voilà ce qui m'a semblé de l'état où j'étais, et je pense aussi que c'est l'histoire de toutes les jeunes personnes de mon âge en pareil cas.[52]

After the first shock of surprise and recognition, the progress of *amour-naissance* is less rapid, for the lover's admiration is not open and bold, but modest and a little timid. Marianne notices that Valville's glances are different from those of the other young men—they are more respectful as well as more flattering.[53] She feels a greater sincerity in his admiration: "The others applauded openly my charms; it seemed to me that he felt them."[54] For the lover at once throws a screen of delicacy over his attentions, lest the newly aroused feelings of the loved one be offended. This tactfulness is recognized and appreciated. From the first moment *amour-tendresse* is based on esteem and respect, and the lover's conduct never deviates from this course.[55] When Marianne is run down by Valville's carriage as she is returning home from church, he takes pains to conceal his feelings, his love revealing itself only in his extreme solicitude for her injury.[56] And Marianne's hesitation in revealing to Valville her residence with Mme Dutour is based on her fear of destroying the respect which he has displayed from the beginning of their acquaintance.

Il y a des attentions tendres et même timides, de certains honneurs qui ne sont dus qu'à l'innocence et qu'à la pudeur; et Valville, qui me les prodiguait tous, aurait pu craindre de s'être mépris, et d'avoir été dupe de mes grâces; je lui aurais du moins ôté la douceur de m'estimer en pleine sûreté de confiance; et quelle chute n'était-ce pas faire là dans son esprit.[57]

Jacob too, when he feels the stirring of tender passion after a long series of light amours, experiences a similar feeling of respect and timidity, shared by his beloved and attested to by her blushes and hesitant glances.[58]

The lover's restraint, however, does not contribute materially to the serenity of his mistress. His timid but ardent glances embarrass her and heighten her agitation. The conflict of feelings throws her into a state of confusion, the disparate elements of which challenge the analytical powers of a Marivaudian heroine. "Never in my life," Marianne confesses, "have I been so agitated. I can't tell you exactly how I felt."[59] And she proceeds to do so in minute fashion, separating her confusion, her pleasure, and her fear, and defining the nature of this experience with perspicuity. Such is the advantage of a sound head in an affair of the heart. Another crisis arises when Valville suspects Marianne of intimacy with M. de Climal. The mingling of sadness and tenderness in his expression stirs her deeply, for she sees its double significance—tribute to her charms and regret at the need to renounce them. She says of her dilemma: "A mingling of pleasure and confusion, that was my state of mind. It was one of those moments of which one can only half seize the import."[60] Jacob describes his perplexity too: "I feared to displease without being clearly aware as yet of my intention to please. The heart is all confusion when it first experiences love."[61]

In addition to their agitation and embarrassment, the lovers of Marivaux move in a dreamy state, a kind of unreal existence referred to by Mme de Lambert in the phrase: "It is as if one were not of the world."[62] This preoccupation in the early stages of love was responsible for the propitious accident of Marianne's being run down by Valville's carriage.

Amour-tendresse also brings with it a sensation of fear, a delicious shudder arising from a new but pleasurable emotion.[63] Recognizing immediately that Valville is in love with her, Marianne knows that her confusion is greater than his because of her inexperience, and that the rush of her feelings may endanger her discretion.

> Et puis dans quel danger n'est-on pas quand on tombe en de certaines mains, quand on n'a pour tout guide qu'un amant qui vous aime trop mal pour vous mener bien![64]

In *amour-tendresse,* however, such fears are short-lived, for the lover's respect and solicitude quickly reassure his mistress. Marianne's injured ankle provokes on the part of Valville a touching display of tenderness, marred later only by his facility in repeating it for another beauty in distress. In time Marianne comes to understand this quality in her lover. She describes him as "naturally very impressionable."[65] Mlle Varthon too, though with certain mental reserves, ascribes to Valville's impulsiveness and ready sympathy the beginning of his affection for her.

Cela a remué cette petite âme faible, qui ne tient à rien, qui est le jouet de tout ce qu'elle voit d'un peu singulier. Si j'avais été en bonne santé, il n'aurait pas pris garde à moi; c'est mon évanouissement qui en fait un infidèle.[66]

This almost childish quality of *amour-tendresse*, a quick pity which leads to tenderness as quickly dissipated, is described elsewhere:

En fait d'amour ce sont des âmes d'enfants que les âmes inconstantes. Aussi n'y à-t-il rien de plus amusant, de plus aimable, de plus agréablement vif et étourdi que leur tendresse.[67]

The confusion past, the woman regains possession of herself and the arts of coquetry appear once more. So Marianne's embarrassment, arising from the necessity of entering the house of a young man with whom she has carried on an innocent flirtation, soon gives way to satisfaction at the advantages of this chance intimacy. With her accustomed subtlety she maintains a pretence of her first confusion, explaining it by reasons quite different from the real ones. Her wit and alert *amour-propre* contrive to produce a simulated embarrassment.

J'agissais donc en conséquence; de sorte qu'on pouvait bien croire que la présence de Valville m'embarrassait un peu, mais simplement à cause qu'il me voyait, et non pas à cause qu'il aimait à me voir.[68]

Vanity too sometimes masquerades as modesty, to conceal the fear of appearing unworthy or ridiculous, of offending taste. Marianne suffers at the thought of revealing to Valville her place of residence and decides to leave his house unaccompanied in spite of the risk of compromising herself with him. She reflects on this motive, which leads her to choose to appear "equivocal rather than ridiculous," to endanger her reputation rather than to admit her humble station in life.

Ne savez-vous pas que notre âme est encore plus superbe que vertueuse, plus glorieuse qu'honnête, et par conséquent plus délicate sur les intérêts de sa vanité que sur ceux de son véritable honneur?[69]

Vanity, she says, is sometimes so strong as to win out even over sentiments of honor.

Qu'importe que notre coeur souffre, pourvu que notre vanité soit servie? Ne se passe-t-on pas de tout, et de repos et de plaisirs, et d'honneur même, et quelquefois de la vie, pour avoir de la paix avec elle?[70]

When at last both lovers are fairly assured that their love is reciprocated, the fact is not conveyed by a bold declaration, but rather by
many small attentions, such as solicitude, marks of respect and esteem,
looks and gestures.[71] There is still no complete liberation of feeling.
Every act is considered in the light of its possible effect on the loved
one, and more is conveyed by attitude than by speech. What Marianne
calls "this silent conversation of the heart" is a highly important step
in the progress of the tender passion; "his every glance bespoke 'I love
you'; and I did not know what to do with my eyes, for they would
have told him the same thing."[72] Ardent but respectful gestures too
are important at this stage.

> Comme les coeurs s'entendent, apparemment qu'il sentit ce qui
> se passait dans le mien; car il reprit ma main qu'il baisa avec une
> naïveté de passion si vive et si rapide, qu'en me disant mille fois:
> Je vous aime, il me l'aurait dit moins intelligiblement qu'il ne fit
> alors.[73]

The certainty of being loved puts an end to Marianne's dissimulation
and throws her into a second confusion, which she attempts again to
conceal in the interests of modesty.[74] Her hand trembles in Valville's,
but she makes an effort to regain her self-possession, and "the spell of
those emotions which held me as if enchanted disappeared."[75] In such
crises the lover must show his delicacy by refusing to take advantage
of the moment of weakness. There is always an interval, says Marianne,
when one needs to be treated gently, when the lover's respect is of
great value. Valville's conduct in this crisis is impeccable and prompts
Marianne to show her gratitude in a perfect definition of *amour-tendresse.*

> Il n'était pas amoureux, il était tendre; façon d'être épris qui, au
> commencement, rend le coeur honnête, qui lui donne des moeurs,
> et l'attache au plaisir délicat d'aimer et de respecter timidement
> ce qu'il aime.[76]

The occupation of the tender heart, she continues, in this waxing
phase of passion, is "to adorn the object of its love with all the dignity
imaginable." There is more charm in this than one would suspect, she
continues; "one would lose in not conforming to it."[77]

After the initial period of hesitancy and the return of self-possession
come the pleasures of discrimination. The balance between the feelings

and the reason has been fairly well maintained even in new and disturbing circumstances; and now the contribution of the head becomes more important in reviewing, prolonging, and elaborating on the impulses of nascent love. In *amour-tendresse* the nature of Marivaudian sensibility consists in gentle emotion filtered through the refining screen of the intelligence. The device of the older Marianne as *raconteuse* results in occasional uncertainty as to the degree in which the emotion of the Marianne of fifteen has been modified by recollection in tranquility. It is admitted that what is long in telling required only a moment to experience.[78] Yet a clear distinction is usually made between the reflections of the older Marianne and the experiences of the younger. In any case, no doubt is permitted that at fifteen Marianne was a precocious analyst of her feelings and a virtuoso in cultivating them, and that her sensibility was a compound of heart and head.

Looking back on her adventure in Valville's house, Marianne explains that the shock of emotion troubled her momentarily, "to a degree which disturbed my reason but did not rob me of it."[79] She considers her sudden loss of poise, her melting into tears at the prospect of Valville's learning her true identity. Attributing this weakness to her extreme youth, she proceeds to examine and enumerate the benefits which she was to reap through her display of emotion. Tears offered the ideal solution to a difficult problem. First of all, tears comforted her and put her more at ease; they suppressed for the moment her *amour-propre* and made her less ashamed to admit the truth about her humble origin. Then too they gave her an air of romantic dignity which made the fact less humiliating and less shocking to aristocratic prejudice. They added to her beauty, ennobled her in the eyes of her lover, and aroused his imagination by letting the "chimeras of love" play over her pathetic figure.

> Il y a de certaines infortunes qui embellissent la beauté même, qui lui préparent de la majesté. Vous avez alors, avec vos grâces, celles que votre histoire, faite comme un roman, vous donne encore. Et ne vous embarrassez pas d'ignorer ce que vous êtes née; laissez travailler les chimères de l'amour là-dessus; elles sauront bien vous faire un rang distingué, et tirer bon parti des ténèbres qui cacheront votre naissance.[80]

With the lover's imagination thus aroused, we have the beginning of what Stendhal describes as crystallization,

> . . . l'opération de l'esprit, qui tire de tout ce qui se présente la
> découverte que l'objet aimé a de nouvelles perfections. . . . Il suffit
> de penser à une perfection pour la voir dans ce qu'on aime.[81]

So misfortune may not only embellish beauty, but also deepen the
lover's attachment through the medium of an aroused imagination.
"If a woman could ever be taken for a goddess," Marianne explains,
"it would be under such circumstances that her lover would believe
her one."[82] The element of mystery hovering about the figure of the
loved one enables the imagination to work unhampered in shaping
her according to the heart's desire.

Realizing this truth instinctively, Marianne, in order to prolong the
uncertainty on which the imagination thrives, tries to conceal her joy
when her insistence upon leaving forces Valville to declare his love.
Silence is her only possible reply, and Valville, sensing the boldness
of his conduct, kisses her hand, an additional *étourderie* which is passed
over without comment, for "between two people in love those are elementary aspects of sentiment which perhaps the mind would notice if
it cared to but which it chooses to overlook to the heart's advantage."[83]

The doubt created by Marianne's hesitancy and silence is soon followed by a partial reassurance, for she parries Valville's direct question
by an avowal of inexperience—"Je ne sais pas ce que c'est que l'amour,
monsieur"[84]—and an expression of gratitude for his *honnêteté*. The
accompaniment to this subterfuge is Valville's constant kissing of her
hand: "We paid no attention to that trifling matter, for we had grown
accustomed to it; that is how things go in love."[85] Marianne grows more
and more evasive, Valville more and more uncertain, until at last he
is driven to a despairing renunciation of hope.[86] Then Marianne's resistance breaks down in another flood of tears, the causes and advantages of which are again carefully examined,[87] and the lover's hope
is restored.

> Les pleurs qu'il me vit répandre le calmèrent tout d'un coup: je
> n'ai jamais rien vu ni de si doux ni de si tendre que ce qui se peignit
> sur sa physionomie; et en effet, mes pleurs ne concluaient rien de
> fâcheux pour lui, ils n'annonçaient ni haine ni indifférence, ils ne
> pouvaient signifier que de l'embarras.[88]

At last Marianne's tears bring her lover to his knees in a transport of
hope and tenderness.

Although the pleasures of love for the *coeur sensible* are many and diverse, its sensations must be enjoyed while they may, for "the flutters of sensibility"[89] are acknowledged even by its devotees to be short-lived. Marianne says: "Of course one must not expect this to last; its grace and dignity are borrowed charms and disappear with the amorous play that lends them to you."[90] Because *amour-tendresse* is a somewhat precarious combination of reason, fancy, and emotion, it is at the mercy of passing events which may easily destroy it or deflect it from its course. Hence each moment must be prized, its sweetness tasted to the full. "How priceless is one minute in the inventory of love!"[91] exclaims the connoisseur Marianne. It is with a complete understanding of the transitory nature of *amour-tendresse* that Marianne explains Valville's infidelity. He has not sufficiently restrained his ardor, and so his affection has cooled, though only momentarily, she hopes. "It is not that his heart has tired of me; it is only a bit satiated with the pleasure of loving from having indulged too ardently in the beginning."[92]

Two plays emphasize in particular the impermanence of tender passion. One, *La Dispute,* is an attempt to prove that constancy is impossible, even in simple natures remote from the temptations and rivalries of salon society.[93] In the other, *La Double Inconstance,* Silvia comments philosophically on the fleeting nature of *amour-tendresse*:

> Lorsque je l'ai aimé, c'était un amour qui m'était venu; à cette heure que je ne l'aime plus, c'est un amour qui s'en est allé. Il est venu sans mon avis, il s'en retourne de même: je ne crois pas être blâmable.[94]

Amour-tendresse thrives on desire, on anticipation. It is the place of the head, by supplementing ingenuousness with tact, to prolong the delicious moments which give this love its charm. Though the conventional goal of *amour-tendresse* is marriage—any other goal would be revolting to it—it is in no haste to arrive. It lingers over each step of nascent affection. Indeed, the sentimental exchange of doubt and reassurance, of pique and self-sacrifice, is dear for its own sake. Marriage would bring an end to it, would transform it into something else, something less sweet to the sensitive heart, which thrives on desire as it never could on fulfillment.[95] The material barriers in the path of budding love—Marianne's humble birth, the objections of Valville's relatives—are not real hindrances but only serve to enrich the attachment. The real obstacles which confront Marivaux's lovers derive from their inner natures and are touching rather than tragic. Most of them spring from *amour-propre* and indicate a wistful desire to maintain dignity and spiritual independence in the face of an overpowering love. The play of sensibility and circumstance in the formative stages of an attachment is characteristic of *amour-tendresse*, setting it apart from passionate love, which rushes headlong toward its goal, and from *amour-goût*, which conforms more rigidly to a pattern. This explains, perhaps, why Marivaux dropped in mid-course his story of Marianne. For after he had invented every conceivable obstacle to the marriage of Valville and Marianne, prolonging their palpitations and postponing the dubious reward, he lost interest in the dénouement and left his tale for another to finish. Madame Riccoboni pays tribute to the true interest and talent of Marivaux when she continues the lovers' trials for another hundred pages, without attempting a solution. Their difficulties are for the most part too trivial to prevent the conventional ending, but its arrival would terminate the most satisfying part of the emotional experience. Marivaux gives his characters every qualification for successful marriage—generosity, taste, mutual respect—except one, forbearance of the commonplace.

It is clear, then, that though the heart guides, the heart must be cultivated in the refinements of *amour-tendresse*. For a heart "bien né," and especially for a woman, this art is learned quickly, almost instinctively. Though Marianne is embarrassed at the thought that Valville is more experienced at love than she, *amour-propre* provides the needed protection, and an alert mind applied to the problem fast makes of her a virtuoso. For Jacob, who certainly is not "bien né," long training is necessary to attain this end. At first the natural man, he makes progress in his sentimental education, learning to simulate tenderness for the benefit of his mistresses and at length experiencing the reality of *amour-tendresse*. I have pointed out that he always makes a distinction between sensuality and sentiment, though at first he is inclined to depreciate the latter. His final initiation into the mysteries of *amour-tendresse* provides the subject matter of Parts VI and VII of the novel. The gradual development of his character through the influence of Parisian society seems completely logical and true to the intentions of Marivaux, and so points to the authenticity of these disputed parts. The fact that the novel was dropped for many years shows again Marivaux's absorption in the many facets of an emotional experience and his lack of interest in the mere matter of conclusion.

Jacob's sentimental education begins with his courtship of Mlle Habert, in which he imitates *amour-tendresse* with a verisimilitude that surprises even himself. The affair with Madame de Ferval, an *amour de vanité*, sweeps him along in a whirlwind of self-esteem. The flattering experience of being sought after by a woman of high social position, by playing upon his vanity, adds to his charm. This affair is followed quickly by another with Mme de Fécour, a *dévote* easily diverted to less pious practices by the appeal of a handsome figure. The comic termination of this affair leaves Jacob's heart untouched and his head considerably wiser in the ways of society women.

At the beginning of Part VI, Jacob discovers through the influence of music that his heart is "sensible." The objection is raised:

> Mais . . . l'on connaît déjà votre âme. Mlle Habert, Mesdames de Ferval et de Fécour vous ont donné occasion de dévoiler aux autres votre penchant pour la tendresse; vous deviez donc dès lors le connaître vous-même.[96]

These "superficial experiences," Jacob explains, did not at all reveal his true nature; "it is commonplace knowledge that in this city the number of one's conquests in no way impairs one's feelings."[97] His meeting with Mme de Vambures, her "noble timidity," her careful observance of the proprieties, her guarded admission of interest, put him in a new situation in which, for the first time, the heart is fully engaged. As the affair progresses, Jacob becomes convinced that any attachment, especially if it is to lead to marriage, must be based on genuine respect and tenderness. His own experience has been his teacher.

> J'avais pris Mademoiselle Habert pour son bien. Je menais une vie douce avec elle; mais mon coeur, comme on le voit, n'y trouvait pas à se fixer. De temps à autre, le charme des sens étourdissait l'âme; cependant, si la tendresse avait toujours eu autant d'empire sur moi que je m'apercevais qu'elle en prenait depuis que je connaissais le fond des sentiments de Mme de Vambures, j'aurais été infailliblement malheureux.[98]

So Jacob is converted to *amour-tendresse*. His last love, though it lacks the spontaneous grace of Marianne's affair, completes Marivaux's exposition in *Le Paysan parvenu* of a variety of loves almost Stendhalian in scope and gives climactic emphasis to the one he considers most worthy of admiration.

The interplay of sensibility and circumstance in the course of *amour-tendresse* leads naturally to the consideration of a less fortuitous outcome of such an attachment. The unfaithful and the neglected lover both figure often in Marivaux's pages, for tenderness, he points out, is a fleeting phase of love, easily felt and easily transferable. The catch and toss of love play is so important in the building up of this delicate relationship that any slip may result in a cooling of affection or possibly a complete break between the lovers. There is danger that the vanity of pleasing, once its goal is achieved, may subside or transfer its attentions elsewhere.

A definite rupture, however, offers an opportunity for the abandoned one to reap a refined vengeance. Here *amour-propre* is called to the severest test, for the deserted lover must convince himself that he is in no way at fault, inconstancy being after all a fundamental trait in human nature.

> Qu'un amant nous quitte et nous en préfère une autre, eh bien! soit; mais du moins qu'il ait tort de nous la préférer; que ce soit la faute de son inconstance, et non pas de nos charmes; enfin, que ce soit une injustice qu'il nous fasse. . . .[99]

In such circumstances it is wise to preserve the appearance that one's own heart is in no way altered. So Marianne says to Valville:

> Je ferai tout pour vous, hors de dire que je ne vous aime plus; ce qui n'est pas encore vrai, et ce qu'après tout ce qui s'est passé, je n'aurais pas même la hardiesse de dire, quand ce serait une vérité.[100]

After Marianne has released her lover to Mlle Varthon, after she has convinced herself of the "superiority" of her soul to his, "a superiority more touching than irritating, more lovable than proud,"[101] she rejoices inwardly in a "sweet and flattering sentiment." By her maintenance of personal dignity in a trying situation, she has demonstrated her nobility of character, she has made it impossible for Valville to forget her, and she is in a position to feel that he is more to be pitied than she. So she can exult:

> C'est que la vengeance est douce à tous les coeurs offensés; il leur en faut une, il n'y a que cela qui les soulage; les uns l'aiment cruelle, et les autres généreuse, et, comme vous voyez, mon coeur était de ces derniers; car ce n'était pas vouloir beaucoup de mal à Valville que de ne lui souhaiter que des regrets.[102]

The vengeance of the sensitive heart contains the same piquant admixture of reason and emotion, of tact and impulsiveness, which marks the tender passion itself.

The tender passion, fragile though its essence is, is in Marivaux's opinion no trifle.

> C'est de l'amour dont il s'agit. Eh bien! de l'amour: le croyez-vous une bagatelle, Messieurs? je ne suis pas de votre avis, et je ne connais guère de sujet sur lequel le sage puisse exercer ses réflexions avec plus de profit pour les hommes.[103]

His study of it affords a keen revelation of human motives and frailties, especially in women. We shall see in following chapters that its ramifications are broad, amounting to considerably more than a personal triumph or a passing sadness. The sweetness of loving and being loved, the delight in one's own emotions and in the sight of others pleasurably moved, the satisfaction to *amour-propre* which results from respectful and tender admiration, dispose the sensitive heart to virtuous thoughts and acts. One pleases by a pretty face, Marianne says; one inspires either love or desire.[104] But for the *âme sensible* this is an elementary pleasure. Greater satisfaction may come through the performance of generous acts, which inspire affection and gratitude. The tender heart, self-confident and successful in its more intimate affairs, grows impatient to extend its influence from the individual to the social group, to embrace all mankind, and so to enjoy in even richer measure the pleasure of its own feelings. It finds in sympathy and generosity toward less fortunate humanity the natural sphere for the expansion of its functions. Such behavior serves a double purpose, for the belief was growing ever stronger that whatever springs from the heart is pleasurable and good. As Shaftesbury pointed out shortly before Marivaux took up his career of letters, the wise union of selfish and altruistic impulses is the surest way to personal happiness. Thus arises the morality of sentiment, and in this semi-egoistic beginning lies perhaps the germ of modern humanitarianism.

VI

AMOUR-PROPRE AND AMOUR-TENDRESSE
IN THE THEATRE

"Il n'y a rien de si varié dans la nature que les joies de l'amour, quoiqu'elles soient toujours les mêmes."

Ninon de Lenclos, *Correspondance authentique*, p. 72.

THE PURPOSE of the present chapter is to illustrate the interplay of *amour-propre* and *amour-tendresse* in the theatre of Marivaux. The novels, because of their wealth of discursive comment, lend themselves to an analytical approach. In the plays, on the other hand, the two themes are so closely interwoven that they cannot readily be studied apart from the situations that give rise to them.

Marivaux's contemporaries were accustomed to complain of the similarity of his plays, and d'Alembert remarked that if an actress always played Marivaux, she would give the impression of never changing her role.[1] Built on the framework of a contest between love and pride, the plays conclude with love victorious. This familiar summarization of Marivaux's theatre is true enough in broad outline, but fails to recognize the complex variations that result in different characters and different situations. The more closely one reads the plays, the more one is struck by their variety as well as by their concentration and unity. Marivaux cultivates his scanty plot of ground as intensively as his contemporaries Pater, Lancret, and Watteau in another medium. This method seems generally characteristic of the rococo art of the Regency period.

Love as represented in the plays is the *amour-tendresse* already analyzed in the novels. It begins with love at first sight, a fact often overlooked by critics, who deny spontaneity to Marivaux's young lovers because they yield reluctantly to their emotions. The usual situation is a chance encounter, an arrested glance, an immediate agitation of two hearts. Lisette and Angélique, walking and reading together, meet Dorante.

> *Lisette.* Il vous salue, nous le saluons; le lendemain même promenade, mêmes allées, même rencontre, même inclination des deux côtés, et plus de livres de part et d'autre; cela est admirable.
>
> *Angélique.* Ajoute que j'ai voulu m'empêcher de l'aimer, et que je n'ai pu en venir au bout.
>
> *Lisette.* Je vous en défierais.[2]

Dorante's meeting with Araminte is more of a *coup de foudre*.

Hélas! Madame, ce fut un jour que vous sortîtes de l'Opéra qu'il perdit la raison: c'était un vendredi, je m'en ressouviens; oui, un vendredi: il vous vit descendre l'escalier, à ce qu'il me raconta, et vous suivit jusqu'à votre carrosse; il avait demandé votre nom, et je le trouvai qui était comme extasié; il ne remuait plus.[3]

The heroes of the plays are frank in admitting their feelings. A typical declaration is as follows:

Je vous y vis, vous vous y démasquâtes un instant, et dans cet instant vous devîntes l'arbitre de mon sort.[4]

The woman is slower to admit her love, perhaps even to recognize it. Silvia, in *Le Jeu de l'amour et du hasard*, feels at once an attraction for Dorante, which she is at a loss to understand because he seems unworthy of her in his valet's costume.[5] Sometimes the confession is made to the *suivante*, who is seldom loath to pass on the information.

Ergaste. Elle m'aime, dis-tu, Lisette? Puis-je me flatter d'un si grand bonheur? Moi qui ne l'ai vue qu'en passant dans nos promenades, qui ne lui ai prouvé mon amour que par mes regards, et qui n'ai pu lui parler que deux fois pendant que sa mère s'écartait avec d'autres dames: elle m'aime!

Lisette. Très tendrement.[6]

A too hasty declaration brings a rebuff from these sensitive souls, who take refuge in the *bienséances* until they are accustomed to a new emotion.

Clarice. Vous m'avouerez, Monsieur, que vous ne mettez guère d'intervalle entre me connaître, m'aimer, et me le dire; et qu'un pareil entretien aurait pu être précédé de certaines formalités de bienséance qui sont ordinairement nécessaires.[7]

In the progress of the affair Marivaux shows his interest in feminine psychology by depicting the conflict between natural inclinations on the one hand and reserve, timidity, and breeding on the other. The barriers fall by infinitesimal degrees. The process is summed up in outline by Arlequin, rustic lover of Silvia, in *La Double Inconstance*.

Les premiers jours, il fallait voir comme elle se reculait d'auprès de moi, et puis elle reculait plus doucement, et puis, petit à petit, elle ne reculait plus; ensuite elle me regardait en cachette, et puis elle avait honte quand je l'avais vue faire, et puis moi j'avais un plaisir de roi à voir sa honte; ensuite j'attrapais sa main, qu'elle me laissait prendre, et puis elle était encore toute confuse, et puis je lui parlais; ensuite elle ne me répondait rien, mais n'en pensait pas moins; ensuite elle me donnait des regards pour des paroles, et puis des paroles qu'elle laissait aller sans y songer, parce que son coeur allait plus vite qu'elle. . . .[8]

The principal difference in Marivaux's treatment of *amour-propre* in the theatre, as contrasted with the novel, is explained by the technical problems inherent in the two mediums. The restricted vehicle of the stage play limits somewhat the full development of character possible in the novel. The heroes and heroines of Marivaux's plays are, like those of the novels, for the most part sensitive souls whose *amour-propre* is omnipresent, many-sided, and perhaps even more expressive through condensation. Its lighter side—vanity, coquetry, love of flattery—and the more serious aspect as well, the suffering of the sensitive ego, are found in the plays. But the type of self-love which, directed through altruistic channels, leads to "contentement de soi-même," does not appear in the theatre. The social and moral problems the latter involves require fuller development than is possible on the stage. Furthermore, this sublimated variety of *amour-propre* is not sufficiently dramatic for the stage. In the plays the characters are less free than are Marianne and Jacob to contemplate their emotions. But their *amour-propre,* revealed both in action and to a lesser degree in introspection, is highly developed enough to form the principal obstacle that love must overcome. The Angéliques, the Silvias, the Aramintes of the comedies are by no means simple maidens, their self-love being nearly as complex as Marianne's. Observing its manifestations in his sister Silvia, Mario remarks: "Cela, c'est l'amour-propre d'une femme, et il est tout au plus uni."[9]

Despite the limitation of the theatre, Marivaux's characters develop, particularly in regard to the life of the feelings. In the classic tragedy the characters appear first at a moment of crisis; we do not witness the formative stages of their development. The great Racinian characters proceed without hesitancy in a course of action determined by their inner completeness.[10] French comedy, even better than French tragedy, displays human beings fully developed, their foibles and vices fixed and evident.[11] What adjustments they make are forced upon them by pressure of society, and they remain fundamentally the same—misers, hypocrites, or fools.

In Marivaux's characters, young and quivering with latent sensibility, we watch the unfolding of the emotional life and the consequent maturing and enrichment of their natures. The plays open most often in tranquil mood—we are not plunged into a full "crise de l'âme." The typical Marivaudian heroine is usually quite sure of herself in the beginning. When disturbing elements arise, she is confident of her ability to cope with them. Yet her assurance is strained or shattered by the rapidity of new emotional experiences. Confusion and complications result from the inability of the characters to understand their feelings. They are at odds with themselves far more frequently than with any outside force, and the struggle resolves itself only when they discern the true nature of the conflict and "see clear in their hearts."[12] In Marivaux's finest plays, the interest lies in the unfolding of self through the experience of nascent love, and the "becoming" constitutes the entire comedy. Marivaux finds the obstacle to this unfolding in *amour-propre*, which in its complexity gives humor and significance to his theatre.

An interesting point of view is expressed in a recent essay by M. Edmond Jaloux,[13] who considers *amour-propre* in Marivaux's theatre to be in reality an indication of excessive modesty[14] in the very young, a fear of untried experiences, an unwillingness to know reality, a reluctance to surrender one's ego to another person—all this coupled with the saddening knowledge that such a surrender is inevitable. M. Jaloux broadens this modesty or reserve into a characteristic of the French nation, a race of individualists, yet at the same time a highly social people, whose behavior in the group tends to formality because of an unwillingness to reveal to the world one's intimate self, to be "different" and so possibly ridiculous.[15] In the ceremonious reserve of Marivaux's young lovers, M. Jaloux sees not a convention of salon society but a protective device of the sensitive soul, whose sense of uniqueness is its most prized possession.

> Réduire ce mécanisme à une formalité de salon, c'est enlever à Marivaux tout ce qu'il a et tout ce qui fait de lui un des plus grands auteurs français, c'est-à-dire cette sincérité perpétuellement douloureuse et cependant si maîtresse d'elle-même qu'on a pu voir une discipline et presque un jeu dans son désordre de sensibilité. . . .[16]

The struggle of the individual to maintain his integrity in the face of the realities of life is, according to M. Jaloux, the important theme of Marivaux's plays. For a woman, the self-surrender involved in love and marriage offers a disturbing problem. Though she may feel a genuine inclination to love, she hesitates to yield to it. She has an almost childish vulnerability to intrusion on her inner life, and it is to protect this inner life that she indulges in "those fierce debates of the inner self, which refuses all that it desires and desires all that it refuses."[17] The Marivaudian heroine avails herself of every weapon: indifference, teasing, hatred, even the pretense of loving another, to postpone the inevitable surrender. This "perverse" behavior is a consequence of the high value she places on her charm, fragility, and sensibility, together with the fear that her qualities may not be fully appreciated.

> Ainsi, chez ces âmes particulières, l'amour-propre et la pudeur ne font qu'un et on ne peut les blâmer qu'en faisant leur éloge et leur retirer quelque chose qu'en reconnaissant leur valeur.[18]

M. Jaloux's identification of *amour-propre* with *pudeur* is an interesting idea which contains a large share of truth. To accept, however, without reserve the theory that *amour-propre* in Marivaux is a complex of inhibitions worthy of Freudian analysis[19] is to commit an error as grave as the commoner one of over-simplification of the theatre. It is difficult to discern any particular abnormality about these young women hovering between adolescence and maturity. Nor can their behavior be divorced from the sophisticated world of the salons, the atmosphere of which enveloped even the very young. The greater the social experience of the heroines, the more reluctant is their surrender and the more skilled are the ruses of their modesty. Furthermore, they cherish the illusion common to youth of all time that they can to a large extent control their destiny, that the misfortunes which they observe about them cannot, must not happen to them. Their resistance to natural impulses—and by no means all of them do resist—results from a combination of much observation and little direct experience, plus an astonishingly clear conception of the kind of worldly happiness they desire for themselves. When these preconceptions are disturbed by an unexpected emotional impact, they resist in ways partly instinctive and partly dictated by the social discipline of preciosity.

Amour-propre as *pudeur* appears in the most attractive women of

Marivaux's plays. Its outward form, in so far as a pattern can be disengaged from the mixture of imitation and instinct, is preciosity, the formalized coquetry of early eighteenth-century society. These women are products of the salons such as Mme de Lambert's, in which wit, intelligence, and delicacy of sentiment combined to produce a "metaphysic of love," softer than that of the seventeenth-century *grandes dames,* but equally fastidious. Since Voltaire's day this phenomenon has been referred to as *marivaudage.*[20] True *marivaudage* always has a double aspect. The game of love is prized as an opportunity to display one's talents. It has also a deeper significance, of which the characters are only partially aware. It is a process of discovering and testing, behind a protective screen, the life of the emotions. The women who display it most markedly are all very young, very reasonable, serene in their self-esteem, and as yet ignorant of any force strong enough to sway them from their senses. Among them are Lucile of *Les Serments indiscrets,* Silvia of *Le Jeu de l'amour et du hasard,* and Hortense of *Le Petit Maître corrigé.*

Lucile is the embodiment of youthful pride and delicacy. She is a *précieuse* in the eighteenth-century manner, whose reserve is a protection for her sensitive feelings. Wise in spite of her years, she has observed that lovers often make very poor husbands. She says to Lisette:

> Je sens en moi un fond de délicatesse et de goût, qui serait toujours choqué dans le mariage. . . . J'ai l'âme tendre, quoique naturellement vertueuse; et voilà pourquoi le mariage serait une très mauvaise condition pour moi. Une âme tendre et douce a ses sentiments, elle en demande; elle a besoin d'être aimée, parce qu'elle aime: et une âme de cette espèce-là, entre les mains d'un mari, n'a jamais son nécessaire.[21]

Courtship is delightful, but its joys are fleeting; after marriage "the goddess becomes human."[22] Lisette finds these observations quite amusing. "Ah, madame," she says, "que vous me charmez! Que vous êtes une Déesse raisonnable."[23]

Silvia, Marivaux's most famous heroine, represents to perfection his conception of young womanhood. It is hard to imagine Marivaux the misogynist creating the Silvia of *Le Jeu de l'amour et du hasard.* Intelligent, witty, serious, and sensitive, she resembles Marianne, with an added gentleness because of her background of family security. She too is a *précieuse* and expresses a strong aversion to marriage. "Songe à ce que c'est qu'un mari,"[24] she says to Lisette, as she portrays the dismal married life of some of her friends. Her fear of being disillusioned and her lover's similar distaste for marriage account for the double disguise on which this familiar play is plotted.

A third *précieuse* is Hortense of *Le Petit Maître corrigé*, a young woman who, while not averse to marriage, esteems herself highly and refuses to be taken for granted. Rosimond, knowing he is to be her husband, is neglectful of her. Hortense demands respect, submissiveness, and a prolonged courtship before she yields. She says of Rosimond:

> Ce n'est pas que j'ai de l'éloignement pour lui; mais si j'aime jamais, il en coûtera un peu davantage pour me rendre sensible. Je n'accorderai mon coeur qu'aux soins les plus tendres, qu'à tout ce que l'amour aura de plus respectueux, de plus soumis: il faudra qu'on me dise mille fois, je vous aime, avant que je le croie, et que je m'en soucie; qu'on se fasse une affaire de la dernière importance de me le persuader; qu'on ait la modestie de croire d'aimer en vain, et qu'on me demande enfin mon coeur comme une grâce qu'on sera trop heureux d'obtenir.[25]

Hortense's attitude might seem like arrogance if we did not know that it reflects a disappointment after the anticipation of happiness. Hortense, in contrast to Lucile and Silvia, has already felt the first pangs of love, and her resistance hides a wounded sensibility and shows a resolve not to surrender herself to an unworthy lover.

The changes wrought in these very positive characters as love weakens their resistance reveal Marivaux's art in unfolding character within the narrow framework of the comedy. Lucile, goddess of reason, begins to lose her poise when she discovers Damis, her rejected suitor, making love to her sister, a plan which she herself had conceived in order to dispose of him. Jealousy and chagrin cause her to admit her true feelings. Reversing her previous declaration, she says:

> La condition la plus naturelle d'une fille est d'être mariée. . . . D'ailleurs, la vie est pleine d'embarras; un mari les partage: on ne sçaurait avoir trop de secours; c'est un véritable ami qu'on acquiert.[26]

Her fresh experience of love does not, however, destroy her clearsightedness, for she admits frankly the power of the desire to please, even in the most "reasonable" woman.

Quand j'y songe, notre amour ne fait pas toujours l'éloge de la personne aimée; il fait bien plus souvent la critique de la personne qui aime; je ne le sais que trop. Notre vanité et notre coquetterie, voilà les plus grandes sources de nos passions; voilà d'où les hommes tirent le plus souvent tout ce qu'ils valent. Qui nous ôterait les faiblesses de notre coeur ne leur laisserait guère de qualités estimables. . . . Pourquoi est-ce que j'aime? Parce qu'on me défiait de plaire, et que j'ai voulu venger mon visage; n'est-ce pas là une belle origine de tendresse?[27]

Silvia as Lisette and Dorante as Bourguignon fall in love at first sight and are stunned by the swift awakening of their emotions. The heroine is caught in a whirl of feelings—surprise, revery, sadness, confusion, pique, and tenderness—all a part of the Marivaudian pattern of nascent love. Trying desperately to regain her original self-assurance, she exclaims to Dorante:

Je ne te hais, ni ne t'aime, ni ne t'aimerai, à moins que l'esprit ne me tourne. Voilà mes dispositions; ma raison ne m'en permet point d'autres. . . .[28]

The straining of love against pride continues without abatement until the valet finally admits that he is Dorante. Silvia, in sore need of this admission,[29] utters the familiar Marivaudian line, "Ah! je vois clair dans mon coeur."[30] But still the incorrigible *précieuse,* she spurns an easy victory. Marivaux seizes this occasion to reveal the insatiability of feminine *amour-propre.* Having recovered from her earlier confusion, Silvia becomes a bold coquette, determined that Dorante must overcome his prejudice of rank and propose to her while she is still Lisette. Silvia, like Marianne, sees herself as a heroine of romance. Dorante, she announces, is to be subjected to the "combat entre l'amour et la raison"[31] beloved of the *précieuses.* Silvia's change from the reasonable young woman to the frightened victim of nascent love and then, made bold by victory, to the accomplished coquette, is a natural evolution. The *pudeur* stage exists only in the early part of her affair with Dorante, and his final capitulation brings from her a cry of triumph, of assertive *amour-propre.*

Vous m'aimez, je n'en sçaurais douter: mais à votre tour jugez de mes sentiments pour vous; jugez du cas que j'ai fait de votre coeur par la délicatesse avec laquelle j'ai tâché de l'acquérir.[32]

Hortense, as the state of her heart becomes increasingly clear, adopts the bold resource of pretending to be in love with Rosimond's friend Dorante. Her lover's indifference does not dismay her. Charm, wit, and intelligence are concentrated on a single aim, to see her lover at her knees. Only then does she reveal her tenderness for him. Her stratagem is an admirable example of the Marivaudian combination of sense and sensibility, a sound head being employed to assure the happiness of a loving heart.

> Je vous ai refusé ma main, j'ai montré de l'éloignement pour vous: rien de cela n'était sincère; c'était mon coeur qui éprouvait le vôtre. Vous devez tout à mon penchant; je voulus pouvoir m'y livrer: je voulus que ma raison fût contente; et vous comblez mes souhaits. Jugez à présent du cas que j'ai fait de votre coeur par tout ce que j'ai tenté pour en obtenir la tendresse entière.[33]

In discussing these resourceful heroines, it is interesting to compare them briefly with the creations of an earlier playwright, Dancourt,[34] whose work lies between that of Molière and Marivaux. His plays are likewise built on intrigues of love, on coquetry, on the pastimes of society, though the *milieu* is usually less aristocratic than is Marivaux's. The plots are amusing and fairly complicated, the study of contemporary manners lively and revealing. But the characters, labeled from the beginning as coquettes, love-sick maidens, ambitious women, or *intrigantes,* remain until the curtain falls without variation from the type. The first act of *L'Eté des coquettes* resembles superficially the opening scene of *Le Jeu de l'amour et du hasard.* Angélique, like Silvia, refuses to marry. But Angélique's reason for hesitating, as contrasted to that of the sensitive Silvia, is pure vanity. "De bonne foi, je n'aime personne; mais je suis ravie d'être aimée, j'en demeure d'accord."[35] She denies the charge of coquetry, preferring to be considered merely curious. "Je me plais à connaître les différents effets que l'esprit et la beauté peuvent produire dans les coeurs."[36] The play proceeds at a rapid pace, with many lovers, many tricks and deceptions, until the final apostrophe:

> Ma foi, vivent les femmes de bon esprit, toutes les saisons leur sont égales, rien ne les chagrine; et jusqu'aux moindres bagatelles, tout leur fait plaisir.[37]

There is a certain charm in the sprightly lines and clever situations; but a casual reading of this and others of Dancourt's plays is sufficient to show the thinness of his characterizations as compared with the discerning psychological development of Marivaux's heroines.[38]

A second type of self-love among Marivaux's women makes *amour-propre* synonymous with *raison*. In this case "reason" is not the self-assurance of youth. It is the judgment of experience, a conclusion reached after careful consideration of the worth of the emotional life as contrasted with a more tranquil existence. Sometimes the attitude of the women of this "reasonable" group is a consequence of real sorrow, such as the death or desertion of husband or lover. With them it is not fear of the unknown but knowledge of reality that deters them from loving again. The older and more sophisticated women of this group discount emotional experiences and prefer, so they think, a companionship of wit or of intellectual interests to one of love. When once more they are aroused, they do not show bewilderment or hesitation, for they understand the significance of their feelings. But reason is challenged by the emotional shock. The latter group, somewhat less appealing, perhaps, than Marivaux's adolescent heroines, are interesting because the resolution of their dilemma is more difficult. Apparently secure in their reasonable attitude, their surrender requires far more complex manoeuvering than in an initial experience of love. Their ultimate surrender is Marivaux's most striking demonstration of the thesis that with women the struggle of the head against the heart is one-sided.

Hortense, of *Le Prince travesti,* is a young widow who has known the joys of *amour-tendresse.* Living proof of the claims of Lucile and Silvia, she has discovered that marriage quickly ends such devoted attentions. Wed to a perfect lover, within four months she loses his love.

> En vérité, tout est perdu quand vous perdez cela. Eh bien! Madame, cet homme dont vous étiez l'idole, concevez qu'il ne vous aime plus, et mettez-vous vis-à-vis de lui: la jolie figure que vous y ferez! Quel opprobre! Lui parlez-vous, toutes ses réponses sont des monosyllabes, oui, non; car le dégoût est laconique. L'approchez-vous, il fuit; vous plaignez-vous, il querelle; quelle vie! quelle chute! quelle fin tragique! Cela fait frémir l'amour-propre![39]

Reason born of experience counts for little, however, when Hortense meets the charming Lélio. In a study of *amour-propre* this play is less significant than others of Marivaux's because the hindrance to love is

an external one, a Princess who also loves Lélio. Resolution of a complicated intrigue rather than the inner struggle of the characters constitutes its principal interest.

La Surprise de l'amour has already been mentioned as an indication
of the quality of *amour-propre* in Marivaux, the hero being in a way
a reflection of the author himself.[40] The Countess, whom Lélio meets
in his retreat, is a rational creature, scorning men and marriage because
of a previous unhappy experience. What is more, she is a coquette and
a tease. To desert a lover, she says, is to perceive his unworthiness and
to "rentrer dans le respect qu'une femme se doit à elle-même."[41] She
taunts him:

> *Lélio.* C'est assurément mettre les hommes bien bas, que de les
> juger indignes de la tendresse d'une femme: l'idée est neuve. . . .
> *La Comtesse.* Moi, monsieur; je n'ai point à me plaindre des
> hommes: je ne les hais point non plus. Hélas! la pauvre espèce! elle
> est, pour qui l'examine, encore plus comique que haïssable.[42]

Clearly understanding his inconsistency, Lélio is soon displaying the
familiar symptoms of the sensitive lover: sighs, hesitation, curiosity,
timidity, impatience. The Countess resists much longer, requiring of
her lover every proof of affection and justifying her coquetry as a conventional pastime. To Columbine she expresses her distaste for marriage, revealing at the same time a hurt long ago inflicted on her *amour-
propre*: "Quoi! je pourrais tomber dans ces malheureuses situations
si pleines de troubles, d'inquiétudes, de chagrins."[43]

Lélio finally declares that in spite of his admiration for the Countess
he does not really love her, but adds: "Je vous avouerai même . . . que
cette conviction m'est nécessaire."[44] This remark sets the Countess
aflutter. What can he mean? After much argument with herself she
reaches the obvious decision: "C'est de l'amour que ce sentiment-là."[45]
Yet the difficulty of melting an *amour-propre* so firmly fortified by reason
as hers results in a lack of warmth in the final declaration. Lélio has
a portrait of the Countess.

> *Lélio.* Il n'y aurait personne qui ne se persuade là-dessus que je
> vous aime.
> *La Comtesse.* Je l'aurais cru moi-même, si je ne vous connaissais
> pas. . . .
> *Lélio.* Ce n'est presque pas une erreur que cela; la chose est si
> naturelle à penser.

La Comtesse. Mais, voudriez-vous que j'eusse cette erreur-là?
Lélio. Moi, Madame; vous êtes la maîtresse.
La Comtesse. Et vous le maître, Monsieur.
Lélio. De quoi le suis-je?
La Comtesse. D'aimer ou de n'aimer pas.[46]

And Lélio the misogynist drops to his knees in the prescribed manner of the eighteenth-century lover.

This play would seem to support M. Trahard's contention that love in Marivaux is so intellectualized that it can hardly be called passion.[47] It reveals the function of *amour-propre* in a sensitive heart which through harsh experience feels the need to enclose its true feelings in a protective covering. The more acute the sensibility, the stronger the protection must be. Love in the theatre of Marivaux, though sincere, is nearly always held in check by the sensitive nature of his characters, who make the most of pride and of conventional modes to avoid a rebuff to their delicate feelings.

The Marquise of *La Deuxième Surprise de l'amour* has enjoyed two years of "the most tender love,"[48] only to be left a widow within a month after her marriage. She meets the Chevalier, who is nursing a broken heart after his mistress has deserted him. They swear eternal friendship on a lofty plane of books and conversation, with no thought of love. But when the Marquise hears that the Chevalier has expressed unwillingness to marry her, her *amour-propre* sustains a shock which drives her to immediate action. It is not reasonable to marry again, she says, but it is even less so to be in a situation where marriage is impossible. The behavior of the Chevalier has lessened her value in the eyes of the world, a foolish but necessary consideration.

> C'est l'opinion qui nous donne tout, qui nous ôte tout; au point qu'après ce qui m'arrive, si je voulais me remarier, je le suppose, à peine m'estimerait-on quelque chose; il ne serait plus flatteur de m'aimer.[49]

She scorns, yet bows to the idea that a woman's reputation is important: "La gloire d'une femme, gloire sotte, ridicule, mais reçue, établie, qu'il faut soutenir et qui nous pare."[50] The Marquise is a *précieuse*, but *pudeur* is a phase she has long outgrown. After an outburst of pique, she sets boldly to the task of winning the Chevalier. With the Marivaudian propensity for analysis of feeling, she considers: Is the Chevalier jealous? Or can he be in love with her after all?

L'est-il, ne l'est-il point? On n'en sçait rien, c'est un peut-être; mais cette gloire en souffre, toute sotte qu'elle est; et me voilà dans la triste nécessité d'être aimée d'un homme qui me déplaît; le moyen de tenir à cela! Oh! je n'en demeurerai pas là, je n'en demeurerai pas là.[51]

Her protestations become more and more suspect, however, as the play goes on through long analyses of *amour* and *amitié* to the final unwinding. For all her assertiveness and reasoned pride, the Marquise has fallen in love, and she proves herself capable a second time of the tenderness of the Marivaudian heroine.

Two others of Marivaux's women should be mentioned briefly here: the Countess of *Le Legs* and the Marquise of *Les Sincères*. Each is a "goddess of reason," the Countess so much so as to be almost forbidding:

> . . . femme qui néglige les compliments, qui vous parle entre l'aigre et le doux, et dont l'entretien a je ne sais quoi de sec, de froid, de purement raisonnable. Le moyen que l'amour puisse être mis en avant avec cette femme![52]

The Countess and the Marquise are mature and sophisticated types, in whom *amour-propre* as reason is so firmly established that to break its hold when their neglected hearts are quickened seems almost impossible. In truth, the heroes of these two plays are the real *âmes sensibles*, their tender feelings being confronted by the marble-like poise of extremely worldly women. The tender Marquis says of the Countess: "Elle est si sensée que j'ai peur d'elle."[53] When Lisette reports to the Countess that the Marquis is showing all the symptoms of love, the Countess surveys her lover's situation with the calm insight of the reasonable mind.

> *La Comtesse.* Hélas! je ne lui en veux point de mal. C'est un fort honnête homme, un homme dont je fais cas, qui a d'excellentes qualités; et j'aime encore mieux que ce soit lui qu'un autre. Mais ne te trompes-tu pas aussi? Il ne t'aura peut-être parlé que d'estime: il en a beaucoup pour moi, beaucoup; il me l'a marquée en mille occasions d'une manière fort obligeante.
>
> *Lisette.* Non, Madame, c'est de l'amour qui regarde vos appas; il en a prononcé le mot sans bredouiller comme à l'ordinaire. C'est de la flamme. . . . Il languit, il soupire.
>
> *La Comtesse.* Est-il possible? Sur ce pied-là, je le plains, car ce

n'est pas un étourdi: il faut qu'il le sente, puisqu'il le dit; et ce n'est pas de ces gens-là dont je me moque: jamais leur amour n'est ridicule. Mais il n'osera m'en parler, n'est-ce pas?[54]

As her passion develops, she becomes increasingly impatient with the reticence of the Marquis and with her own reserve which causes it. Desperate and frustrated, she exclaims:

Qu'on me dise en vertu de quoi cet homme-là s'est mis dans la tête que je ne l'aime point! Je suis quelquefois, par impatience, tentée de lui dire que je l'aime, pour lui montrer qu'il n'est qu'un idiot. . . .[55]

Yet the Marquis never feels sufficiently at ease to speak freely. At one point he tries to make her guess with whom he is in love, an easy solution to the *impasse*. A love affair become a guessing game causes M. Trahard to suspect the genuineness of the feeling.[56] This is a justifiable criticism of *Le Legs*, in which wit and reason preponderate to the end; but it is not possible to condemn all of Marivaux's theatre as a *jeu d'esprit*.

The Marquise in *Les Sincères* is the most formidable of the "reasonable" heroines. A product of Marivaux's mature years (1739), the play sparkles with wit and is one of the most admired works in his theatre.[57] The Marquise, a feminine Alceste, professes to admire sincerity more than any other human quality. She and Ergaste have embraced the cult of frankness, which they employ in carrying on a Platonic affair. The Marquise scorns her devoted suitor Dorante, who woos her, with far greater sincerity, in the language of tender passion. After hearing his sighs and protestations, she exclaims: "M'aimez-vous beaucoup? ne m'aimez-vous guère? faites-vous semblant de m'aimer? C'est ce que je ne sçaurais décider."[58] She appeals to Ergaste for a frank estimate of her charms. Ergaste replies that she is the most lovable of women, though perhaps not the most beautiful. This is the *coup de grâce* to the fortress of haughty pride, which is now transformed into an exigent desire to please, to be admired and loved. Observing her displeasure, Ergaste apologizes, admitting that in spite of his sincerity he may of course be mistaken. The Marquise snaps: "Quand on a le goût faux, c'est une triste qualité que d'être sincère."[59] At last, convinced of Dorante's devotion, she recognizes that her agile fencing with Ergaste was never love, and at the same time she learns of his affair with Araminte. While the two marriage contracts are being drawn up, the Marquise laughs: "Ah! Ah! Ah! nous avons pris un plaisant détour pour arriver là,"[60] a Marivaudian detour which has exposed a very vulnerable femininity.

Another type of *amour-propre* rests on prejudices of wealth or social position. It is a form of snobbery which Marivaux satirizes in *L'Ile des Esclaves* and *L'Ile de la Raison*.[61] It figures, as we have seen, in *Le Jeu de l'amour et du hasard*, where prejudice of rank struggles against nascent love. In this play, however, it is less important than elsewhere because the lovers are merely masquerading as servants. A late play, *Le Préjugé vaincu* (1746), is built entirely on the theme of social inequality. Here the problem of breaking down the prejudice is a simple one, for the heart has its say almost from the first. Angélique says of her lover:

> Dorante est aimable; mais malheureusement il lui manque de la naissance, et je souhaiterais qu'il en eût. J'ai même eu besoin quelquefois de me ressouvenir qu'il n'en a point.[62]

The "reasonable" heroines of Marivaux's theatre are sometimes affected by social prejudices, but they soon recognize the absurdity of their attitude. Araminte, the heroine of *Les Fausses Confidences,* is introduced as a veritable goddess of reason. A young widow, she handles both material and sentimental affairs with cool assurance. Those who observe her closely, however, express some doubt as to the stability of her reasonableness, if ever her emotions are aroused. Dubois has told Dorante, her lover, that she is extremely reasonable. He continues:

> Tant mieux pour vous, et tant pis pour elle. Si vous lui plaisez, elle en sera si honteuse, elle se débattra tant, elle deviendra si faible, qu'elle ne pourra se soutenir qu'en épousant.[63]

This is an accurate description of the course of her feelings and her conduct in the ensuing struggle of heart against head. When Dubois reveals to Araminte his master's feeling for her, a hopeless passion because of his poverty, Araminte protests, in spite of her confusion, that such an obstacle to love is unreasonable.

> *Dubois.* Vraiment oui; Monsieur Dorante n'est point digne de Madame. S'il était dans une plus grande fortune, comme il n'y a rien à dire à ce qu'il est né, ce serait une autre affaire; mais il n'est riche qu'en mérite, et ce n'est pas assez.

Araminte. Vraiment non, voilà les usages; je ne sais pas comment je le traiterai; je n'en sais rien, je verrai.[64]

Araminte is soon engaged in a struggle against her own emotions and convictions, against family prejudices and conniving servants, and against the hesitancy of her lover, who will not risk declaring himself until he is sure that her reason is in full retreat. The character of Araminte is perhaps the most complex to be found in Marivaux's theatre, for she combines intellect, preciosity, and pride with tenderness, open-mindedness, and sympathy. Standing midway between Silvia and Lucile, whose charm lies in their immaturity and capability of development, and the older Marquises and Countesses, who please through their sophisticated coquetry, she represents the feminine ideal of a transitional period between the age of reason and the age of sentiment.[65]

It requires a careful reading of Marivaux to find a woman who represents the pure coquette, bent on proving by many conquests the irresistibility of her charms. The heroines are too susceptible themselves to dispose at caprice of the susceptibility of their lovers. We have seen, however, that few of his heroines are above indulgence in coquetry. One alone stands out as the embodiment of *amour-propre* as *coquetterie*, the Countess of *L'Heureux Stratagème*. Frontin says of her: "Ce coeur-là, je crois que l'amour y campe quelquefois; mais qu'il n'y loge jamais."[66] Of her lover she remarks breezily: "Ce n'est pas que je n'estime Dorante; mais souvent ce qu'on estime ennuie."[67] An advocate of the single standard, she excuses her inconstancy by saying that man's requirements are unreasonable, if not actually impossible.

> Si vous les en croyez, il n'y a plus pour vous qu'un seul homme qui compose tout votre Univers. Tous les autres sont rayés; c'est autant de morts pour vous, quoique votre amour-propre n'y trouve point son compte, et qu'il les regrette quelquefois. . . .[68]

There follows a delightful bit of sparring between the Countess and the Marquise. Accused of being a coquette, the Countess replies that her friend is not innocent of the same fault, but because she is unsuccessful she hides it more carefully. To this the Marquise answers that had she not spurned his love, the Chevalier would not now be paying court to the Countess. The Countess retorts: "Je ne chicanerai pas ce dédain-là; mais quand l'amour-propre se sauve, voilà comme il parle."[69] When the Countess's intrigues leave her burdened with a lover whom she does not want and in danger of losing Dorante, she begins to doubt the worth of such conquests. "Misérable amour-propre des femmes," she exclaims. "Vanité d'être aimé! Voilà ce que vous me coûtez!"[70] She would pay dearly for her coquetry, were not the matter resolved artificially by the revelation that the Chevalier's courting is a trick to bring her to her senses.

A study of the heroines of Marivaux would not be complete without a glance at another group, who through education or background lack the sophisticated self-love evidenced in most of his women. Though they have a natural modesty, neither pride nor coquetry is a serious obstacle to the course of their love. Because of their essential simplicity, they are impatient of any obstacle which hinders the free expression of their feelings. They prove how largely *marivaudage* is the product of a peculiar environment, for displaying the least of it, they have likewise been the least exposed to the *milieu* which engenders it. One or two of them are among the most charming of Marivaux's heroines.

Silvia, the shepherdess who falls in love with Arlequin, is a naïve but sensible creature, who finds preposterous the deception and hedging usual between lovers. Warned that it is bad tactic to reveal her true feelings, she complains: "Voilà qui est étrange: on devrait bien changer une manière si incommode; ceux qui l'ont inventée n'aimaient pas tant que moi."[71] Her speech to Arlequin is piquant satire on the eighteenth-century style of love-making.

> Là, là, consolez-vous, mon amant, et baisez ma main, puisque vous en avez envie; baisez, mais écoutez, n'allez pas me demander combien je vous aime; car je vous en dirais toujours la moitié moins qu'il n'y en a. Cela n'empêchera pas que dans le fond je ne vous aime de tout mon coeur: mais vous ne devez pas le sçavoir, parce que cela vous ôterait votre amitié; on me l'a dit.[72]

La Double Inconstance shows in higher development the awakening of love in a simple nature. Silvia, in love with Arlequin, unwittingly attracts the Prince; the latter kidnaps her, hoping to persuade her to become his wife. Her ingenuousness seems to him her greatest charm.

> Les autres femmes qui aiment ont l'esprit cultivé, elles ont une certaine éducation, un certain usage, et tout cela chez elles falsifie la nature; ici, c'est le coeur tout pur qui me parle: comme ses sentiments viennent, elle me les montre, sa naïveté en fait tout l'art, et sa pudeur toute la décence.[73]

Though she is not flattered by the prospect of a royal marriage, it soon appears that she is not without the most universal form of *amour-propre*, the desire to please. Overhearing the women of the court, who remark that she is too ordinary ever to become a queen, Silvia lets this insult weaken her resistance to the Prince's suit. Soon her feelings for the Prince begin to take a turn. Urged on by the wish to refute court gossip, she renounces her rustic lover without a pang, once she is assured that his feelings will not be hurt. The importance of the play in a study of *amour-propre* lies in its support of the claim of Marianne that the desire to please is innate in all women and has no need to be developed through education.

Three of these artless heroines all bear the appropriate name Angélique. Angélique of *La Mère confidente* is a carefully sheltered maiden who nonetheless has had clandestine meetings with Dorante, arranged by the sly Lisette. Naturally shy and modest, she tries various subterfuges to convince herself that her conduct is proper. She says to Lisette: "Une autre fois, quand vous lui direz de venir, du moins ne m'avertissez pas; voilà tout ce que je vous demande."[74] Her mother, guessing the situation, persuades Angélique to confide in her and urges greater discretion. But when Angélique senses her mother's opposition to Dorante, inner obstacles of modesty and timidity are cast aside in a burst of rebellion. Angélique begs Dorante to forgive her for seeming to reject him, using her mother's warning as an excuse for her behavior.

> Excusez l'embarras où se trouve une fille de mon âge, timide et vertueuse. Il y a tant de pièges dans la vie! j'ai si peu d'expérience! serait-il difficile de me tromper, si on voulait? Je n'ai que ma sagesse et mon innocence pour toute ressource, et quand on n'a que cela on peut avoir peur: mais me voilà bien rassurée. . . .[75]

With Angélique, as with the other young women of this group, modesty is a very feeble obstacle to the progress of love.

Angélique of *L'Ecole des mères* is likewise naïve and inexperienced, the result of a strict upbringing. She has lived in seclusion from the world, and her reserve is obviously superimposed upon a naturally tender and open nature. In the following conversation with her lover, she does not regret the accidental revelation of her feelings, though her training would never have allowed such freedom of expression under ordinary circumstances.

Eraste. Il m'a paru que vous m'aimiez un peu.

Angélique. Non, non, il vous a paru mieux que cela: car j'ai dit bien franchement que je vous aime; mais il faut m'excuser, Eraste, car je ne savais pas que vous étiez là.

Eraste. Est-ce que vous seriez fâchée de ce qui vous est échappé?

Angélique. Moi, fâchée! Au contraire, je suis bien aise que vous l'ayez appris sans qu'il y ait de ma faute; je n'aurai plus la peine de vous le cacher.[76]

L'Epreuve, one of the gems of Marivaux's theatre,[77] has as its Angélique "une simple bourgeoise de campagne," who openly confesses her love for the rich Lucidor, for, as he says, "son coeur, simple, honnête et vrai, n'en sait pas davantage."[78] Wishing to make sure that she loves him for himself rather than for his wealth, Lucidor puts her to the test of hearing several other proposals and even of offering her as husband a rich bourgeois of Paris. Angélique, believing that she has been tricked into confessing her love to one who does not return it, is overwhelmed with shame and feels her love turning to hatred. The "dupe of her good faith,"[79] she nevertheless quickly forgives Lucidor when she learns his real feelings and the reason for his experiment. It may be doubted whether the love of Lucile or Silvia—certainly not that of the countesses and marquises—in similar circumstances, would have survived this harsh affront to *amour-propre.*

From a study of the Marivaudian heroines, it appears that in all except the most naïve, *amour-propre* serves as a mask or *persona,* which is dropped, at least in part, as the character attains full emotional self-realization. Marivaux's women are individualists, content in their ego. They believe themselves to be calm and reasonable creatures, able to face the world with clear-eyed assurance. After an emotional shock, there comes a denial and a retreat into themselves until an adjustment can be made to the new experience. Sometimes this adjustment comes quickly, but more frequently the illusion of freedom from domination of the feelings lasts long enough for the characters to become embroiled in a maze of amusing complications, which must be resolved before the final surrender.

With the more worldly heroines this behavior is, in varying degrees, imitative, instinctive, and rational. It is the product of the prevailing fashion of preciosity, of an instinctive defense of the ego, and of a deliberate defense of a preconceived notion of worldly happiness. The love impulse is hampered, but never in the end thwarted, by the reserves of convention and *amour-propre*. In a conventional age even adolescence reflects the tense and brilliant atmosphere of the salons and has about it something intellectual, almost *recherché*, against which emotional development must contend. The "goddesses of reason," by virtue of their wider experience, represent a deliberate choice of conduct. The coquettes as well understand their behavior and the value of the goal in view. For all of them, these "last *précieuses*," life seems to offer an opportunity for selection, the possibility of control of their destiny. The essence of Marivaux's theatre lies in the breaking down of the imitative and rational elements of this behavior and of the more obstinate phases of *amour-propre* through the awakening of the emotions, either in nascent love or in love repeated.

In the intent surveillance by *amour-propre* over the feelings, the sophisticated heroines of Marivaux's theatre differ somewhat from Marianne, who likewise experiences first love. Though *amour-propre* and reason form an ever-present check on her behavior, she gives freer expression to her feelings, whether of joy or grief, than do these more conservative young women. Nothing like her emotional outpourings in the presence of Madame de Miran is to be found in the theatre of Marivaux. Marianne's feelings are richer and more varied, and her pride in them more outspoken. She expresses her faith in the emotions as guides to truth and as indices of natural goodness. Her pride in the beauty of her feelings, in her altruistic sentiments, introduces another form of *amour-propre* and points as well to an age when *amour-propre* will no longer be a check but a spur to emotional expression. More clearly than Lucile and Silvia she heralds a new age, in which the feelings will be freed from inner or outer restraints. Yet when these bars go down completely, sentiment becomes *sensiblerie*, as in the plays of Nivelle de La Chaussée and the dramas of Diderot. Not until de Musset do we find again such fine sensitivity in the emotional life, the interest in youth as a fleeting but lovely period with its reserves as well as its *élans*. And with de Musset, a hundred years have passed, bringing a new style in feelings as well as in manners. In him there is more passion, more disillusionment, more scepticism, and more poetry. In Marivaux all this is foreshadowed, but restrained by classic measure.

THE MORALITY OF SENTIMENT

"La réflexion peut faire l'homme de probité; mais la sensibilité fait l'homme vertueux. La sensibilité est la mère de l'humanité, de la générosité; elle sert le mérite, secourt l'esprit, et entraîne la persuasion à sa suite."

L'Encyclopédie, "Sensibilité—Morale," XXX, 767.

THE high classic age, from about 1660 to 1675, is characterized externally by a patterned procedure in all forms of human endeavor. Perhaps no other society of modern times has been so single-minded in its adherence to fixed standards and so successful in imposing stability, however short-lived, on a world of change and variation. Yet the very perfection of the pattern hastened reaction.[1] If we accept the idea of a classic-romantic pendulum,[2] the period of Marivaux would show the early swing away from the ideals of classicism toward a greater freedom in life and literature. The late seventeenth and early eighteenth centuries are marked by a shifting of standards, a change from "stability to movement," and by the rise of a new mentality which questioned traditional values. The classic forms persist during this time, but attacks on them grow bolder. The moral and religious doctrines of the classical period, perhaps because they failed to represent the practice of a rich, idle, and worldly aristocracy, were first to be called in question. Evidences of this reaction have been pointed out in Chapter I. Deism had its champions in the salon of Mme de Lambert. More numerous still were those members who, like Mme de Lambert herself, hesitated to put aside the prop of orthodox religion but sought a moral principle more in keeping with social realities than the authoritarian ethics of Pascal and Bossuet. This salon represents the new lay morality and is not hostile to the morality of sentiment. Heart and head at first work together to evolve new standards, both rational and sentimental. Marivaux, sensitive recorder of the social conditions of the day, reflects both currents, though the voice of the heart speaks more clearly in him than in Mme de Lambert.

Lanson describes the seventeenth century as splendidly rather than profoundly Christian. But in spite of the *libertin* current, there was no direct attack on the principles of established religion, and great literature was for the most part Christian in inspiration. Pessimism marks the great classic writers, particularly those who fell under the influence of Port-Royal. The teachings of the church set the moral tone for the age, which is characterized by "a sad way of viewing things human, by an absence of all hope in the future of humanity."[3] Yet in actuality men no longer practiced Christian asceticism. Doctrine and conduct were increasingly at variance.[4] From the weakening of faith and the awareness of the discrepancy between belief and practice spring a new concept of happiness and a new optimism, embodied in both the rational and the sentimental moralities of the opening century.

As a friend of Fontenelle and a frequenter of the salons, Marivaux kept abreast of the most liberal thought of his time. He was not himself a systematic thinker. He looked upon life with the eye of the artist and the psychologist rather than of the philosopher. Yet he could not be indifferent to ideas that were raising the intellectual temperature of his associates, and we know from *Le Spectateur français* that he had a lively interest in social, moral, esthetic, and religious questions. The "social comedies," *L'Ile des Esclaves, L'Ile de la Raison,* and *La Colonie,* deal in half-comic, half-serious vein with problems of rank and wealth and even with the question of woman's rights. In the novels, as preoccupied as he is with analysis of emotional response, there are many implications of general ideas, for no imaginative writer who deals with the stuff of human life can avoid them. Sometimes Marivaux goes farther and states his attitudes explicitly. Among the clearest and most insistent of these attitudes in the two novels is his evident disapproval of an authoritarian religion and an authoritarian ethics. Not only does his recording of the social life of the time reflect this breaking down of authority, but through ridicule and through the pleadings of his protagonists Marivaux makes clear his preference for freedom rather than dogma in moral and religious matters.

Marivaux puts into the mouth of Jacob, his peasant hero, a frank but indulgent appraisal, quite unclassical in spirit, of man's fundamental nature.

> On est ce qu'on est, et le monde n'y a que voir. Après tout, qu'est-ce qu'on fait dans cette vie? un peu de bien, un peu de mal; tantôt l'un, tantôt l'autre; on fait comme on peut, on n'est ni des saints ni des saintes. Ce n'est pas pour rien qu'on va à confesse, et puis qu'on y retourne; il n'y a que les défunts qui n'y vont plus; mais pour des vivants, qu'on m'en cherche.[5]

Jacob represents the resistance of the average man to arbitrary restrictions of conduct. He prefers to act on impulse, under the stress of emotion, not according to a code. He is an amiable opportunist, disarming in his frankness. Explaining why his plans for a second marriage are well advanced soon after his wife's death, he says: "Dans tout le cours de ma vie, il a semblé que j'étais né pour renverser les lois ordinaires."[6] His reflections on the state of religion in France, at first deferent to the established order, become increasingly bold as he learns to rely on his own reason. A young country boy recently arrived in Paris, he apologizes for criticizing a venerable institution.

> J'eus même honte d'avoir poussé si loin mes idées; je les croyais contraires à ce principe de soumission absolue que j'avais sucé avec le lait.[7]

But he outgrows this attitude.[8] Obedience to authority, he perceives, is too often an external and mechanical observance which is not allowed to interfere with self-interest. The most selfish and eccentric behavior is often masked under a show of piety.

> Qu'est-ce donc que la religion aujourd'hui dans ce royaume? Ce n'est donc plus qu'un masque dont chacun décide le grotesque selon son caprice. . . . Qui sait encore si l'intérêt n'est pas l'âme de cette nouvelle conduite?[9]

Religion in France is founded on a "prejudice of blind obedience," an obedience superficially accepted and actually defied. This equivocal behavior may be observed both in priests and in penitents. Would it not be better to put aside entirely this false and pretentious piety, this strict obedience to the letter of religion but not to the spirit, and to allow one's heart and conscience to guide? Jacob respects true piety as he does any sentiment that comes warmly from the heart. He is not heterodox. His shrewd intelligence and his desire to rise in the world prompt him to conform, but he makes no pretense at devoutness. His frankness is contrasted with the behavior of hypocrites and devotees, whose cant and deception Marivaux delights to expose.

Marivaux ridicules society women, and *bonnes bourgeoises* as well, who submit every detail of their lives to the rule of "directors of conscience." The latter are portrayed unsympathetically; if they do not actually exploit gullible penitents for selfish ends, they overreach their function as spiritual guides and meddle in the minutest detail of private life, sometimes alienating husband and wife, sister and sister.[10] Jacob says of these directors:

Cet usage est sans doute louable et saint en lui-même; c'est bien fait de le suivre, quand on le suit comme il faut, et ce n'est pas de cela que je badine; mais il y a des minuties dont les directeurs ne devraient pas se mêler aussi sérieusement qu'ils le font, et je ris de ceux qui portent leur direction jusque-là.[11]

The Habert sisters meekly submit to direction of this kind, though not without an occasional breach in the pattern of piety. Marivaux describes a quarrel between the two sisters. Hearing an uproar above, Jacob cannot believe his ears. A quarrel is out of the question, for he believes them incapable of thus offending God. Catherine, the servant, corrects him emphatically.

"Ce sont les meilleures filles du monde," she says, "cela vit comme des saintes; mais c'est justement à cause de leur sainteté qu'elles sont mutines entre elles deux; cela fait qu'il ne se passe point de jour qu'elles ne se chamaillent sur le bien, sur le mal, à cause de l'amour de Dieu qui les rend scrupuleuses." Catherine is obliged to intervene in the argument. "Je gage que c'est quelque cas de conscience qui leur tourne le cerveau." "Bon!" says Jacob, "Un cas de conscience! Est-ce qu'il n'y a pas un casuiste avec elles? Il peut bien mettre le holà; il doit savoir la Bible et l'Évangile par coeur." "Eh! oui!" replies Catherine, "mais cette Bible et cet Évangile ne répondent pas à toutes les fantaisies musquées des gens, et nos bonnes maîtresses en ont je ne sais combien de celles-là."[12]

In contrast with this bickering is the hearty scorn of the *bonne bourgeoise* Mme d'Alain for the prying type of director and for religious scrupulosity.

Faites comme moi; je parle de Dieu tant qu'on veut, mais je ne donne rien; ils sont trois ou quatre de sa robe qui fréquentent ici: je les reçois bien; bonjour, monsieur; bonjour, madame; on prend du thé, quelquefois on dîne; la reprise de quadrille ensuite, un petit mot d'édification par-ci par-là, et puis je suis votre servante; aussi, que je me marie vingt fois au lieu d'une, je n'ai pas peur qu'ils s'en mettent en peine.[13]

Jacob sees the follies of the world but does not disdain it. He reflects the new notes of tolerance and optimism, born of the desire to be happy on this earth.[14] His hearty lust for life leads him to condone the sins of the flesh.[15] Nor does he reproach himself harshly for certain acts not strictly honorable but contributing to his rise in life. His treatment of the servant girl Geneviève, whose ill-gotten money he accepts though his "honor" will not allow him to marry her, is not according to all the rules of probity. As usual he is engagingly direct:

> Cet argent qu'elle m'offrait n'était pas chrétien; je ne l'ignorais pas, et c'était participer au petit désordre de conduite en vertu duquel il avait été acquis; c'était du moins engager Geneviève à continuer d'en acquérir au même prix. Mais je ne savais pas encore faire des réflexions si délicates; mes principes de probité étaient encore fort courts.[16]

After all, the good use to which he put the money, Jacob thinks, goes far to justify the means.

> Il y a apparence que Dieu me pardonnera ce petit gain, car j'en fis un très bon usage; il me profita beaucoup; je m'en servis pour apprendre l'écriture et l'arithmétique, avec quoi, en partie, je suis parvenu dans la suite.[17]

If poverty excuses such peccadillos, prosperity, Jacob realizes, does not. As soon as he can afford it, his virtue flourishes. And at all times, he feels, the goodness of his intentions protects him from the charge of immorality. In his promptness to follow the urges of his heart, in his generosity and quick sympathy, he portrays the natural man, at times erring, but essentially incorruptible.[18]

The concept of retribution, of this world as a testing place for another, has little place in the consciousness of Marivaux's characters except perhaps on the deathbed. What they are immediately concerned with is their personal happiness, a full and pleasurable existence. Their Christianity is not authoritarian and ascetic but sentimental, of gentle not heroic mold. There is no Polyeucte among them. It is always the softer side of Christian faith that Marivaux stresses. The death of M. de Climal, the only striking instance in the novels of fear of retribution, loses its harshness in a warm flood of penitence. Under a pious exterior Climal, Marivaux's celebrated Tartuffe, has been a seducer. But now on his deathbed he makes a full confession of his sins and seems, as the priest suspects, almost to enjoy self-abasement and remorse. The priest assures him of the mercy of God and of the sweetness of forgiveness.

Voici les merveilles de la grâce; je suis pénétré de ce que je viens d'entendre, pénétré jusqu'au fond du coeur. . . . Puisque vous pleurez, Dieu vous aime, et ne vous a pas abandonné. . . . Gémissez donc, monsieur, gémissez, mais en lui disant: O mon Dieu, vous ne rejetez point un coeur contrit et humilié. Pleurez, mais avec confiance, avec la consolation d'espérer que vos pleurs le fléchiront, puisqu'ils sont un don de sa miséricorde.[19]

Climal leaves a part of his fortune to Marianne, and this affords her the opportunity to forgive, to display the noble generosity of the *belle âme*. Though she has suffered from his wickedness and will profit by his death, Marianne is so touched by this edifying scene that she grieves as if over the loss of a dear friend.

J'ai beau être pauvre; le présent que vous me faites, si vous mourez, ne me consolera pas de votre perte; je vous assure que je la regarderai aujourd'hui comme un nouveau malheur. Je vois, monsieur, que vous seriez un véritable ami pour moi, et j'aimerais bien mieux cela, sans comparaison, que ce que vous me laissez si généreusement.[20]

Thus religion is a source of moral reclamation, of consolation and forgiveness, of pity and sympathy. Although it retains the traditional trappings, it loses its sternness in its blending with sensibility, as Leslie Stephen points out. After stating that it would be absurd to assign any precise philosophical meaning to sentimentalism, which is more a social than an intellectual phenomenon, Stephen adds that the movement "indicates certain tendencies which are connected with the development of thought."

The modern sentimentalism may, perhaps, be defined as the effeminate element of Christianity. The true sentimentalist accepts all that appears to be graceful, tender, and pretty in the Gospels, and turns away from the sterner and more masculine teaching which enables a religion to rule the world, as well as to amuse our softer hours.[21]

So modified, it gives rise to agreeably pathetic scenes, in which the sensitive heart finds opportunity for self-expression.

But religious values are seldom in the foreground in Marivaux's writings. Indeed, in the comedies they are entirely absent. He is far more interested in moral values set up on purely human standards. Conduct and character, not pious observances, determine a man's worth. Belief in the natural goodness of the heart, together with love of humanity and a desire to improve its lot, constitutes the morality of sentiment, which in Marivaux has one of its earliest and fullest expressions in imaginative literature. Jacob, without the poetry and the passion, is an early Jean-Jacques.

Though Marivaux, like Mme de Lambert, did not reject reason and decorum as aids to virtue, he embraced to a greater extent than she the conception of the heart as guide, the new morality of sentiment, in which "consciousness is ceasing . . . to be a check on the impulses of the individual and becoming a moral *sense,* a sort of expansive instinct for doing good to others."[22] The fullest and most influential exposition of the morality of sentiment in the early eighteenth century appears in the writings of Anthony Ashley Cooper, third Earl of Shaftesbury (1671-1713).[23] Shaftesbury enjoyed a wide vogue in England, where he influenced not only the poets, dramatists, and novelists of the school of sensibility, but also the neo-classicist Alexander Pope. Later this influence was extended to the continent. "His very wide influence throughout Europe," says Cazamian, "is an element in the international contagion of sensibility as a philosophical principle."[24]

Among the French writers personally acquainted with Shaftesbury were Pierre Bayle and Leclerc, who met him in Holland, and Pierre Coste and Des Maizeaux in London. In 1708 a French translation appeared of the *Letter concerning Enthusiasm,* and in 1710 Coste translated the *Essay on the Freedom of Wit and Humor.* Previous to 1709 there was no mention of Shaftesbury in any French periodical. In 1709 *Le Journal des Savants* carried an article on the *Letter concerning Enthusiasm,* and Leclerc discussed the same work in *La Bibliothèque choisie.* In 1710 the *Essay on the Freedom of Wit and Humor* was translated, and comments on it appeared in *Les Nouvelles de la République des Lettres,* in *La Bibliothèque choisie,* and in *Le Journal des Savants.* Leclerc, who maintained a warm friendship for Shaftesbury, continued through 1711 to publish articles and reviews of his works, including thirty pages devoted to a detailed *résumé* of the *Enquiry concerning Virtue and Merit.* In 1720 Des Maizeaux translated Leibnitz's *Remarks on a Letter concerning Enthusiasm* and published it in a *Recueil de diverses pièces.* In this work Leibnitz comments favorably on the theory of the beauty of virtue, Shaftesbury's central idea. After this there was silence until 1745, when Diderot translated the *Enquiry.*[25] Venturi, however, mentions the importance of the "subterranean action" of

Shaftesbury's ideas in France in the first half of the eighteenth century,[26] though a widespread interest in him is not discernible until Diderot's translation introduced him to the philosophers of the Enlightenment, among whom Diderot himself and Rousseau became the principal disciples.[27]

It is probable that Shaftesbury's theory of the moral sense, of an innate conscience that spontaneously distinguishes between the good and the bad, was known to members of Mme de Lambert's salon. However that may be, there is a close parallelism between the morality of sentiment sketched by Mme de Lambert herself and the ideas of the English moralist.[28] Though I have not been able to ascertain whether Marivaux read Shaftesbury, he was quite possibly familiar with the theory of the moral sense through his salon associations and through the above-mentioned articles and reviews. The fact that his moral ideas, both implicit and explicit, are not always consistent, that he sometimes appears to hesitate between a rational and a sentimental morality, though inclined by temperament toward the latter, would suggest that he was not acquainted at first hand with the full text of a treatise so persuasive and dogmatic as Shaftesbury's *Enquiry*, not available in French translation until 1745. Marivaux was given to random observation and reflection rather than to theorizing and to study of the moral philosophers. Whether he was a reader of Shaftesbury or not, however, it is certain that sentimental and humanitarian ideas bearing a close resemblance to Shaftesburian ethics were current in the society he frequented. Many of Shaftesbury's ideas may be found in the writings of Pierre Bayle, whose friendship with the English philosopher we have already noted.[29] Bayle's belief in an innate moral sense—"Il y a des idées d'honneur dans le genre humain, qui sont un ouvrage de la nature, c'est-à-dire de la Providence générale"[30]—and his theory of the influence of the emotions on conduct—"Le véritable principe des actions de l'homme n'est autre chose que le tempérament, l'inclination naturelle pour le plaisir, le goût que l'on contracte pour certains objets, le désir de plaire à quelqu'un. . . ."[31] received expanded and enthusiastic presentation in the writings of Shaftesbury. The roundabout infiltration of Bayle's ideas into France, through the medium of the English deistic writers, emphasizes the cosmopolitan character of these ideas and makes exact identification of sources often difficult. This continues to be true throughout the history of the French deistic movement

There seems to be no question but that the contributions of the French *précurseurs*, Bayle, Fontenelle, and Perrault, were not felt directly to any great extent by the later French school, but first crossed the Channel, only to return, greatly augmented by Toland, Collins, and their followers, to the welcoming arms of Voltaire and d'Holbach.[32]

Though Marivaux cannot be unreservedly classed among the deists, his acceptance of certain of their ideas as to the role of the feelings in human relationships marks him as a transitional figure between the rationalistic morality of the late seventeenth century and the eighteenth-century morality of sentiment. Many of his characters display the sentimental virtuosity admired and advocated by Shaftesbury.

Shaftesbury, one of the early deists, identifies God with the principle of harmonious order in the universe. Man's place in the well-planned scheme of things is an important one: as Nature's proudest creation, he is himself divine. The theological conception of a corrupt and groveling humanity, burdened with original sin and faced with problematical redemption, yields before the optimistic notion of a creature essentially noble and good.

With the establishment of man's divinity, external checks to his behavior are deprecated. Hell, the devil, the last judgment, are offensive conceptions, at least to the "liberal, polished, and refined part of mankind," and should be retained only for the "vulgar," who fail to grasp their true position in the universal order. Man's real guide to conduct lies within himself, in the moral sense, which for Shaftesbury is a natural and hence a divine instinct. Man possesses a native power to discern right and wrong, an ability denied him by the theological doctrine of depravity. It is natural for him to hate vice and to love virtue.

> The heart cannot possibly remain neutral, but constantly takes part one way or other. However false or corrupt it be within itself, it finds the difference, as to beauty and comeliness, between one heart and another, one turn of affection, one behavior, one sentiment, and another; and accordingly, in all disinterested cases, must approve in some measure of what is natural and honest, and disapprove what is dishonest and corrupt.[33]

For the superior individual, then, the "virtuoso," the moral sense takes the place of religious sanctions and rewards. It instinctively approves excellence in conduct and is closely associated with the esthetic sense, which spontaneously recognizes excellence in art. This infallible inward sense, through which we apprehend the universal harmony, is the basis of both moral and esthetic perceptions. Virtue is best served by a cultivation of taste in conduct, as one cultivates taste in art. The virtuoso in morals seeks to make life an art by effecting a harmony between the egoistic and the social impulses. There is no essential conflict between virtue and self-interest. To be good does not involve a sacrifice, for exercise of man's naturally altruistic instincts gives pleasure. What is beneficial and pleasurable to others is likewise beneficial and pleasurable to oneself. "To be wicked and vicious," Shaftesbury says, "is to be miserable and unhappy . . . every vicious action must be self-injurious and ill."[34] He continues:

> To have the natural affections, such as are founded in love, complacency, good-will, and in a sympathy with the kind or species, is to have the chief means and power of self-enjoyment. . . . How much the natural affections are in themselves the highest pleasures and enjoyments, there should, methinks, be little need of proving this to anyone of human kind who has ever known the condition of the mind under a lively affection of love, gratitude, bounty, generosity, pity, succour, or whatever else is of a social or friendly sort.[35]

The self-passions—love of life, resentment of injury, pleasure, ambition, love of praise, indolence—when immoderate, "must be the certain means of losing us the chief enjoyment of life, and raising in us those horrid and unnatural passions, and that savageness of temper, which makes the greatest of miseries and the most wretched state of life."[36] This harmonizing of natural or social affections and self-affections is Shaftesbury's great interest. Love of humanity should be man's ruling passion, the measure of his virtue, "which of all excellences and beauties is the chief, and most amiable. . . ."

> That single quality . . . beneficial to all society, and to mankind in general, is found equally a happiness and good to each creature in particular, and is that by which alone man can be happy, and without which he must be miserable.[37]

It would be false to impute to Marivaux an optimism so bland and sweeping as Shaftesbury's. In the first place his enthusiasm for man's prospects of happiness is limited by the realization of the misery that external events beyond control often bring to the most virtuous.[38] In the second place, his views of man's fundamental nature, though just as tolerant, are not so consistently flattering. Even in the best of men, Marivaux observes, the bad is mixed with the good, and it is often impossible to say which of the two, the goodness or the badness, is the more "natural." Society, as Jacob notes, sometimes corrupts; but the heart has its waywardness too. It is the wayward heart, "the heart of a man, of a Frenchman who has really existed in our time,"[39] which is responsible for the infidelity of the hitherto charming hero of *Marianne.*

> Faites-vous ici un spectacle de ce coeur naturel, que je vous rends tel qu'il a été, c'est-à-dire avec ce qu'il a eu de bon et de mauvais; vous l'avez d'abord trouvé charmant, à présent vous le trouvez haïssable, et bientôt vous ne saurez comment le trouver.[40]

Valville is not a monster; he is simply an ordinary man. His weakness and changeableness are symptoms of the instability of all things human.[41]

This sense of the equivocal nature of good and bad in humanity, which evidently springs from direct observation and not from dogmatic theory, appears throughout Marivaux's works, from *Le Spectateur français* and the plays to the novels, and accounts no doubt for the inconsistency of Marivaux's judgments on the moral nature of man. In rare and isolated instances it is possible to find in his works support for the two extreme views of Calvin and Rousseau, as well as for intermediate positions. For Marivaux, consistency was no hobgoblin. As a moralist his opinions remain in a state of flux, influenced doubtless by his moods as he wrote, as well as by observation, reading, and reflexion. His most pessimistic judgments are to be found in *Le Spectateur français,* and it may be significant that this was written in 1722-23, not long after the Law crash in which he lost his entire fortune. Here we find him expressing the theological doctrine of depravity: "It is true that we are all born wicked; but we bring this wickedness with us as a monster that must be combatted."[42] At the other extreme, we find him writing in 1725 a "philosophical" play, *L'Ile des Esclaves,* in which, in the congenial environment of a desert isle, masters and slaves are purged of the injustices toward each other perpetuated by an artificial society and return to a state of innocence. In a touching scene of reconciliation, all class distinctions are stripped away and they recognize their common heritage.[43]

Perhaps the best available clue to Marivaux's true position is Diderot's remark: "Listen, my friend, if you consider the matter closely, you will find that in everything our true opinion is not that from which we have never vacillated, but that to which we most habitually return."[44] The implied or explicit estimate of man's moral nature to which Marivaux most habitually returns is this: some men are born with a disposition to virtue, some to vice; but all men have a conscience which enables them to distinguish between good and bad. The persistence of virtue amidst the numerous temptations to wrong-doing with which the world surrounds us testifies to the strength of this innate sense of justice.

> Il faut que les hommes portent dans leur âme un furieux fonds de justice, et qu'ils aient originairement une bien forte vocation pour marcher dans l'ordre, puisqu'il se trouve encore d'honnêtes gens parmi eux.[45]

Conscience may manifest itself in two ways: rationally or instinctively. In the first case, the moral issue presents itself to the consciousness as an idea of justice or obligation, and reason becomes the corrective of anti-social impulses.

> Nous sommes frappés de la nécessité qu'il y a d'observer un certain ordre, qui nous mette à l'abri des effets de nos mauvaises disposi-tions; et la raison, qui nous montre cette nécessité, est le correctif de notre iniquité même.[46]

There are some individuals, however, in whom the disposition to virtue is so strong that conscience operates instinctively, thus eliminat-ing in most instances the need for reasoning with oneself before the act. Virtue is "in the blood," as Mme de Miran says of Marianne, or one is "naturally honorable," as Jacob says of himself.

The conscience as a rational agency stems from the moral theory of the seventeenth century. The conscience as an instinctive agency an-ticipates Rousseau's morality of sentiment. As will be shown in Chapter IX, Marivaux never completely substitutes feeling for reason in the moral choice. His heroine Marianne is both "sensible et raisonnable." In this respect as in many others he is a transitional figure. But his most glowing tributes are reserved for the character in whose being virtue is so firmly implanted that instinct can be trusted to guide him aright: "an instinct which guides us and makes us act without reflec-tion, when we are confronted with a touching spectacle."[47] This sense varies among men, being more fully developed in some than in others. Marivaux's "virtuoso" is the *bon coeur,* or the *belle âme,* whose social responses are instinctive and sure because they spring from the promptings of the heart. The good hearts form an *élite,* an aristocracy based on fineness of feeling rather than on intellect or birth. Marivaux does not present his *bon coeur* as part of an abstract philosophical system; he studies him in his setting, as he moves among men. We see the functioning of the "moral sense" in a hundred different situations where its beauty is calculated to arouse the admiration of the reader. It is only one step from Marivaux's consciousness of the beauty of virtuous acts, impressed on the reader throughout *Marianne,* to the identification of the beautiful and the good in later writers of the sensibility movement, such as Diderot and Rousseau.[48]

Both Marianne and Jacob are *bons coeurs,* so esteemed by themselves and others. Just as Marianne possesses natural taste which leads her unerringly to prefer the exquisite in dress, manners, and material surroundings, so she is endowed with a moral sense which prompts generous and noble conduct. This gift wins for her the warm admiration of Mme de Miran.

> Je puis vous assurer que, par son esprit, par les qualités de l'âme, et par la noblesse des procédés, elle est demoiselle autant qu'aucune fille, de quelque rang qu'elle soit, puisse être . . . et ce que je vous dis là, elle ne le doit ni à l'usage du monde, ni à l'éducation qu'elle a eue, et qui a été fort simple; il faut que cela soit dans le sang, et voilà à mon gré l'essentiel.[49]

For the *bons coeurs,* nature's favorites, virtue involves—except in rare instances where the egoistic passions are most strongly engaged[50]—no effort at self-restraint, no difficult act of will conquering instinct, but a *laisser-aller* of the heart. Of course the fact that Marivaux's characters are creatures of sentiment rather than passion minimizes the temptation to wrong-doing and spares them moral conflict. Jacob possesses a fund of natural kindness, a spontaneous sympathy which leads him to respond immediately at sight of human suffering.

> Qu'on ne soit point étonné de cette générosité. Je voyais d'honnêtes gens dans le besoin; et, quoique l'orgueil et la cupidité me sollicitassent vivement, ces passions ne s'étaient point encore rendues maîtresses de mon coeur. Elles sont violentes, j'en conviens; mais la nature, qui se faisait entendre, n'eut point de peine à les terrasser.[51]

Likewise the good heart is instinctively repelled by mean or vulgar motives. Threat and intimidation cannot persuade Marianne to give up her lover. But where ignoble motives are powerless, gratitude toward those who have loved and aided her prompts her to make the sacrifice. She is compelled through the persuasion of the heart, not through external force or menace. Jacob is shocked by the proposal of M. de Fécour that he intercede favorably for him with the charming and unfortunate Mme de Dorville. "J'irais parler d'amour à une personne que je ne connais point, et cela pour vous! Mon coeur ne peut s'y résoudre."[52]

Fortunately for these noble hearts, they are part of a scheme of things in which virtue and self-interest usually coincide, at least in the long run.[53] Marianne's conduct is admirably candid and sincere in circumstances where a clandestine love affair would be neither unprecedented nor unpardonable. She places in the hands of Mme de Miran her unopened love letters. She tells of a mysterious visitor, the forerunner of family opposition to her marriage; to remain silent would have been a cause of shame to her, and poor tactics as well. The realization of the utility of virtue, however, is posterior to the act itself, which, according to the metaphysics of the good heart, must be spontaneous.

> Et puis, me direz-vous, vous ne couriez aucun risque à être franche; vous deviez même y avoir pris goût, puisque vous ne vous en étiez jamais trouvée que mieux de l'avoir été avec Mme de Miran, et qu'elle avait toujours récompensé votre franchise.
>
> J'en conviens, et peut-être ce motif faisait-il beaucoup dans mon coeur; mais c'était du moins sans que je m'en aperçusse, je vous jure, et je croyais là-dessus ne suivre que les purs mouvements de ma reconnaissance.[54]

Jacob's refusal to be a party to the evil designs of M. de Fécour gives him a two-fold pleasure, for "his heart assured him" that such high-minded conduct would advance him much farther than would the material assistance of the rich financier.[55]

Goodness of heart, with its attendant social sympathies, is not contingent upon noble birth. Marianne and Jacob, forced to make their way unaided by wealth or position, are constantly reminded of the rareness of true virtue, which prizes intrinsic rather than superficial worth. When Marianne takes refuge in the convent, the prioress listens politely to her story, but Marianne senses a lack of genuine kindness: "It seemed to me that her heart had given no sign of life."[56] M. de

Fécour is unmoved by Mme de Dorville's pleadings in behalf of her husband. Jacob finds that to Fécour poverty and distress are ideas devoid of any reality. "He must have been naturally hard-hearted, for I believe that prosperity can completely callous only such hearts as that."[57] Some men, however, conceal genuine sympathy beneath a crusty exterior, as in the case of M. Bono, the only member of a group of courtiers and financiers to be touched by the piteous situation of Mme de Dorville, the embodiment of virtue in distress. M. Bono is a "natural man," unspoiled by the refinements of polite society, simple and direct, brusque but kind. Marivaux presents him as an example of what a man of position could be if he made the most of his advantages. Too often the great man is proud and indifferent, affable only to those who can serve him, disdainful of those whom he could serve. He is portrayed in the first paper of *Le Spectateur français* as a courtier whose moral sense is all but stifled by worldly preoccupations. Marivaux feels that if the courtier could see himself through the eyes of the man whom he has offended, his vanity would melt away and he would recognize their fundamental equality.

> Vous vous amusez, dans un auteur, des traits ingénieux qu'il emploie pour vous peindre. Le langage de l'homme en question vous corrigerait; son coeur, dans ses gémissements, trouverait la clef du vôtre; il y aurait dans ses sentiments une convenance infaillible avec les sentiments d'humanité dont vous êtes encore capables.[58]

Sometimes Marivaux chooses to awaken this latent virtue in a hardened heart, as in the repentance of M. de Climal on his deathbed.

Yet in this imperfect world, everyone except a few irreclaimables respects and loves the good heart. "Virtuous people are rare," says Marianne, "but those who esteem virtue are not."[59] For the sensitive heart the spectacle of natural goodness is the cause of its warmest rhapsodies and effusions. Marianne describes her benefactress Mme de Miran as possessing "a goodness of heart which sends my heart into transports when I think of it, and which I never remember without weeping through tenderness and gratitude."[60] In the scene before the minister of justice, one of Marivaux's most striking *tableaux* of sensibility, it is Marianne's goodness of heart, aided by her beauty and her tears, that touches the relatives, banded together to exclude her from their group. The minister is the first to relent:

Je vous déclare que je ne m'en mêle plus. A quoi voulez-vous qu'on remédie? A l'estime que Mme de Miran a pour la vertu, à l'estime qu'assurément nous en avons tous? Empêcherons-nous la vertu de plaire?[61]

Amid a general flutter of hearts and handkerchiefs, all experience the "melting feeling,"[62] which, according to Rousseau, never fails to accompany the sight of virtue, generosity, and charm.

The good heart is not the exclusive property of one social class. Rare always, it is found as often among the lowly as among the proud. Though Marivaux seems to promise for Marianne a noble lineage, she appears throughout the book as a nameless orphan, ennobled only by her beauty of character. It is this virtue in humble circumstances that appeals to Mme de Miran and to Mme Dorsin and causes the minister to exclaim: "The nobility of your parents is uncertain, but that of your heart is undeniable, and I should prefer the latter if it were necessary to choose."[63] Jacob brings with him to the city the solid virtue of the peasant: "God made me simple and candid, and friendly to worthy people."[64] In his early novel, *Les Effets surprenants de la sympathie,* Marivaux praises the natural kindness of the peasants and the beauty of the simple life. In the story of the nun, interpolated in *La Vie de Marianne,* a peasant family receives the friendless Mlle de Tervire, whose rich and ambitious relatives have cast her aside. In the humble cottage of the farmer Villot she is warmly welcomed. "One is immediately attracted to goodhearted people; whatever they are, they are friends in all stations of life."[65] The natural goodness of peasants and simple folk, admired by Rousseau and George Sand, finds here an early counterpart.

For the good hearts it is not enough merely to act on their generous impulses; at the same time they must enjoy their goodness. The egoistic pleasure which accompanies all emotional experience in the sensitive soul reaches its highest pitch when the heart vibrates with sympathy or generosity. Virtue is a never-failing source of sweetness and consolation to those who possess it.[66] Marianne is flattered by the attention her beauty attracts, but prizes more highly her good heart. This inner satisfaction becomes in its turn a motive for virtuous behavior. The nun comments: "One must be honest for oneself, though often those with whom one is speaking do not deserve that one be so for them."[67] Jacob too finds in his goodness an endless source of self-satisfaction; "I applauded myself for my affection for her, as a praiseworthy feeling, as a virtue."[68] The promptings of his heart always guide him aright, he feels.

> J'ai peu de lumières pour distinguer le bien et le mal; mais quand mon coeur me dit: fais telle chose, je la fais, et je ne me suis point trouvé jusqu'à présent dans le cas de le regretter."[69]

These words may be considered an early manifesto of the morality of sentiment. Sensibility is substituted for self-restraint; an impulse of the heart serves as excuse even for questionable acts. In the same spirit Rousseau said of Mme de Warens, "Her conduct was reprehensible, but her heart was pure."[70] And Rousseau himself, his heart overflowing with love of mankind, placed his children in a foundling hospital. Jacob, like Rousseau, senses his individuality and is impatient of outer restraints. His comment on his life, "Dans tout le cours de ma vie, il a semblé que j'étais né pour renverser les lois ordinaires,"[71] is only slightly more tempered than the ringing assertion, "Je suis autre."

Marivaux, like Shaftesbury, believed in a deliberate cultivation of the moral sense. In this he is less primitivistic than Rousseau, who saw in civilization the corrupter of the good heart. This variance in attitude may possibly be attributed to their differing fortunes in the social life of the day. Where Rousseau was unable to succeed and consequently retired in disgust, Marivaux held a small but well-established place and so was able to observe more dispassionately the interplay of interests between the individual and the group. Marivaux admits that natural virtue may suffer to some extent by contact with worldly surroundings—"I left my village only three or four months ago, and I have not yet had time to be corrupted and to become wicked"[72]—but for the most part social experience stimulates and refines the responses of the good heart by providing it with a wider sphere of activity and more frequent opportunities to indulge in egoistic-altruistic pleasure. When he first arrives in Paris, Jacob's moral instincts, though fundamentally right, lack refinement and delicacy.[73] His moral sense develops rapidly, however, as his social horizon widens. He laments that poverty prevents him from responding more fully to the generous impulses called forth by the sight of human suffering.

> Il est bien triste de ne pouvoir rien, quand on rencontre des personnes dans l'affliction. . . . Je n'ai de ma vie été si touché que ce matin; j'aurais pleuré de bon coeur, si je ne m'en étais pas empêché.[74]

Naturally good, Jacob improves as his fortune brightens, so that in prosperity he is truly admirable. But though he makes progress, he fails to attain the heights of virtuosity that Marianne, a woman, does. He is the *bon coeur*, she the *belle âme*. In her an instinctive preference for the good and the beautiful is combined with an eagerness to refine and develop her natural gifts. This knowledge of her inner excellence enables her to face the world courageously and to win its admiration.

Je n'étais rien, je n'avais rien qui pût me faire considérer; mais à ceux qui n'ont ni rang ni richesses qui en imposent, il leur reste une âme, et c'est beaucoup; c'est quelquefois plus que le rang et la richesse, elle peut faire face à tout.[75]

VIII

MARIVAUX'S HUMANITARIANISM

"Lorsqu'on me parle de personnes douées d'une grande sensibilité, ce qui m'intéresse, c'est de savoir si cette sensibilité s'applique à elles ou bien à d'autres."
Pensées du Président Benoît-Champy.

AMONG the social relationships in which the generous impulses of the good heart find expression, is friendship. It is a favorite theme of Mme de Lambert, who speaks of friendship in nearly the same terms she uses to describe tender love.[1] For her it is a natural impulse; the first movement of the heart, she says, was to unite with another heart.[2] She describes the pleasures of confidence, the charm of revealing one's soul to one's friend, of reading in his heart.[3] A gentle and moderate sentiment, it is appealing to the sensitive soul, which shuns passion. Women, according to this early feminist, have a greater talent for it than do men.[4]

Marivaux, who throughout his long life proved himself a devoted friend of both men and women, presents in his novels surprisingly few instances of disinterested friendship. Nor does he devote a single essay of *Le Spectateur français* to a discussion of this theme. The friendship between Clarice and Caliste, in *Les Effets surprenants de la sympathie*, is sustained from beginning to end by an ulterior motive, Clarice's desire to hear of her beloved even from the lips of a rival and to enjoy the "charme imposteur" of vicarious feeling.[5] But because Clarice is a beautiful soul, she is able to offer her friend genuine sympathy and affection, to which Caliste responds rather tardily by praise of Clarice's virtues after her death.[6] Marianne, though she has many admirers of both sexes and of all ages, lacks young friends who share her interests. Her intimacy with Mlle de Fare, Valville's cousin, after a promising beginning, is interrupted by the disclosure of Marianne's humble origin.[7] Though Mlle de Fare remains faithful in spite of Marianne's "disgrace," Marivaux does not develop the friendship further. Marianne and Mlle Varthon, a young English girl who is placed in the convent by her widowed mother, exchange vows of eternal friendship and engage in an intimate "commerce de coeur." In the beginning it is a spontaneous affection, equally effusive on both sides. Marianne says:

> Je me pris pour elle de l'inclination la plus tendre. La sienne pour moi, disait-elle, avait commencé dès qu'elle m'avait vue; elle n'avait senti de consolation qu'en apprenant que je demeurerais avec elle.[8]

But it is a very short-lived intimacy, interrupted by rivalry in love and by Marianne's discovery of the unworthiness of Mlle Varthon. Her warmest affection of this kind is for the nun, Mlle de Tervire, into whose friendship no rivalry can of course enter, whose admiration for Marianne is whole-hearted, and who because of similar youthful experiences is able to occupy the position of adviser to Marianne.

One friendship which Marivaux develops rather fully is that between Jacob and Dorsan. Jacob saves the life of the nobly born and influential Dorsan and is in turn aided in his career. Such a relationship is particularly pleasing to the good heart because of its abundant opportunity for exercising the expansive sentiments of generosity and gratitude. Jacob's brave deed is rewarded with a burst of gratitude on the part of Dorsan.[9] Their friendship grows rapidly, and Dorsan takes responsibility for Jacob's success in the world.

Mon cher La Vallée, votre fortune n'est plus votre affaire, c'est la mienne; c'est l'affaire de votre ami, car je suis le vôtre, et je veux que vous soyez le mien.[10]

He shows the most delicate consideration for Jacob upon his introduction to aristocratic society.[11] Dorsan firmly believes that virtue is not a matter of birth but creates its own aristocracy.[12] Jacob's material benefits from this friendship support the Shaftesburian conception of the fundamental harmony between the social and the self-affections.

It is frequently said that the eighteenth century admired fidelity outside the marriage relation rather than in it.[13] Liaisons of long duration, such as that of Voltaire and Mme du Châtelet, were accepted and honored. But a husband or wife whose affection gave signs of permanence and exclusiveness became an object of ridicule.[14] Marivaux frequently satirized the manners of the *beau monde* in regard to marriage. One of his characters comments: "We know quite well that the heart is a kind of *hors d'oeuvre* in marriage."[15] Fidelity is looked upon as a decidedly provincial virtue;[16] at least in Parisian society it is less constricting.

C'est une fidélité galante, badine, qui entend raillerie, et qui se permet toutes les petites commodités du sçavoir-vivre.[17]

Farmer Blaise, having inherited a sum of money, plans to settle in Paris. Discussing their new mode of life, he says to his wife: "Nous aimer, femme! morgué! il faut bian s'en garder; vraiment, ça jetterait un biau coton dans le monde."[18]

La Chaussée, whose *Préjugé à la mode* was a *succès de larmes* of the year 1735, has his *petits marquis* poke fun at a uxorious husband who has retired to the country to seek uninterrupted domestic happiness:

> C'est un homme perdu, noyé dans son ménage, . . .
> Ce n'est point là le but que le sexe envisage
> Lorsqu'au nôtre il veut bien se laisser assortir;
> C'est d'entrer dans le monde, et non pas d'en sortir.[19]

It is not safe, however, to assume that this represents the prevailing attitude of the French toward family life in the eighteenth century. In its extreme form such conduct was confined to a small group of aristocrats, whose artificial mode of existence tended to stifle the natural affections. The absence in literature during this period of scenes of filial or conjugal affection can possibly be accounted for as a continuance of the reticence of the classic age toward the revelation of one's inner feelings. Sainte-Beuve, in characterizing the *Souvenirs* of Mme de Caylus as a perfect expression of the "pure urbanity" of the early eighteenth century, comments on the lack of childhood memories in her writings.

> Ces races aristocratiques et fines, douées d'un tact si exquis et d'un sentiment de raillerie si vif, ou n'aimaient pas ces choses simples, ou n'osaient pas le laisser voir. Leur esprit, nous le connaissons de reste et nous en jouissons; mais où est leur coeur?[20]

In his novels, as well as in his theatre, Marivaux is not concerned with the high aristocracy. He declares in *La Vie de Marianne* that it is not his purpose to "paint the feelings of the human heart in high station."[21] Perhaps he finds in the lives of the more highly privileged classes too great a uniformity of action and sentiment. At any rate, he interests himself in the lesser nobility of Paris and the provinces, in the middle classes, and in the common people. He portrays the untutored goodness of heart of Mme Dutour and of Mme d'Alain as well as the more refined emotional nature of Marianne and her foster mother, Mme de Miran. In the wide sphere of his observation we find, together with frequent scenes of domestic infidelity or indifference, many examples of tender and devoted family life. Marivaux, then, has his place among the initiators of that "intimate and domestic sensibility,"[22] which produced in the course of the century many amenities as well as absurdities in life and literature.

The psychology and the ethics of family life interested Marivaux deeply, as numerous domestic scenes in the plays and novels, as well as papers in *Le Spectateur*, show. The nun's tale, which Marivaux considered important enough to cause suspension of Marianne's adventures for more than a hundred pages, is based entirely on difficulties which arise from cross-currents of emotion within the family circle. The story contains many moving scenes: a pitiful child neglected by its mother,[23] a mother who forgives her disobedient son on his deathbed,[24] a harsh father who relents at the sight of his grandchild,[25] a long separated mother and daughter drawn together by instinctive sympathy ("la voix du sang")[26]—tableaux which anticipate the ripe age of sensibility. In *Le Paysan parvenu* Jacob, now M. de la Vallée and on the way to fortune, is overjoyed to meet his brother, who is in less fortunate circumstances. His good heart quickly transforms joy and sympathy into action, for he is convinced that sympathy alone is more often a cheap satisfaction of one's *amour-propre* than an expression of real generosity.[27]

Marivaux, like Mme de Lambert, was interested in the education of children,[28] his approach, however, being nearer to Rousseau's than was that of Mme de Lambert, who posed, at least on the surface, as a strict disciplinarian. Marivaux believed in the power of love in guiding a young child and considered a child who showed fear and constraint in the presence of his parents to be badly educated.[29] His play *L'Ecole des mères* shows that unnatural restrictions placed on youth do not hold long once the emotions are awakened. The gentle education of the child Marianne by the *curé* and his sister develops her natural talents for virtuous and resourceful living, whereas neglect and harsh treatment during childhood sow fear and chagrin in the heart of Mlle de Tervire. Four issues of *Le Spectateur français* (*feuilles* 21, 22, 24, 25) present a novelette—unfinished, as usual—the story of a man who after the loss of health and fortune retires to the country with his wife and children. The tale exalts filial affection, praises the simple virtues, and condemns the material standards of court and town. In this picture of ideal family life, a mother's affection for her son is the only force necessary to obtain obedience and reciprocal affection.[30]

Marivaux believed that when the question of marriage arises, the child's happiness should be placed before any considerations of name or fortune. His plays afford many instances of sympathetic parents whose wishes either accord with or give place to those of their children. M. Orgon is the "père raisonnable et généreux" who contrasts with the Harpagons and Orgons of the older theatre. He consents indulgently to his daughter's wish to appear in disguise before her suitor. "Va, dans ce monde, il faut être un peu trop bon pour l'être assez."[31] Mme Argante offers herself to her daughter as a friend rather than as a parent. "Te voici dans un âge raisonnable, mais où tu auras besoin de mes conseils et de mon expérience."[32] Other parents, less tractable at first, are either ignored or quickly won over.[33]

Marivaux presents Mme de Miran as an ideal parent, for once she has consented to a marriage which the world will certainly regard as highly irregular, she shares the joy of the young couple.

> Je suis moi-même sensible à la joie que je vous donne à tous deux. Le ciel pouvait me réserver une belle-fille qui fût plus au gré du monde, mais non pas qui fût plus au gré de mon coeur.[34]

In the nun's tale the father's opposition to his son's wishes brings lasting sorrow to several members of the family. In his novels as well as in his theatre, Marivaux is a consistent advocate of marriage based on love. Even Jacob, though his first venture is a marriage of convenience, heartily approves of the love match for others.[35]

The ideal family atmosphere for Marivaux is a loving yet respectful familiarity, a tone of gentleness and easy *badinage*. He ridicules formality in family relationships: the addressing of the father as *monsieur*, the repression of spontaneous demonstrations of affection.[36] Above all, Marivaux sees the family as a powerful institution for preserving virtue and morality through its supreme influence on youth during the formative years. This end is largely attained through appeal to the sentiment of gratitude.

Gratitude offers one of the strongest provocations for the outpourings of the sensitive soul. Indeed, *reconnaissance* is one of the earliest delimitations of the word *sensibilité* after its original signification, "la faculté de sentir."[37] The *curé's* sister, before her death, points out to Marianne that the memory of her childhood training should be a lifelong inspiration for noble conduct.

> Je vous ai élevée dans l'amour de la vertu; si vous gardez votre éducation, tenez, Marianne, vous serez héritière du plus grand trésor qu'on puisse vous laisser: car avec lui, ce sera vous, ce sera votre âme qui sera riche.[38]

Later, the tender relationship between Mme de Miran and Marianne affords the latter frequent opportunity to display her versatility in gratitude. Whether she is presented with a purse, an apartment, or a husband, her response is immediate and eloquent. The beauty of her thankfulness calls forth ecstatic exclamations from Mme de Miran and her friend Mme Dorsin. "Eh, ma fille . . . qui est-ce qui n'aurait pas le coeur bon avec toi, cher enfant? Tu m'enchantes."[39] Their admiration creates a sense of obligation which spurs this virtuoso in generous emotions to out-do her previous efforts, even to indulge in conspicuous self-sacrifice. She will gladly renounce all her rosy future rather than displease her foster mother.[40] Between the two chief objects of her affection, her heart has never wavered.

> C'est le coeur de ma mère qui m'est le plus nécessaire, il va avant tout dans le mien; car il m'a fait tant de bien, je lui ai tant d'obligations, il m'est si doux de lui être chère![41]

The appreciation her gratitude calls forth proves to Marianne the sweetness of this emotion and enables her to experience the familiar "contentement de soi-même," privilege of the sensitive heart. An orphan who has won for herself a mother, Marianne exemplifies the full flowering of sensibility in the family relationship.[42]

The role of the good heart in friendship and in family relations, an indication of the more open expression of personal feeling which characterizes the age of sensibility, is less remarkable than the more expansive tender-heartedness that embraces all mankind—or at least the deserving part. Marivaux's share in this dawning social consciousness and his relation to the humanitarian movement of the early eighteenth century remain to be considered.

Marivaux's observing and reflective interest in the complexity of social relationships convinced him that human lives are interdependent, that no man's happiness is entirely self-determined or existent apart from the happiness of others. His creed is perhaps expressed by Marianne, grateful recipient of numerous benefactions from good hearts touched by her misfortunes: "Nous avons tous besoin les uns des autres; nous naissons dans cette dépendance, et nous ne changerons rien à cela."[43] Long before his major novels were written Marivaux had begun to voice in his journalistic writings his sympathy for human suffering, his disapproval of a social group which valued wealth and rank above nobility of character, and his impatience with the apathy of influential persons who made no move to assist the less fortunate. His plays are frequently the vehicle for social criticism, often through random comments of the characters, but in a few instances through plot and central idea. One finds in the theatre many references to prejudices of rank. Maître Pierre remarks: "D'un sang noble? Queu guiable d'invention d'avoir fait comme ça du sang de deux façons, pendant qu'il viant du même russiau!"[44] Arlequin refuses the title of nobility offered him by the Prince: "Mon honneur n'est pas fait pour être noble; il est trop raisonnable pour cela."[45] Later he reminds the Prince that high rank carries with it certain obligations. "Allez, vous êtes mon prince, et je vous aime bien; mais je suis votre sujet, et cela mérite quelque chose."[46] Marivaux ridicules the ambition of the middle classes to climb the social ladder. Mme Argante is angry because her daughter refuses to marry the Count.

> Ma fille n'a qu'un défaut, c'est que je ne lui trouve pas assez d'élévation; le beau nom de Dorimont et le rang de comtesse ne la touchent pas assez; elle ne sent pas le désagrément qu'il y a de n'être qu'une bourgeoise. Elle s'endort dans cet état, malgré le bien qu'elle a.[47]

Araminte, however, far more tolerant than her mother, voices the familiar Marivaudian note of distress at the sight of injustice to deserving people.

> Il est vrai que je suis toujours fâchée de voir d'honnêtes gens sans fortune, tandis qu'une infinité de gens de rien en ont une éclatante; c'est une chose qui me blesse. . . .[48]

The so-called "social comedies," behind their fantastic settings, contain sharper criticism of manners and institutions of Marivaux's day than do the comments of the characters in the "surprises of love." In *L'Ile de la Raison* (1727) Spinette describes the conduct of her mistress in the following terms:

> . . . Orgueil sur la partie de la naissance. Qui sont-ils ces gens-là? de quelle maison? et cette petite bourgeoise qui fait comparaison avec moi? Et puis cette bonté superbe avec laquelle on salue des inférieurs; cet air altier avec lequel on prend sa place; cette évaluation de ce que l'on est et de ce que les autres ne sont pas.[49]

L'Ile des Esclaves (1725), discussed in respect to Marivaux's belief in natural goodness,[50] satirizes the manners of the nobility, their coquetry, their lack of consideration for those less privileged than they. The servants conceive an ambitious plan to reform their masters.

Nous vous jetons dans l'esclavage, pour vous rendre sensibles aux maux qu'on y éprouve; nous vous humilions, afin que, nous trouvant superbes, vous vous reprochiez de l'avoir été. Votre esclavage, ou plutôt votre cours d'humanité dure trois ans. . . . . Vous êtes moins nos esclaves que nos malades; et nous ne prenons que trois ans pour vous rendre sains, c'est-à-dire, humains, raisonnables, et généreux pour toute votre vie.[51]

But the "course in humanity" breaks down through the pity of the servants for their masters' unhappy state.

How widespread Marivaux assumes the social sympathies to be, may be seen from an examination of the characters he presents in his novels. Marianne, her friend Mlle de Tervire, the nuns in her convent, her benefactresses Mme de Miran and Mme Dorsin, her lover Valville, even humble folk like the *lingère* and the innkeeper's wife, are endowed with generous sentiments. From beginning to end of *La Vie de Marianne,* there are numerous instances of spontaneous sympathy called forth by Marianne's charm and her pathetic plight. From the day when as a foundling she is adopted by the *curé* and his sister, to the scene before the minister of justice which gains to her side an entire family, she is the inspiration for altruistic emotion. Her lover in fact has an excess of this virtue. Valville's proneness to sympathize with damsels in distress loses temporarily for Marianne both her lover and her pleasing prospects. A more disinterested sympathy is evidenced by the innkeeper's wife who succors Tervire's ill and penniless mother. Her deed calls forth admiration and the desire to emulate her charity:

Nous nous sentîmes attendries pour cette femme, qui, dans une adventure aussi douloureuse, avait su moins disputer que pleurer; nous donnâmes de grands éloges à la bonne action de notre hôtesse, et nous voulûmes toutes y avoir part.[52]

It is Jacob's ready sympathy which constitutes his surest claim to the distinction of *âme sensible.* In the early days in Paris, this devoted valet remained faithful to his impoverished mistress when the rest of her household had deserted her. "Pour moi," he says, "pénétré . . . de tout ce que je voyais, j'allai me présenter à Madame, et lui vouai un service éternel, s'il pouvait lui être utile."[53] This gracious act comes as a happy and amusing contrast to a series of *fourberies.* Jacob's generosity gains steadily in range and quality. Indeed, the steps of his career are marked by a succession of sympathetic impulses, followed by quick action, which usually results in unforeseen material advantage. His prompt assistance to Mlle Habert when she has a fainting spell on the Pont Neuf ends in his marriage and his first step upward on the way to fortune. As his capacity for doing good increases, Jacob frankly admires his *bon coeur* and basks in the warmth of his generous emotions.[54]

Among Marivaux's *bons coeurs* sympathy and generosity go hand in hand. Like Marivaux himself, Jacob is constantly amazed at the indifference of men of wealth who have in their hands the power to alleviate suffering.[55] When he is in a position to do so, he proves himself so magnanimous that the adjective *parvenu* in his case loses entirely its pejorative sense. Another example of generosity, leading to exaggerated self-sacrifice, is that of Mlle de Tervire, who, after years of abject poverty, finding herself assured of a comfortable income, relinquishes it without hesitation because of sympathy for the family of her benefactress.[56]

Thus sympathy and generosity frequently lead to benevolence, of which the novels provide a number of instances. Marivaux is careful, however, to distinguish false benevolence, humiliating to the receiver, and true benevolence, prompted by genuine sympathy and guided by delicacy and tact. Marianne's sensitive nature quickly notes the spirit in which benefactions are made, and she shudders before the indifferent and perfunctory manner of M. de Climal's first assistance to her (before he has discovered the charms of this needy orphan). Her remarks on the spirit of true generosity are striking in an age when charity was most often a routine duty, more rarely a part of *noblesse oblige*—as Mme de Lambert suggests it should be—and almost never the expression of a sincere desire to alleviate human suffering.

> Est-ce qu'on est charitable à cause qu'on fait des oeuvres de charité? Il s'en faut bien. Quand vous venez vous appesantir sur le détail de mes maux . . . quand vous venez me confronter avec toute ma misère, et que le cérémonial de vos questions, ou plutôt de l'interrogatoire dont vous m'accablez marche devant le secours que vous me donnez, voilà ce que vous appelez faire une oeuvre de charité? Et moi je dis que c'est une oeuvre brutale et haïssable, oeuvre de métier et non de sentiment.[57]

She points out that consideration for the feelings of those whom one assists wins the recompense of gratitude. She is amazed at the blindness of most people in not recognizing the potentialities of this simple approach.

Il est vrai que, si les hommes savaient obliger, je crois qu'ils feraient tout ce qu'ils voudraient de ceux qui leur auraient obligation: car est-il rien de si doux que le sentiment de reconnaissance, quand notre amour-propre n'en répugne point? On en tirerait des trésors de tendresse; au lieu qu'avec les hommes on a besoin de deux vertus, l'une pour vous empêcher d'être indignée du bien qu'ils vous font, l'autre pour vous en imposer la reconnaissance.[58]

True benefactions are always accompanied by this consideration for the sensibilities of others. Madame de Miran, paragon of virtues, shows infinite delicacy in her efforts to befriend Marianne lest her charity prove humiliating to her ward. Marianne exclaims:

On ne saurait payer ces traits de bonté-là. De toutes les obligations qu'on peut avoir à une belle âme ces tendres attentions, ces secrètes politesses de sentiment sont les plus touchantes.[59]

Aware of her utter dependence on her "chère mère," Marianne is touched by this tact and thoughtfulness.[60] And Mme de Miran is in turn overcome by the nobility of Marianne's nature, which makes it impossible for her to accept gifts unless she is assured of the loving-kindness which goes with them.[61] Dorsan's benefactions to Jacob lead the latter, like Marianne, to discourse on true generosity.

Il faut l'avouer, si les bienfaits ont un droit inaliénable sur notre sensibilité, le plus ou le moins de ce droit se prend dans la manière de les répandre. Souvent on donne mal; le bien mal donné perd la plus grande partie de ses attraits. Un homme est dans la misère; son état implore des secours; on veut bien les lui donner; mais on l'humilie par les demandes réitérées auxquelles on l'expose, ou on le fatigue par des remises qui l'accablent, loin de le soulager. Doit-il avoir obligation quand on lui donne enfin? Oui, s'il pense bien: le service mérite la reconnaissance; mais celui qui donne doit-il la réclamer? Non, sans doute; ce qu'on donne de cette façon n'est plus à soi; c'est une faveur que celui qui la reçoit a achetée; c'est donc son acquisition, et non pas un don.[62]

The lengthy portrait of Mme Dorsin in *La Vie de Marianne*, the best authenticated of many sketches of Marivaux's contemporaries scattered through the novels, stresses the quality of noble generosity so much admired by the author. It is quite generally acknowledged to represent

Mme de Tencin, past the adventurous age and now a noble and beneficent lady. Marivaux, who had reason to show gratitude to Mme de Tencin, paints her in Mme Dorsin as one who, having once performed a service, feels that the initial act compels repetition, that the obligation rests with her rather than with the one whom she befriends.[63]

The numerous instances of sympathetic and generous behavior in Marivaux's writings bear witness to a sincere love of mankind in this reserved and fastidious author. It is noticeable, however, that in nearly every instance where Marivaux's characters rally to the aid of persons in distress, they are drawn by an appealing quality in the unfortunate which makes generous acts easy and pleasant. These good hearts sometimes attempt, it is true, to discover a broader basis for their social sympathies. Mme de Miran offers "reason and humanity"[64] as the explanation for her generous conduct, but this abstraction loses significance in special cases, in which the pleasure of giving aid is the immediate motive.

> Je la protège; je lui ai fait du bien, j'ai dessein de lui en faire encore; elle a besoin que je lui en fasse, et il n'y a point d'honnêtes gens qui n'enviassent le plaisir que j'y ai, qui ne voulussent se mettre à ma place. C'est de toutes les actions la plus louable que je puisse faire; il serait honteux d'y trouver à redire, à moins qu'il n'y ait des lois qui défendent d'avoir le coeur humain et généreux.[65]

Disarming as her argument is, it is reasoning of the heart rather than of the head. Such generosity depends on a warm personal relationship between giver and receiver.

In a single instance in the novels Marivaux portrays a character whose benevolence seems capable of transcending personal relationships and embracing all mankind. M. Bono, mentioned above as the only one of a group of rich financiers to be moved by the plea of Mme de Dorville for her sick husband,[66] is indeed the modern humanitarian in embryo. Gruff and unprepossessing in manner, practical and sentimental at the same time, he reminds one not a little of a retired Chicago business man turned philanthropist. The difference is that Bono is a bit more philosophical. He has a wide view of human distress and of man's inhumanity to man. It is true that, like Mme de Miran, he is most deeply moved when youth, beauty, and virtue are added to the picture of distress. "Vous êtes donc bien triste, pauvre jeune femme?"[67] he asks the pretty young woman whose husband has lost both health and means of support.

After his promise of assistance, he continues to question Madame de Dorville about her unhappy life. He scoffs at her reason for selecting a noble but impoverished suitor rather than a rich *bourgeois*, the nobleman having rescued her from a wolf while the *bourgeois* fled from the scene at top speed. This argument, Bono finds, is more appropriate in a novel than in real life.

> Votre mari était excellent pour tuer des loups; mais on ne rencontre pas toujours des loups sur son chemin, et on a toujours besoin d'avoir de quoi vivre.[68]

He is eager for this gracious person to have comfort and protection. But M. Bono is also capable of a more impersonal attitude toward philanthropy. He has considered in its broader aspects the problem of human suffering and the means of alleviating it. He says:

> Il faut bien secourir les gens qui sont dans la peine. Je voudrais que personne ne souffrît, voilà comme je pense; mais cela ne se peut pas.[69]

He is a man of good will, a philanthropist within the limited sphere possible under the *ancien régime*, ready to do good when he sees the opportunity, and as such he may be considered the forerunner of the modern humanitarian.

Because of the active charity he is known to have practiced throughout his life[70] and the evidence of certain of his writings, socialistic leanings have been ascribed to Marivaux. Larroumet offers this opinion and even feels called upon to present an apology for Marivaux, an apology which at the same time explains the quality of Marivaux's social sympathies.

> S'il s'est trompé, c'est par excès de sensibilité pour ceux qui souffrent, de colère généreuse contre ceux qui jouissent au dépens de leurs semblables. Cette sensibilité, cette tendresse pour les humbles et les petits, si rare encore au moment où il écrivait, servirait d'excuse à des erreurs plus graves. Elles suffisent pour assurer aux oeuvres morales de Marivaux . . . toujours l'estime et parfois l'admiration de ceux qui consentiront à les parcourir.[71]

Marivaux's allegedly socialistic writings, however—his half-jesting advocacy of the abolishment of class distinctions in *L'Ile des Esclaves*, his sympathy for a man who is scorned because a good character is his only claim to distinction,[72] even his bitter denunciation of the rich who flaunt their wealth when others are starving[73] (protests against actual abuses

of the time seen as well by Fénelon, La Bruyère, and the Abbé de Saint-
Pierre)—pale beside the incendiary words of Rousseau and later revolu-
tionary thinkers. Marivaux remains essentially a conservative who accepts the existing order as a decree of divine Providence.[74] The social
order is a plan devised perhaps deliberately to remind men of their in-
terdependence and their duty to help one another. Yet it is a scheme
all to the advantage of the rich, and so it lays upon them heavy obligations.

> Cette inégale distribution des biens . . . lie nécessairement les
> hommes les uns aux autres, il est vrai: mais le commerce qu'elle forme
> entr'eux n'est-il pas trop dur pour les uns, et trop doux pour les
> autres? et cette différence énorme qui se trouve aujourd'hui entre le
> sort du riche et celui du pauvre, Dieu, qui est juste autant que sage,
> n'en serait-il pas comptable à sa justice, s'il n'y avait pas quelque
> chose qui tînt la balance égale, si le bonheur du riche ne le chargeait
> pas aussi de plus d'obligations?[75]

Marivaux does, however, venture to question the divine plan when he
sees how poorly the rich man carries out his responsibility. He excuses
his boldness by saying that his complaint grows out of a sense of "impuis-
sante médiocrité," the result of his poverty and consequent inability
to satisfy his desire to help others.

> Juste ciel! Quels sont donc les desseins de la Providence dans le
> partage mystérieux qu'elle fait des richesses? Pourquoi les prodigue-
> t-elle à des hommes sans sentiment, nés durs et impitoyables, pendant
> qu'elle en est avare pour les hommes généreux et compatissants, et
> qu'à peine leur a-t-elle accordé le nécessaire?[76]

Yet Marivaux never poses as a social reformer. He has no *Discours sur
les origines de l'inégalité,* no *Contrat social.* He asks for no sacrifice
of privilege on the part of the aristocracy but simply for a more active
benevolence. He proposes no drastic social reforms nor even any systematic philanthropic projects.[77]

Humanitarian impulses then are for Marivaux a function of the good
heart, easily touched, responsive to suffering in the world, and above
all finding pleasure in its altruistic emotions. It is to the *bon coeur*
that he makes his appeal. His familiar story of the young girl faced with
the alternative of begging in the street or selling herself to a rich man

closes with an appeal to the spirit of pity and generosity among men, strengthened by glowing praise of the pleasure of true charity.

Il y serait entré je ne sais quelle douceur de vous trouver dans l'ordre, hors de reproche, et comme en état de vous regarder avec quiétude et confiance: il s'y serait mêlé je ne sais quel sentiment de votre innocence, je ne sais quelle suavité, que l'âme respire alors, qui l'encourage et lui donne un avant-goût des voluptés qui l'attendent. Oui, voluptés; c'est le nom que je donne aux témoignages flatteurs qu'on se rend à soi-même, après une action vertueuse . . . jamais l'âme n'en a satiété; elle se trouve, en les goûtant, dans la façon d'être la plus délicieuse et la plus superbe: ce ne sont point des plaisirs qui la dérobent à elle-même: elle n'en jouit pas dans les ténèbres; une douce lumière les accompagne, qui la pénètre, et lui présente le spectacle de son excellence. Voilà les plaisirs que vous avez sacrifiés à l'avilissement des plaisirs du vice.[78]

This exaltation of the joy of doing good, this personal pleasure in altruistic acts, has been depreciated as in reality a "disguised selfishness."[79] It is, of course, quite possible to explain the generous acts of Marianne and Jacob on this basis. Marivaux's recognition of *amour-propre* as a strong motive of conduct may be compared with the thesis of Mandeville, who, like Shaftesbury, was a near contemporary of Marivaux. Mandeville sees all virtue as springing from a thirst for praise, as selfishness masquerading. To account for the moral virtues of the Greeks and Romans he asserts that "what carried so many of them to the utmost pitch of self-denial was nothing but their policy in making use of the most effectual means that human pride could be flattered with."[80] No man, he says, is wholly proof against "the witchcraft of flattery, if artfully performed and suited to his abilities."[81] When reminded that many noble and generous actions have been performed in silence, he replies that pity, which prompts most of such actions, "is as much a frailty of our nature as anger, pride, or fear."[82] Of all our weaknesses it most resembles virtue, but being a natural impulse it may produce either good or evil. "Whoever acts from it as a principle, what good soever he may bring to the society, has nothing to boast of but that he has indulged a passion that has happened to be beneficial to the public."[83]

Marivaux, though he sees clearly and often smiles at the motive behind much "virtuous" behavior, is inclined to accept pity, generosity, and honesty as to the credit of the human race, no matter from what source they spring. Mandeville's explanation of humanitarian impulses as a function of *amour-propre* seems particularly applicable to Jacob, whose good deeds, prompt and unpremeditated though they seem to be, turn him too often into a boastful hero, offering to himself and demanding from everyone else admiration for his *bon coeur*. Marianne, though in retrospect she is frank in recognizing a double motive in many of her actions, appears to be more genuinely touched, more truly generous than Jacob. In spite of the ever-present "vanity of pleasing," she is more nearly the embodiment of Shaftesbury's "beautiful soul," one who has attained the desirable balance between selfish and altruistic emotions.   Individual efforts to relieve injustice and suffering, regardless of the motive which prompts them or the allotment of satisfaction to giver or receiver, lie at the base of the modern humanitarian movement.[84]

Many forces contributed to the rise of the humanitarian movement in the early eighteenth century. Deistic and philosophic thought searched for an explanation of evil in the universe and, with the setting up of purely human standards of morality, sought the way to eliminate or at least ameliorate injustices. Science too was destroying the ancient ideas of hereditary superiority among classes and races. Increased travel was breaking down barriers between nations and establishing a feeling of kinship among men. The newly enriched middle classes, trained for peaceful pursuits rather than for war, were eager for the sympathy and support of the lower classes in order to insure continued prosperity. Most important of all was the situation among the upper classes, who were beginning to feel the need for a change of interest.[85] The new philanthropy was in large part an emotional reaction against formalism in manners and thinking, a reaction which, as we have seen, substituted *amour-tendresse* for *galanterie* and demanded a greater intimacy in family relationships, more flexible standards in art and morals, a more personal religion.

The word *sécheresse* appears with noteworthy frequency in descriptions of eighteenth-century society.[86] Life had become artificial, hedged in at every turn by rigid formulas. Particularly for the women of the aristocracy an idle and patterned existence was growing irksome.[87] The first release came through a freer expression of sentiment in personal relationships; this was soon extended to mankind in general.[88] Often enough humanitarianism did little more than provide a fresh thrill for an effete aristocracy. Taine considers the glow of warmheartedness which spread over the age to indicate no actual change in manners, but rather a new affectation:

> . . . des effusions, des rêveries, des attendrissements qu'on n'avait point encore connus. Il s'agit . . . d'être humain, d'avoir un coeur, de goûter les douceurs et les tendresses des affections naturelles, d'être époux et père, bien plus d'avoir une âme. . . .[89]

He finds it always an intellectualized emotion, an idyll played in the salons. Marivaux seems to have hoped that this temperamental altruism might be encouraged to express itself in ways socially useful. But such acts of benevolence as he portrays are palliatives only, incomplete and shortsighted, with no definite program. They are significant only as timid beginnings of a movement that was later to spread over Europe and America. The sensitive heart, with its expansive social sympathies, was an initiator of humanitarian conduct, which in its early development was inextricably mixed with sensibility. Later the movement found more stable support in the rationalistic spirit and endured when its own exaggerated manifestations had perished through ridicule.[90]

Living in a transitional age, Marivaux remains free from the extreme form of sentimental altruism which appeared in mid-century. There is little in his work which goes beyond a desire to relieve suffering in deserving cases which cross his path. He is neither the theorist of nor the participant in movements of social reform. Conservative and fastidious, he recoils from the bold schemes of younger men of his day.[91] Though he seems at times to long for a better order of things, he believes such hopes to be visionary. Social inequalities have this advantage at least, that they stimulate the social virtues, through the exercise of which the *âme sensible* attains emotional self-realization. To flinch before the spectacle of human suffering, to play the good Samaritan, to view with complacency the happy results of one's random and capricious acts of generosity—such experiences are an end in themselves to the sentimental humanitarian. Marivaux's belief in an innate moral sense, his predilection for characters whose altruistic impulses are prompt and irresistible, and his emphasis on the voluptuous pleasure which results from yielding to such impulses mark his humanitarianism as personal and sentimental rather than rational. The quality of his humanitarianism is determined and limited by his sensibility.

SENSE AND SENSIBILITY

"In life, courtesy and self-possession, and in the arts style, are the sensible impressions of the free mind, for both rise out of a deliberate shaping of all things, and from never being swept away, whatever the emotion, into confusion and dullness." William Butler Yeats.

In the foregoing chapters an attempt has been made to define the positive aspects of sensibility in Marivaux's writings and to trace the extent to which the author anticipated characteristics of the full-fledged movement of sentimentalism of the second half of the eighteenth century. We have seen how a new conception of the ideal man, toyed with in the salon of Mme de Lambert, takes shape in the "sensitive heart" of Marivaux's theatre, of *La Vie de Marianne,* and, to a lesser extent, of *Le Paysan parvenu*: a character of effeminate disposition, finding the essence of its humanity in the feelings rather than in the reason or the will. Self-conscious and self-admiring, this character preserves its integrity in all circumstances through a fastidious pride and delights in the beauty of its emotional responses. In love it substitutes tenderness for passion, expressing itself in variety and delicacy of feeling rather than in intensity and self-forgetfulness. Believing that its relations with others should be characterized by warmth and spontaneity, the sensitive heart tends to rely on its feelings as moral guide, prizing particularly the virtues of sympathy, gratitude, generosity, and benevolence.

The purpose of the present chapter is to indicate the limitations of Marivaux's sensibility and its transitional nature.

Marivaux's position as a transitionalist in the movement of sensibility is partly determined by the absence in his writings of certain aspects of romantic sentimentalism. There is in his works no romantic love of nature—no colorful description of the out-of-doors, no pathetic fallacy. What references to nature we find are as bleak and casual as Molière's famous stage-setting: "Le théâtre représente un lieu champêtre, et néanmoins fort agréable."[1] A garden or a summer house may provide background for vivid scenes in the novels, but the characters give little attention to their surroundings, and descriptive elements are few and bare. Sometimes they express a positive aversion to rural life. Lisette in *Le Dénouement imprévu* says to Mlle Argante:

Que de repos vous allez avoir à sa campagne! Plus de toilette, plus de miroir, plus de boîte à mouches. . . . Il n'y a là que de bons gros coeurs, qui sont francs, sans façon, et de bon appétit.[2]

And the dénouement is brought about by the lover's yielding to his mistress's dislikes.

> *Eraste,* [à genoux.] Je vous adore; et puisque vous haïssez la campagne, je ne sçaurais plus la souffrir.[3]

Marivaux is a city author,[4] an indoor author, preoccupied with the intimate lives of people in comfortable interiors. The broad horizons, the "something green" that Rousseau contributed to literature are not to be found in Marivaux. Nature for him, as for the great classicists, is human nature, not the world of woods and mountains soon to be rediscovered by all Europe.

Primitivism, though anticipated in Marivaux, is viewed only as a piquant theory. A passage in *Les Effets surprenants de la sympathie* takes the opposite point of view, stressing the benefits brought to a tribe of savages by the presence of a white man who teaches them to cook their food and to care for the sick.[5] *L'Ile des Esclaves* is the most striking instance of his playing with the theory of primitive virtue and the corrupting effect of civilization. Here he seems to be in the direct line leading from Montaigne to Diderot and Rousseau. But though Marivaux finds many faults with the society of his day, he is far from advocating a "return to nature." Any such movement would have seemed reactionary to him. As pointed out earlier, he accepts only with limitations the doctrine of natural goodness, though he portrays many people whose natural instincts are good. Mme Argante says reprovingly to her daughter, "Les passions seraient bien à leur aise, si leur emportement rendait tout légitime."[6] Marivaux's *bons coeurs* and his *âmes sensibles* improve by cultivation, by reasonable guidance of the feelings into channels where they may develop to best advantage. He holds with Mme de Lambert that morality is "not intended to destroy nature but to perfect it."[7] Here again his position appears to be a moderate one; he approves neither of primitivism nor of over-civilization. His attitude is stated in these lines from *Réflexions sur les hommes,* written in 1750:

> Il faudrait donc, pour le bonheur des hommes, qu'ils ne fussent ni trop ignorants ni trop avancés.
>
> Trop d'ignorance leur donne des moeurs barbares; le trop d'expérience leur en donne d'habilement scélérates.
>
> La médiocrité de connaissances leur en donnerait de plus douces.[8]

Children have little place in the novels of Marivaux, and praise of the innocent bliss of early years appears in no instance. Marianne, in describing her childhood, says: "I shall be brief, for I imagine that all these details are boring to you; they are not particularly interesting, and I am eager to get on to other things."[9] The joys of family life are portrayed to some extent, but young people are far more interesting to Marivaux when they have reached adolescence and are ready to experience the adventures of self versus society than in less developed stages of their lives.

In Marivaux there is no romantic nostalgia. He does not look to the past or to the future for a more congenial world; nor does he long for the remote and the unattainable. Though recognizing its faults, he accepts as it is the society of his day, content with the prospect of gradual reform. Marivaux, like Fontenelle, believes that the present is the best time, the inheritor of all the good from older civilizations.[10] The variety of the spectacle of his own day satisfies him. His is no *mal du siècle* attitude. Nor does he attempt to recreate the atmosphere of the past, whether it be pagan antiquity or the Christian middle ages. Chateaubriand and Hugo are still to come, and their romantic idealizations of older times would probably be incomprehensible to Marivaux.

Though he attacks certain types, such as the hypocrite and the selfish rich, Marivaux is not a social reformer and moral revolutionist. He is in the vanguard among sentimental humanitarians, and he advocates certain "causes," such as saner education of children, greater freedom for women, and a mild form of redistribution of wealth. But he is far from being a propagandist or a crusader. He presents his ideas in artistic form, never as tracts for the times. His sharpest attack on the evils of the social structure, presented in the divagations of a fascinating beggar whom he calls "the needy philosopher," is dropped suddenly after the sixth chapter. The humanitarian novels of Hugo and George Sand contain far more ardent pleadings for the improvement of suffering humanity than do the novels of Marivaux.

A further limitation of Marivaux's sensibility is the absence of enthusiasm in his writings. For Diderot "l'homme sensible obéit à l'impulsion de la nature et ne rend que le cri de son coeur."[11] Venturi compares Shaftesbury and Diderot: "C'est sur un sentiment chargé de germes spéculatifs et artistiques que roule une grande partie de l'oeuvre des deux écrivains: l'enthousiasme."[12] Though the word has many connotations in both writers, its most common meaning is a "yielding to the intimate laws of their personality."[13] Diderot admired the informal, enthusiastic tone of Shaftesbury's writings. Shaftesbury's exaltation of virtue as the basis of happiness, his praise of friendship, love of country, and humanitarian sentiments, and above all his idea of man as a part of nature's well-ordered plan, find a sympathetic response in Diderot. In Shaftesbury's enthusiasm, Venturi says, Diderot found "the apology and the exaltation of the moral value of living and concrete experience as opposed to abstract schemes, the apology and the exaltation of the moral value of abandonment to the most intimate and profound part of our being."[14] I have pointed out in an earlier chapter certain similarities between Shaftesbury and Marivaux in respect to the belief in an innate moral sense and the beauty of virtue. But Marivaux never presents these ideas with the unreserved faith of the enthusiast. His natural conservatism makes intellectual or emotional enthusiasm distasteful to him. The analysis of feeling in the light of reason is too characteristic a Marivaudian procedure to admit the unbounded enthusiasm for the emotional life to be found in Diderot and Shaftesbury. To analyze a feeling, one must at some time have experienced it. But Marivaux's characters analyze themselves with a subtlety incompatible with the impetuosity of the enthusiast. Jacob, when he discovers that he is impressionable to music, gives way for a few moments to the pure delight of a new emotional experience. But emotion is quickly tempered by interest in this new aspect of his nature. Instead of the soaring passages of Diderot on music, we have the moderate pleasure of a man who tries to fit this new experience into the familiar pattern of his life.[15] Marivaux's sensibility is not a quest of "strange emotional adventure." It is not yet an escape from reality but an attempt to enrich reality by a new awareness of the feelings and a play of the intelligence over them. It introduces an element of novelty and exhilaration into conventional society sometimes on the verge of being bored. The new experiment in feeling prepares the way for coming revolution, but does not yet threaten to overthrow reason and moderation.

The reader who approaches *La Vie de Marianne* after an acquaintance with *Julie, Delphine, or René* is struck by the impression that, though Marianne would have recognized her kinship with these later *âmes sensibles,* she would have had her reserves, her misgivings about them as of a company somewhat inordinate. She would have found in them the excess of her own qualities. In other words, the sensibility of Marivaux has a moderation of tone that sets it apart from later phases of the movement. Chief among these tempering influences are common sense, a critical turn of mind, manifesting itself in irony, and a bent toward realistic portrayal of manners. The first two are heritages from the classical period, and the third is both a continuation and an anticipation. The clarity of Marivaux's insight into human nature is classical,[16] but the extension of his observation to the minutia of the emotional life and to all classes of society, with a new emphasis on the relation between environment and character, anticipates the modern realistic and psychological novel. As powerful an advocate of the life of sentiment as Marianne is, it seems clear that much of the sensibility of Marivaux's novels is simply a dispassionate reproduction of the manners of his time. The detachment of the realist is more evident in *Le Paysan parvenu,* in which Jacob finds himself in the midst of a society deliberately "ornamenting" its passions, but even Marianne, writing years afterward, is capable of standing aloof from her "movements of the heart." The realism, the irony, and the common sense of Marivaux distinguish him from writers wholly committed to the doctrine of sensibility, whose zeal knows little moderation. And yet the curious intermittence of these qualities shows him hesitating, half-sceptic and half-believer, before the vision he has caught of "la vie sentimentale."

Among these tempering influences the ironic spirit is the least constant. If it were habitual, of course, it would result in the virtual negation of sensibility, which demands for its existence a certain amount of good faith. Irony is more in evidence in the comedies than in the novels. Yet even in the novels it appears often enough to indicate a hesitant aloofness of the critical intelligence before some youthful follies of the life of feeling. In this respect particularly lies the value of Marivaux's device of the older *raconteur.* Marianne and Jacob, from the vantage point of age and experience, comment tenderly but somewhat ironically on their vanished youth. Marianne, describing her versatile coquetry, compares the past to the present and says wryly: "My pretty little face was the cause of many a folly, though you would scarcely believe it to judge by my appearance today."[17] When Climal offers to buy her a new outfit, though she suspects his motive, she is torn between honor and cupidity. After considerable debate with her conscience, she decides that she can accept the gift, for after all, Climal does not really love her and so she is not taking advantage of his weakness.[18] The older Marianne smiles at her adeptness in winning these inner struggles.

On croit souvent avoir la conscience délicate, non pas à cause des sacrifices qu'on lui fait, mais à cause de la peine qu'on prend avec elle pour s'exempter de lui en faire.[19]

Jacob, reviewing in detail the arguments for and against his liaison with Geneviève, says:

On trouvera peut-être un peu longues les représentations que me faisait l'honneur; mais c'est qu'il a besoin de parler longtemps, lui, pour faire impression, et qu'il a plus de peine à persuader que les passions.[20]

This intervention of irony makes sprightly the long digressions analyzing states of feeling and keeps emotional passages from becoming maudlin.

Marivaux's ironic bent makes him more keenly aware than are most writers in the vein of sensibility of the fugitiveness of delicate feeling. "All things pass and nothing remains." The older Marianne realizes how time and events belie vows of eternal friendship, of eternal love. She says of her story: "I am telling you facts as they happen in accordance with the instability of things human, and not adventures of the imagination."[21] "To be the plaything of the most terrible events," she says again, "is only a matter of living on earth."[22] Marivaux's characters indulge in no romantic avowal of the eternal preservation of their passion, no plea that nature share and remember their joys. Rousseau and Lamartine would be incomprehensible to them. A feeling, at the moment sincere, can be forgotten in an hour, or replaced by another, quite different and equally sincere. Marianne's tears and sighs over the death of Climal do not prevent her from enjoying very shortly afterward the flattering attentions of lover and friend.[23] After the first shock of surprise, she views Valville's infidelity as something to be expected in the natural course of events. Valville is after all only "a man, a Frenchman, and a contemporary of the lovers of his time," who had loved her "from the first moment with a tenderness as swift as it was ardent (a tenderness ordinarily of short duration, like those fruits that pass quickly because they have ripened too early)."[24]

A further limitation to Marivaux's sensibility is his realism, his aptitude for presenting people accurately in their *milieu*. Few of his characters have the autonomous personality of the ideal *âme sensible*. The heroines of the plays, with a few exceptions already noted, are clearly the product of salon atmosphere, and their conduct is determined by the code of a social group. Marianne, with her power of self-absorption, is strong enough to resist external influences not in harmony with her inner self, as is shown during her stay with Mme Dutour. Those in high station, such as Mme Dorsin, Mme de Miran, and Jacob's friend Dorsan, enjoy an economic freedom which sometimes enables them to overcome the vices and limitations of their class. But for the most part Marivaux's characters are firmly planted in an environment with which they are inseparably connected and from which they take their color; the quality of their sensibility is determined by it. Thus in the upper middle class, as depicted in *Le Paysan parvenu*, sensibility is shown to be little more than a deliberate effort to "ornament the passions" and to make the idle hours pass more agreeably. The good heart of a Mme Dutour, on the other hand, is coarsened by the vulgarity of lower middle class environment. Jacob, who passes successively through several *milieux*, takes color from all of them, each adaptation contributing a new *persona* to his "collective personality."

Marivaux's accurate portrayal of manners and character in the lower as well as in the upper ranks of society places him among the founders of the realistic novel. Jacob and Marianne, who tell in the first person their respective stories, allege their concern for truthfulness. Marianne makes it clear that she is telling the real story of her life.[25] Valville, she points out, is no monster invented to spin a tale. He is an ordinary man, and the world is full of others like him.[26] Jacob insists that his is not "a story fabricated for pleasure."[27] Such statements are the stock-in-trade of the novelist, but they are nevertheless in keeping with Marivaux's method. Although Marivaux does not attempt Balzac's detailed reproduction of material surroundings, some of his descriptions, spare as they are, create as vivid a sense of atmosphere as that of the pension Vauquer. The *ménage* in which Jacob is first employed, with its backstairs gossip and the easy ways of master and mistress, is vivid and distinctive. The casualness of Madame in her love affairs, together with her frankness and generosity, makes her a "caractère sans façon," who, as Jacob says, "led this kind of life as naturally as one drinks and eats."[28] The Habert living room furnishes another example of perfect fitness between characters and their surroundings.[29] The famous street brawl in *La Vie de Marianne*, in which Mme Dutour disputes with a coachman over the amount of a fare,[30] is one of the earliest naturalistic descriptions of the *bas peuple* in French literature and makes Marivaux the link between Scarron and Furetière in the seventeenth century and the modern realistic novelists. This passage was condemned by some critics of the day, whose tastes were offended by the author's excursion into domains hitherto excluded from "literature."[31] Nor has the criticism of this strain in Marivaux entirely passed away in recent times. Brunetière, sworn enemy of naturalism, censures Marivaux for the language of Mme Dutour and for the coarseness of Mme d'Alain and concludes: "Doubtless Marivaux, beneath all his preciosity, retained a fundamental vulgarity."[32] Fleury finds the coachman scene inappropriate in a novel so subtle and delicate in tone as *La Vie de Marianne*.[33] The sharp flavor of reality in Marivaux shows the versatility of an author who can turn easily from the study of "sensitive souls" in refined surroundings to the portrayal of sturdier creatures, such as Geneviève and Catherine, Mesdames Dutour and d'Alain, M. Bono, and Jacob himself. They live for us in speech and background, in gesture and facial expression, as well as in thought and feeling.

Marivaux's common sense is manifested in his satire of extravagant language and affected manners and in the spirit of comedy with which he treats zealotry or excessive abandonment to feeling. He exposes affectation pitilessly. Jacob, in beginning his story, says that men are not duped by pretentious conduct; they recognize the lack of real merit for which it is a substitute.[34] When he appears in society in company with the Comte de Dorsan, he sees through the artificiality which requires that speech be at variance with real feeling.

> Je ne connaissais point ce grand air du monde qui oblige la bouche à n'être presque jamais d'accord avec le coeur. Je savais encore moins qu'une belle femme ne devait plus parler sa langue maternelle, qu'elle en devait trouver les expressions trop faibles pour rendre ses idées, et que, pour y suppléer, la mode voulait qu'elle employât des termes outrés, qui souvent dénués de sens, ne peuvent servir qu'à mettre de la confusion dans les pensées, ou qu'à donner un nouveau ridicule à la personne qui les met en usage.[35]

In contrast with such preciosity, which Marianne had expected to find in a world so far removed from her own, she comments on the naturalness of manners and speech that prevails in the home of Mme Dorsin.

> Ils ne disaient rien que de juste et que de convenable, rien qui ne fût d'un commerce doux, facile et gai; j'avais compris le monde tout autrement que je ne le voyais là (et je n'avais pas tant de tort):

je me l'étais figuré plein de petites règles frivoles et de petites finesses polies; plein de bagatelles graves et importantes, difficiles à apprendre, et qu'il fallait savoir sous peine d'être ridicule, toutes ridicules qu'elles sont elles-mêmes.

Et point du tout. . . .

Il me semblait que cette politesse était celle que toute âme honnête, que tout esprit bien fait trouve qu'il a en lui dès qu'on la lui montre.[36]

Marivaux's common sense led him to adopt a conservative attitude toward religion, appropriate to a man of breeding. D'Alembert says of him: "While far from being devout, he was even farther from disbelief."[37] He despised extremes of any kind, atheists and zealots alike sharing his scorn. In an early paper of *Le Spectateur français* he censured Montesquieu for his attack on established religion in *Les Lettres persanes*.[38] But excess of religious enthusiasm was equally offensive to him, and each of the great novels contains a portrait of at least one *faux dévot*, as well as several less detailed sketches. In the scenes where these characters appear, Marivaux displays a gift for comedy worthy of Molière. The dinner at the home of the Haberts, where *gourmandise* is glossed by piety, and the quarrel that results from excess of zealotry in these maiden hearts shows the ridiculous extremes to which misguided enthusiasm leads.[39] When Jacob has married Mademoiselle Habert, he comments on the frenzy of his wife's affection, so disproportionate to his own:

Pour aimer comme elle, il faut avoir été trente ans dévote, et pendant trente ans avoir eu besoin de courage pour l'être; il faut pendant trente ans avoir résisté à la tentation de songer à l'amour, et trente ans s'être fait un scrupule d'écouter ou même de regarder les hommes, qu'on ne haïssait pourtant pas.[40]

When she asks him whether his love for her is equal to hers for him, he refers mockingly to the part which the sister and her religious director had in their marriage, their excess of scruple almost driving the couple into each other's arms.

La bonne querelle, m'écriai-je; et que ce bon directeur a bien fait d'être si fantasque! Comme tout cela s'arrange! Une rue où l'on se rencontre, une prière d'un côté, une oraison d'un autre, un prêtre qui arrive et qui vous réprimande . . . une division entre deux filles pour un garçon que Dieu envoie; que cela est admirable!

Et puis vous me demandez si je vous aime? Eh! mais cela se peut-il autrement! ne voyez-vous pas bien que mon affection se trouve là par prophétie divine, et que cela était décidé avant nous? Il n'y a rien de si visible.[41]

Mme de Ferval, Jacob's first acquaintance among society women, is a *fausse dévote,* whose piety is quickly thrown to the winds when she finds other emotional outlets. Jacob says of her:

Elle avait des grâces naturelles. Par-dessus cela, elle était fausse dévote, et ces femmes-là, en fait d'amour, ont quelque chose de plus piquant que les autres. Il y a dans leurs façons je ne sais quel mélange indéfinissable de mystère, de fourberie, d'avidité libertine et solitaire, et en même temps de retenue, qui tente extrêmement.[42]

Other scenes in *Le Paysan parvenu,* too lengthy to be detailed here, ridiculing the scrupulosity, the fanaticism, and the backsliding of the *fausses dévotes,* their unctious interviews with plump and rosy "directors of conscience," whose voracious appetite is as impressive as their piety, reach the high-water mark of comedy in Marivaux and show his scorn of the hypocrisy he sees in excess.[43]

In a less comic vein is the case of M. de Climal in *La Vie de Marianne.* Hearing Climal and the priest congratulating themselves on their generous assistance to her, Marianne comments:

Imaginez-vous qu'on avait épluché ma misère pendant une heure, qu'il n'avait été question que de la compassion que j'inspirais, du grand mérite qu'il y aurait à me faire du bien, et puis c'était la religion qui voulait qu'on prît soin de moi; ensuite venait un faste de réflexions charitables, une enflure de sentiments dévots.[44]

The excesses of Climal are not confined to his enthusiasm for charitable acts. On his deathbed he is reprimanded by the priest for his extreme penitence and self-denunciation.[45]

Marivaux also ridicules those whose goodness of heart is over-exuberant, undisciplined by taste and common sense. The garrulous Mme Dutour, who befriends Marianne, overflows with good intentions, but her tactlessness nullifies their value for her sensitive charge.[46] Mme d'Alain, in *Le Paysan parvenu,* is described as "such a good woman that a little weeping always carried the day with her."[47] Elated by a confidence entrusted to her by Jacob and Mlle Habert, she cannot refrain from telling everyone in the house that she knows a secret. Her

uncontrolled goodness of heart is treated more tolerantly, however, than
is Mme Dutour's, possibly because the whole tone of *Le Paysan* is lustier
than is that of *Marianne*.

> Son zèle et sa bonté n'en savaient pas davantage, et c'est assez
> là le caractère des meilleures gens du monde. Les âmes excessive-
> ment bonnes sont volontiers imprudentes par excès de bonté même;
> et, d'un autre côté, les âmes prudentes sont assez rarement bonnes.[48]

This appraisal of Mme d'Alain is a key to Marivaux's position in the
movement of sensibility. It shows his distrust of excess, whether on the
emotional or the rational side, and his feeling for the need of a balance
between zeal and discretion, between heart and head.

Marivaux advocates cultivation of both heart and head as the surest
basis for personal happiness. The most admirable characters of his
theatre, Araminte of *Les Fausses Confidences,* Hortense of *Le Petit
Maître corrigé,* Silvia of *Le Jeu de l'amour et du hasard,* possess sense
and sensibility in just proportion. Marianne is the best example of
this combination. She is at once wise and impulsive ("sage et neuve,"
as Marivaux says elsewhere); the interpenetration of heart and head
is so prompt and complete that her feelings are quickly converted into
sentiments—feelings, that is, not only become articulate but purged of
whatever is gross and excessive. Feeling is the motive force in conduct,
but before it issues in acts, it is adjusted to circumstances by taste and
discernment. Although warmth of feeling is the quality that Marianne
most admires, she stresses the value of a fine intelligence to direct it.
This is the basis of her comparison of her two benefactresses. The kindness of Mme de Miran is limited by whatever need obviously presents
itself; she is incapable of penetrating beyond self-evident facts in a
situation. "Voilà ce que produisait la médiocrité de ses lumières; son
esprit bornait la bonté de son coeur."[49] Mme Dorsin, on the other hand,
was able to envisage far more than reserve or timidity would allow one
to reveal to her.

> Tout ce que vous n'osiez lui dire, son esprit le pénétrait; il en
> instruisait son coeur, il l'échauffait de ses lumières, et lui donnait
> pour vous tous les degrés de bonté qui vous étaient nécessaires.[50]

That Marivaux's characters are heirs of an age of reason is shown
in another way. After their acts they are prone to analyze their behavior in accordance with a kind of rationale of sensibility. Baldly put,

they are persuaded that sensibility pays. The charge that Marianne is a cool and calculating little hussy (Saintsbury, for instance) is based on this kind of mental activity, but to make the charge is to overlook the fact that calculation does not precede but follows the act. Only rarely does Marianne entertain considerations of prudence before her response. Once she admits a "gesture of calculated prudence" which "cost her dearly."[51] But in most instances the sincerity of her feelings removes the suspicion that she is an adventuress. When reminded that emotional displays have always worked to her advantage in her relationships with Mme de Miran, she agrees, but she denies consciousness of any ulterior motive. "Je croyais là-dessus ne suivre que les purs mouvements de ma reconnaissance."[52] The balance sheet of sensibility is drawn up after the results are known, and it is consistently on the credit side. Marianne's tears, for instance, enjoy a great success, as in the scene in which her noble conduct moves the three hearts closest to her.

> Vous voyez que mon affaire devenait la leur, et ce n'était point là être si à plaindre: je n'étais donc pas sans secours sur la terre; on ne m'y faisait point verser de larmes sans conséquences.[53]

For every expenditure of emotional energy there is, almost invariably, a commensurate return. The absence of superabundant and inconsequential sensibility in Marivaux[54] is evidence that the man of reason has not yet been lost in the man of feeling. Even sensibility must recommend itself to reason.

Marivaux's ideal character, then, is described by the phrase "tendre et raisonnable"[55] or "sensible et raisonnable."[56] Marivaux believes that the feelings and the reason are reconcilable and that experience in social and private life will result in the attainment of a working balance between the two functions. One is not born to such delicate perfection; even those "nés sensibles" profit from the cultivation of both mind and feelings. The process of maturing is largely that of compensating for the underdevelopment of one or the other of these faculties. In the plays, it is more often the heart that needs cultivating, to free it from the bonds of convention. The problem of self-education is reversed for the leading characters of the two novels. From the very beginning of his career in Paris, at the age of eighteen, Jacob's common sense stands him in good stead; but his emotional responses are limited and crude. It is his sensibility that wants cultivating. While pity and generosity

are quick to show themselves and to verify his claim to natural goodness of heart; tenderness and the refinements of sentiment are as yet
unknown to him, his peasant practicality in affairs of the heart being
foremost in determining his conduct. He repulses the proposition of
the servant Geneviève, though its material advantages are attractive,
on the ground that such an arrangement is contrary to the *moeurs* of his
village.[57] Sagacity, at the service of ambition, approves his marriage
with Mademoiselle Habert, well-to-do but more than twice his age,
and his adventures with the influential Mesdames de Ferval and de
Fécour. He is inclined at first to feel that sentiment is superfluous in
love, an adornment perhaps, but oftener than not, an obstacle to the
practical aspects of an affair. But even in the early days, he is poten-
tially an *âme sensible*. When he meets Mme de Vambures, his heart
knows for the first time the trepidations and delights of the tender
passion.[58] Possibly it is true that he is successful enough now to indulge
for the first time in the luxury of tenderness, but it is true as well that
he is for the first time in a position to understand it. His affair with
the Duchess follows, though in less detailed portrayal, the pattern of
Marianne's love. It is the fulfilment of his sentimental education, and
so completes the apparent plan of Marivaux to have Jacob achieve success both materially and sentimentally.

When, on the other hand, Marianne comes to Paris at fifteen, her
sensibility is already highly developed; her mind, though "not to be
despised," is slower to mature.

> J'étais remplie de sentiment; j'avais le coeur plus fin et plus avancé
> que l'esprit, quoique ce dernier ne le fût déjà pas mal.[59]

Marianne makes more rapid progress than Jacob in achieving the desirable equilibrium of sense and sensibility. This fine equilibrium is,
I believe, unparalleled in the literature of sensibility. Marivaux goes
as far as he can in upholding the predilections of a rational age while
conceding the primacy of the heart. He is thus a transitional figure between an age of reason and an age of feeling. The synthesis of the
rational and the emotional that he effected, however, might be considered an end as well as a beginning.

How is it that Marivaux, in whom so much of the classical age survived, became the first important representative in literature of the
movement of sensibility? Was he one of those men of genius whose
clairvoyance enables them to become the mouthpiece of as yet uncon-

scious aspirations, and of whom Jung says: "They are the first in their time to divine the deeply moving mysterious currents, and to express them according to the limits of their capacity in more or less speaking symbols"?[60] It would, I believe, be both unnecessary and misleading to assume that Marivaux was a prophetic genius of this sort. It would be unnecessary because, as we have seen, the ideal of the sensitive heart had already been foreshadowed in the salon society in which Marivaux moved. It would be misleading because there is no evidence that, in Jung's words, "his work transcends his personality."[61] The clarity of his vision and the adequacy of his symbols denote the completely self-conscious artist, who selects from his *milieu* the phenomena that appeal to his interests and satisfy the needs of his personality. Contemporary estimates of Marivaux as a man are disappointingly meager but agree in ascribing to him a sensitive *amour-propre*, quick to take offense, and at the same time a real sympathy for the sufferings of others. Fear of ridicule would explain the lack of warmth that d'Alembert observed, while granting that Marivaux had "moments of sensibility."[62] Timidity contending with the wish to "shine" in society may account for both Marivaux's umbrageous silences and the forced audacity of his occasional startling singularities of expression, observed by Fontenelle.[63] All this suggests a sensibility which, at disadvantage in a society of witty and logical minds, would seek freer expression in imaginative creations.

Jacob probably speaks for his creator when he says, "Everyone has his own way of expressing himself, which comes from his way of feeling."[64] This comment touches upon the interrelation between sensibility and style and leads to the inevitable question of *marivaudage,* a term frequently applied, with varying degrees of derogation, to Marivaux's manner. Used by later writers to cover all varieties of preciosity, affectation, or eccentricity, it was employed by Marivaux's contemporaries to describe what they considered his predilection for reading profundity into trivialities, his hair-splitting effort at delicate distinctions, and his undue straining for wit and originality. It implied a double criticism, both of subject matter and style. Voltaire found in Marivaux's plays "much metaphysics and little naturalness," and remarked that *honnêtes gens* could scarcely be expected to understand them.[65] "Forgive me if I speak affectedly (fais des pointes)," he says again; "I have just read two pages of *Marianne*."[66] At the time of Marivaux's death, condemnation of his "neologisms" and "artificiality," censure often

tinged with personal venom, absorbed his critics to such an extent that
they made little effort to inquire into the significance of his way of
writing. Voisenon, calling him "the caricature of M. de Fontenelle,"
says, "He made a style for himself which no one would wish to imitate."[67]
Collé, accusing him of monotony and dullness, says of his work: "The
valets, the servants, even the peasants, bear the mark of the affected
style for which he has been so justly criticized both in his novels and in
his comedies."[68] Grimm's comment is particularly scathing:

> Il avait un genre à lui, très-aisé à reconnaître, très-minutieux, qui
> ne manque pas d'esprit ni parfois de vérité, mais qui est d'un goût
> fort mauvais et souvent faux. M. de Voltaire disait de lui qu'il pas-
> sait sa vie à peser des riens dans des balances de toiles d'araignée;
> aussi le marivaudage a passé en proverbe en France. Marivaux avait
> de la réputation en Angleterre, et s'il est vrai que ses romans ont
> été les modèles des romans de Richardson et de Fielding, on peut
> dire que, pour la première fois, un mauvais original a fait faire des
> copies admirables.[69]

Even d'Alembert, whose *Eloge* is the outstanding contemporary effort
at a just appraisal of Marivaux, speaks of "the strange neologisms which
mar even his best productions."[70]

What is the explanation of this "singularity" of manner, the object
of scorn and hostility among Marivaux's contemporaries, particularly
in his later years? Jacob sees in style the reflection of one's way of feeling. With Marivaux it is more than that. His "unique" mode of expression results not only from his singularities of feeling but from his
attempts to reproduce realistically the hidden and devious paths of the
emotional life he saw about him, to explain the motives for conduct
of a formal and self-conscious society hovering on the verge of a new
freedom in feeling and behavior. This era was a fleeting one. Soon after
the accession of Louis XV, certainly with the advent of La Chaussée's
comedies, it drew to a close. Marivaux alone among writers gave adequate expression to that moment of transition between two ruling illusions—the life of reason and the life of feeling—when the habits of analysis inherited from the one had not yet given way before the enthusiasm
of the new. His attempts to clarify the complexities of the feelings led
to lengthy analyses, which a lady among Marivaux's acquaintances
likened to walking "a hundred leagues on a single floor board."[71] The
bold and readily comprehensible effects of passion did not interest

Marivaux. Fontenelle, in his *Réflexions sur la Poétique,* describes the sphere which Marivaux was to make peculiarly his own:

> Tout le monde connaît les passions des hommes jusqu'à un certain point; au-delà, c'est un pays inconnu à la plupart des gens. . . . Combien les passions ont-elles d'effets délicats et fins qui n'arrivent que rarement, ou qui, quand ils arrivent, ne trouvent pas d'observateurs assez habiles?[72]

Exploration of this little charted realm requires a new medium of expression, and Marivaux's painstaking effort to supply it awakened the criticism of his contemporaries.

At various times during his career Marivaux sought to justify his position. Always sensitive to criticism, he replied, not without bitterness, to the charge that he "ran after wit" and that his writings were "unnatural." Naturalness in writing, Marivaux holds, lies in the expression of one's individual viewpoint rather than in an attempt to imitate either ancient or modern authors.

> . . . en un mot, penser naturellement, c'est rester dans la singularité d'esprit qui nous est échue, et ainsi que chaque visage a sa physionomie, chaque esprit aussi porte une différence qui lui est propre. . . .[73]

The sixth essay of *Le Cabinet du philosophe* (1734) is a thorough-going attempt at self-justification. If an author thinks badly, his irrationality will be reflected in his style, and criticism of his thinking will be in order. On the other hand, the extreme nicety of his thinking may account for the accusation of "guindé" or "recherché" brought against his style.

> L'homme qui pense beaucoup approfondit les sujets qu'il traite: il les pénètre, il y remarque des choses d'une extrême finesse, que tout le monde sentira, quand il les aura dites; mais qui, en tout temps, n'ont été remarquées que de très-peu de gens: et il ne pourra assurément les exprimer que par un assemblage et d'idées et de mots très-rarement vus ensemble.[74]

Marivaux emphasizes that an author's way of thinking is responsible for his style. And when his thoughts are about the complicated maze of the emotional life, the style cannot be simple and direct. Jacob speaks once more for Marivaux when he points out the difficulty of an exact reproduction:

. . . surtout dans les choses où il est question de rendre ce qui
se passe dans l'âme, cette âme qui tourne en bien plus de façons
que nous n'avons de moyens pour les dire, et à qui du moins on
devrait laisser, dans son besoin, la liberté de se servir des expressions
du mieux qu'elle pourrait, pourvu qu'on entendît clairement ce
qu'elle voudrait dire, et qu'elle ne pût employer d'autres termes sans
diminuer ou altérer sa pensée.[75]

This truth, recognized by Sainte-Beuve with certain reservations[76] and
by an increasing number of more recent critics,[77] is perhaps made
clearer by the foregoing study of the quality of Marivaux's sensibility.
The blindness of his contemporaries is due, apart from personal antago-
nisms, either to their failure to recognize the nature and the importance
of Marivaux's contribution, or to their absorption in the more practical and immediate problems of the philosophic movement. There were
a few who acknowledged his achievement. L'Abbé Prévost comments
that an author who seeks to develop the faculties of the heart as carefully as Descartes and Malebranche had developed those of the mind,
will necessarily employ terms and figures as extraordinary as his dis-
coveries.[78]

The sensitive hearts of Marivaux appear to be not only a projection
of himself and his individual vision of the world, but also a portrayal,
on a broader scale and more consistently than any predecessor, of manifestations of sensibility in the actual society of his youth. Aside from
personal disposition, the attraction of these social manifestations to
Marivaux can be explained by his interests as a moralist, a psychologist,
and an artist. In the life of feeling, moderated by reason and common
sense, Marivaux found a new basis for morality. In such divergent
spheres as love, family relationships, religion, and humanitarianism,
Marivaux considers man's feelings, in most cases, to be worthy guides.
They are an index to natural goodness, and above all, a source of happiness.

Marivaux's interest as a psychologist is everywhere evident in his
penetrating analysis of feeling. He regards the feelings as the surest clues
to man's essential nature. "For my part," Marivaux remarks, "I think
that the feelings alone can give us a sure idea of ourselves."[79] His tracing
of the intricate functioning of *amour-propre* and *amour-tendresse* and
his analysis of motives in terms of individual psychology show an almost
scientific intensity and thoroughness. Little interested in the broad gen-

eralities of human conduct, he is absorbed in observing the differences among men, in recording each detail and variation. He says:

> Et de ce que les hommes ont toujours les mêmes passions, les mêmes vices et les mêmes vertus, il ne faut pas en conclure qu'ils ne font plus que se répéter.
>
> Il en est de cela comme des visages; il n'y en a pas un qui n'ait un nez, une bouche, et des yeux; mais aussi pas un qui n'ait tout ce que je dis là avec des différences et des singularités qui l'empêchent de ressembler exactement à tout autre visage.[80]

These "differences and singularities" come everywhere to the eye of a realistic observer like Marivaux, and they appear even in his minor characters; but it is in the complex emotional life of the sensitive Marianne that he finds the richest medium for his powers of psychological analysis.

For Marivaux, it is from examining the multiciplicity of the feelings that man is seen to be the being "divers et ondoyant" who challenges the psychologist and the artist. He welcomes the phenomena of sensibility, as he sees them in Mme de Lambert's salon and elsewhere, because, introducing an element of self-conscious artistry into living, they appeal to his instinct as a creative writer. The interplay of *amour-propre* and *amour-tendresse* in Marivaux's plays introduces a new element of variety into French comedy. Although his novels show little evidence of structural plan (it was to be many years before the novel was regarded as a form of art), separate scenes manifest the skill of the artist in shaping complex materials to give unity of impression. His admiration for the sensitive heart is in part esthetic, based on the spectacle it offers in its variety of response to circumstances. Thus sensibility becomes for Marivaux the material of the creative writer, constituting the most important element in his artistic view of life.

BIBLIOGRAPHY

The Works of Marivaux

Marivaux, Pierre Carlet de Chamblain de, *Oeuvres complettes*, Paris, Veuve Duchesne, 1781, 12 vols.

―――― *Oeuvres complètes*, Edition Duviquet, Paris, Hautcoeur et Gayet jeune, 1825-30, 10 vols.

―――― *Les Effets surprenans de la sympathie, ou les Avantures de * * * *, Paris, chez Pierre Prault, 1713-14, 5 vols.

―――― *La Vie de Marianne*

1re	partie, Pierre Prault, 1731		
2me	"	, Prault père, 1734	
3me	"	, Prault fils, 1735	
4me	"	, " ",	1736
5me	"	, " ",	1736
6me	"	, " ",	1736
7me	"	, " ",	1737
8me	"	, à la Haye, chez Gosse et Néaulme,	1737
9me	"	, Fleuron Triangulaire,	1741
10me	"	, " "	, 1741
11me	"	, à la Haye, chez Jean Néaulme,	1741
12	"	, (apocryphe) en Hollande,	1745

―――― *La Vie de Marianne*, Paris, Garnier, 1912? Also 1933.

―――― *Le Paysan parvenu*, Paris, Prault père, 1734-36, 5 vols. (In Library of Congress)

―――― *Le Paysan parvenu, ou les Mémoires de M. * * * *, chez Prault père, 1735, 4 vols.

―――― *Le Paysan parvenu*, in 4 vols. Parts 1-4, Paris, Prault père, 1736; Part 5, Prault, 1736; Parts 6, 7, 8, La Haye, H. Scheuleer, 1756. (In Harvard University Library)

―――― *Le Paysan parvenu*, in 2 vols., Paris, chez la Veuve Duchesne, 1764. (In Columbia University Library)

―――― *Le Paysan parvenu* and *La Vie de Marianne*, Paris, Garnier, 1865, 2 vols.

―――― *Le Paysan parvenu*, Paris, Garnier, 1912?

―――― *La Provinciale*, edited by Paul Chaponnière, Genève, S.A. des Editions Sonor, 1922. (First published anonymously in *Mercure de France*, April, 1761).

―――― *Le Spectateur français*, Introduction et notes de Paul Bonnefon, La Collection des chefs-d'oeuvre méconnus, Paris, Bossard, 1921.

―――― *Théâtre complet*, with introduction by Edouard Fournier, Paris, Laplace et Sanchez, 1878.

―――― *Théâtre choisi*, with Eloge de Marivaux by M.F.A. de Lescure, Paris, Firmin-Didot, 1883.

General Reference Works

Aldington, Richard, "Marivaux and Marivaudage," *North American*, CCXVI (1922), 254-58.

d'Alembert, Jean Le Rond, *Oeuvres philosophiques, historiques et littéraires*, Paris, chez Jean-François Bastien, 1805, 18 vols.

d'Argenson, René Louis de Voyer de Paulmy, Marquis, *Mémoires*, Paris, Boudouin frères, 1825.

Babbitt, Irving, *Rousseau and Romanticism*, Boston and New York, Houghton Mifflin, 1919.

Bachaumont, Petit de, et Pidansat de Mairobert, *Mémoires secrets pour servir à l'histoire de la République des Lettres, depuis 1762 jusqu'à nos jours (1762-1787)*, Londres, J. Adamson, 1777-1787.

Baker, Ernest A., *A History of the English Novel*, London, H. F. and G. Witherby, 1930. 10 vols.

Baldensperger, F., *Sensibilité musicale et romantisme*, Paris, Les Presses françaises, 1925.

Baldwin, Edward C., "Marivaux's Place in the Development of Character Portrayal," *Publications of the Modern Language Association*, XXVII (1912) 168-187.

Bernbaum, Ernest, *Anthology of Romanticism and Guide through the Romantic Movement*, Thomas Nelson and Sons, New York, 1929, 5 vols.

Bertaut, Jules, *La Jeune Fille dans la littérature française*, Paris, Michaud, 1911.

Birkhead, Edith, "Sentiment and Sensibility in the Eighteenth Century Novel," in *Essays and Studies by Members of the English Association*, Oxford, Clarendon Press, 1925.

Boulan, Emile, *Figures du dix-huitième siècle: Le Sage, Fontenelle et Mme de Lambert*, Leyde, A. W. Sijthoff, 1920.

Bourgeois, F. "La Société et l'art français au XVIIIe siècle," in *Revue des Cours et Conférences*, dec., 1921; mars, 1922.

Bricaire, Nicolas de la Dixmerie, *Les Deux Ages du goût et du génie français, sous Louis XIV et sous Louis XV*, Amsterdam, chez Barthelemi Vlam, 1770.

Broglie, Emmanuel de, "Mme de Lambert," in *Le Correspondant*, 10 et 25 avril, 1895.

Brunetière, F., *Les Epoques du théâtre français (1636-1850)*, Paris, Calmann-Lévy, 1892.

―――― *Etudes critiques sur l'histoire de la littérature française*, Paris, Hachette, 1887-91.

―――― *Histoire de la littérature française classique*, 3rd. ed., Paris, Delagrave, 1921, 3 vols.

Buchner, Margaret L., *A Contribution to the Study of the Descriptive Technique of Jean-Jacques Rousseau*, Baltimore, The Johns Hopkins Publications, 1937.

Buffier, Le Père, *Traité de la société civile*, Paris, P. Gifart, 1726.

Casati, Ennemond, "Hérauts et Commentateurs de Shaftesbury en France," *Revue de la Littérature Comparée*, 1934.

―――― "Quelques Correspondants français de Shaftesbury," *Revue de la Littérature Comparée*, 1931.

Cayrou, Gaston, *Le Français classique: lexique de la langue au XVIIe siècle*, Paris, Didier, 1923.

Cazes, Albert, *Pierre Bayle, sa vie, ses idées, son influence, son oeuvre*, Paris, 1905.

Chaponnière, Paul, "Marivaux vu par l'abbé Trublet," *Revue d'Histoire Littéraire de la France*, 1928, pp. 78-84.

Chateauminois, Marie, "Eloge de Marivaux," in *Revue Politique et Littéraire*, 8 mai, 1880.

Clergue, Helen, *The Salon: A Study of French Society and Personalities in the Eighteenth Century*, New York and London, G. P. Putnam's Sons, 1907.

Collé, Charles, *Journal et Mémoires* (1748-1772), Paris, Firmin-Didot, 1868, 3 vols.

Cousin, Victor, *La Société française au XVIIe siècle selon Le Grand Cyrus*, Paris, Didier, 1858, 2 vols.

Crébillon *fils, Oeuvres*, Paris, Le Divan, 1930, 5 vols.

Dallas, Dorothy Frances, *Le Roman français de 1660 à 1680*, Paris, Librairie J. Gamber, 1932.

Dancourt, Florent Carton, *Oeuvres de théâtre*, à Paris, aux dépens des Libraires Associés, 12 vols, 1760.

Debu-Bridel, Jacques, "La Préciosité, conception héroïque de la vie," *Revue de France*, 15 sept., 1938.

Descartes, René, *Oeuvres*, Paris, L. Cerf, 1897-1910, 12 vols.

Deschamps, *Marivaux*, Paris, Hachette, 1897.

Desnoiresterres, G., *Les Cours galantes*, Paris, E. Dentu, 1860-64, 4 vols.

Diderot, Denis, *Lettres à Sophie Volland*, Paris, Editions de la Nouvelle Revue Française, 1930, 3 vols.

—— *Oeuvres complètes*, Edition J. Assézat, Paris, Garnier, 1875-77, 20 vols.

Du Bled, Victor, *La Comédie au dix-huitième siècle*, Paris, Lévy, 1893.

—— *La Société française du XVIe au XXe siècle*, Paris, Perrin et Cie., 1900-1913, 9 vols.

Duclos, Charles Pinot, *Oeuvres*, Paris, A. Belin, 1820-21, 3 vols. *Considérations sur les moeurs de ce siècle*, Vol. I.

Ducros, Louis, *La Société française au XVIIIe siècle*, Paris, A. Hatier, 1933 (2nd edition).

Du Peloux de Saint-Romain, Charles, vicomte, *Répertoire général des ouvrages modernes relatifs au XVIIIe siècle français* (1715-1789), Paris, E. Grund, 1926.

Dupont, Paul, *Houdar de la Motte*, Paris, Hachette, 1898.

Durry, Marie-Jeanne, "Quelques Nouveautés sur Marivaux," *Revue des Cours et Conférences*, 30 déc., 1938; 15 jan., 15 fév., 15 mars, 1939.

Encyclopedia of the Social Sciences, edited by R. A. Seligman and Alvin Johnson, New York, Macmillan, 1930-35, 15 vols.

Encyclopédie, ou dictionnaire raisonné des sciences, des arts et des métiers, par une Société de gens de lettres, mis en ordre par Diderot; et quant à la partie mathématique, par d'Alembert. Paris (et sous l'indication de Neufchâtel), 1751-72, 28 vols. in fol., dont 11 de pl.

Fénelon, *Oeuvres*, précédées d'études sur sa vie, par Aimé-Martin, Paris, chez Lefèvre, 1835, 3 vols.

Feugère, A., "Rousseau et son temps: la littérature de sentiment au XVIIIe siècle," *Revue des Cours et Conférences*, 36me année, 1934-36.

Fleury, Jean, *Marivaux et le marivaudage*, Paris, Plon, 1881.

Folkierski, W., *Entre le classicisme et le romantisme*, Paris, Champion, 1925.

Fontaine, André, *Les Doctrines d'art en France; peintres, amateurs, critiques, de Poussin à Diderot*, Paris, H. Laurens, 1909.

Fontenelle, *Oeuvres*, Amsterdam, chez François Chanquion, 1764, 12 vols.

Fouillée, Alfred, *La Psychologie du peuple français*, Paris, Alcan, 1927.

Fredrick, Edna C., "Marivaux and Musset: Les Serments indiscrets et On ne badine pas avec l'amour," *Romanic Review*, XXXI, *259-264*, Oct., 1940.

Friedell, Egon, *A Cultural History of the Modern Age*, New York, Alfred A. Knopf, 1933, 3 vols.

Funck-Brentano, F., *Figaro et ses dévanciers*, Paris, Hachette, 1909.

Gaiffe, F., *Le Drame en France au XVIIIe siècle*, Paris, Colin, 1910.

Gautier, Théophile, *Histoire de l'art dramatique en France*, Leipzig, Durr, 1858-59, 6 vols.

Gide, André, *Oeuvres*, Paris, Editions de la Nouvelle Revue Française, 1933-39, 15 vols. Vol. VII, "Les Dix Romans français que. . . ."

Gill, W. A., "Henry James and His Double," *The Atlantic Monthly*, C (1907), 458-66.

Giraud, Charles, *La Maréchale de Villars et son temps*, Paris, Hachette, 1881.

Gohin, F., *Les Transformations de la langue française pendant le XVIIIe siècle (1740-1789)*, Paris, Belin frères, 1903.

Goncourt, Edmond de et J. de, *L'Amour au XVIIIe siècle*, Paris, E. Dentu, 1875.

——— *L'Art du XVIIIe siècle*, Paris, Charpentier, 1859, 3 vols.

Goncourt, Edmond de, *La Femme au XVIIIe siècle*, Paris, Flammarion, 1935, 2 vols.

Gosse, Edmund, *A History of Eighteenth Century Literature*, New York, Macmillan, 1929. (First edition, 1888).

Gossot, E., *Marivaux moraliste*, Paris, Didier, 1881.

Green, F. C., *French Novelists: Manners and Ideas from the Renaissance to the Revolution*, London, J. M. Dent and Sons, 1928.

——— *Minuet*, London, J. M. Dent and Sons, 1935.

Grimm, C., "La Question Marivaux-Richardson," *Revue de la Littérature Comparée*, 1924.

Grimm-Diderot, *Correspondance littéraire*, Paris, Garnier frères, 1877, 16 vols.

Guérard, Albert Léon, *The Life and Death of an Ideal*, New York and London, C. Scribner's Sons, 1928.

Guyer, Foster E., *The Influence of Ovid on Chrétien de Troyes*, University of Chicago Libraries, 1921.

Hazard, Paul, *La Crise de la conscience européenne (1680-1715)*, Paris, Boivin et Cie., 1935, 3 vols.

——— *Etudes critiques sur Manon Lescaut*, Chicago, The University of Chicago Press, 1929.

——— *Quatre Etudes*, Oxford University Press, 1940.

Hearnshaw, F. J. C., *The Social and Political Ideas of Some Great French Thinkers of the Age of Reason*, New York, F. C. Crofts, 1930.

Hénault, Charles Jean François d', *Mémoires,* Paris, E. Dentu, 1885.

Hermand, Pierre, *Les Idées morales de Diderot,* Paris, Presses Universitaires de France, 1923.

Hourticq, Louis, *De Poussin à Watteau,* Paris, Hachette, 1921.

Houssaye, Arsène, *Galerie de portraits du XVIIIe siècle,* Paris, Charpentier, 1848.

Hughes, Helen Sard, "Translations of the Vie de Marianne," *Modern Philology,* 1917, pp. 491-512.

Jaloux, Edmond, "Marivaux," *Nouvelle Revue Française,* avril, 1936.

Janin, Jules, *Chefs-d'oeuvre dramatiques du XVIIIe siècle,* Paris, Laplace, 1872.

────── *Histoire de la littérature dramatique,* Paris, Lévy, 1855.

Jones, Silas Paul, *A List of French Prose Fiction from 1700 to 1750,* New York, The H. W. Wilson Company, 1939.

Jourdain, Eleanor F., *Dramatic Theory and Practice in France, 1690-1808,* London, Longmans Green and Co., 1921.

Jung, C. G., *Psychological Types,* New York, Harcourt Brace, 1933.

La Chaussée, Nivelle de, *Oeuvres,* Paris, Prault, 1754, 5 vols.

La Fontaine, Jean de, *Oeuvres,* Paris, Hachette, 1883-97, 11 vols.

La Harpe, J.-F., *Le Lycée ou Cours de Littérature.* In *Oeuvres,* Paris, chez Pissot, 1778.

Lalou, René, *Défense de l'homme,* Paris, Kra, 1926.

Lambert, Thérèse de Marguenat de Courcelles, marquise de, *Oeuvres,* A. Auguste, chez Conrad Henri Stagé, Paris, 1764. First complete edition, Lausanne, 1747.

La Motte, Houdar de, *Oeuvres,* Paris, Prault l'aîné, 1754, 10 vols.

Lanson, G., *Histoire de la littérature française* (19me édition), Paris, Hachette, 1912.

────── *Hommes et livres,* Paris, Lecène, 1895.

Lanson, G., "Origines et premières manifestations de l'esprit philosophique dans la littérature française de 1675 à 1748," *Revue des Cours et Conférences,* XVII, 2me série, 1909.

────── *Nivelle de La Chaussée et la comédie larmoyante,* Paris, Hachette, 1887.

La Perrière, H. de, "La Marquise de Lambert," in *Mémoires de l'Académie de Troyes,* mai, 1935, pp. 207-256.

La Porte, l'Abbé de, *Essai sur la vie et les ouvrages de M. de Marivaux,* in *Oeuvres complettes de Marivaux,* Paris, Veuve Duchesne, 1781. Vol. 1.

La Rochefoucauld, François de, *Maximes,* Paris, Flammarion, 1926.

Larroumet, Gustave, *Marivaux, sa vie et ses oeuvres,* Paris, Hachette, 1882.

Le Breton, A., *Le Roman français au XVIIe siècle,* Paris, Hachette, 1890.

────── *Le Roman français au XVIIIe siècle,* Paris, Lecène, 1898.

LeCouvreur, Adrienne, *Lettres,* Paris, Plon, 1892.

Legouis, Emile, *The Early Years of William Wordsworth,* London, J. M. Dent, 1921 (2nd edition).

Legouis, Emile and Cazamian, Louis, *A History of English Literature,* New York, Macmillan, 1930.

Legros, R. P., "Diderot and Shaftsbury," *Modern Language Review,* 1924.

Lemaître, Jules, *Impressions de théâtre,* Paris, E. Dentu, 1892, 11 vols.

Lenclos, Ninon de, *Correspondance authentique*, Paris, E. Dentu, 1886.

Lenient, G., *La Comédie en France au XVIIIe siècle*, Paris, Hachette, 1888, 2 vols.

Lenoir, R., *Les Historiens de l'esprit humain*, Paris, Alcan, 1926.

Le Sage, Alain René, *Oeuvres choisies*, Amsterdam, et se trouve à Paris, Rue et Hôtel Serpente, 1783, 15 vols.

Lesbros de la Versane, Louis de, *Esprit de Marivaux, et Analectes de ses ouvrages, précédés de la Vie historique de l'auteur*, Paris, Veuve Pierres, 1767.

Lescure, M. de, *Etude critique de Mme de Lambert*, en tête des *Oeuvres morales de Mme de Lambert*, Paris, Librairie des Bibliophiles, 1883.

Lettres d'une religieuse portugaise, Edition Eugène Asse, Paris, G. Charpentier, 1883.

Lichtenberger, A., *Le Socialisme au XVIIIe siècle*, Paris, Alcan, 1895.

Lièvre, Pierre, "Les Fausses Confidences," *Mercure de France*, CCLXXV (1937), 588-91.

Loménie, M. de, "De l'influence des salons sur la littérature du XVIIIe siècle," *Revue des Cours Littéraires*, 26 déc., 1863; 2 jan., 13 fév., 11 juin, 1864.

Mackenzie, Henry, *The Man of Feeling*, with introduction by Henry Morley, New York, Cassell and Co., 1886.

Magendie, Maurice, *La Politesse mondaine et les théories de l'honnêteté, en France, au XVIIe siècle, de 1600 à 1660*, Paris, Alcan, 1925.

———— *Le Roman français au XVIIe siècle, de l'Astrée au Grand Cyrus*, Paris, E. Droz, 1932.

Magne, Emile, *Ninon de Lenclos*, Paris, Emile-Paul frères, 1925.

Marais, Mathieu, *Journal et Mémoires sur la Régence et le règne de Louis XV*, Paris, Firmin-Didot, 1863-68, 4 vols.

Marmontel, J.-F., *Mémoires d'un père pour servir à l'instruction de ses enfants*, Edition Maurice Tourneux, Librairie des Bibliophiles, 1891, 3 vols.

Masson, Pierre-Maurice, *Mme de Tencin*, Paris, Hachette, 1909.

Meyer, E., *Marivaux*, Paris, Boivin et Cie., 1921.

Michelet, Jules, *Histoire de France*, Paris, Chamerot, 1860-66, 16 vols. Vol. XV, *La Régence*; Vol. XVI, *Louis XV*.

Molière, *Oeuvres*, Edition Eugène Despois, Paris, Hachette, 1873, 13 vols.

Monglond, A., *Histoire intérieure du préromantisme français*, Grenoble, B. Arthaud, 1929, 2 vols.

Montesquieu, Charles Louis de Secondat de, *Lettres persanes*, Ed. rev. et annotée . . . par Henri Barckhausen, Paris, Hachette et Cie., 1913, 2 vols.

Montgomery, Frances K., *La Vie et l'oeuvre du père Buffier*, Paris, Association du doctorat, 1930.

Mornet, Daniel, *Origines intellectuelles de la révolution française*, Paris, Armand Colin, 1933.

———— *La Pensée française au XVIIIe siècle*, Paris, Armand Colin, 1929.

———— *Le Romantisme en France au XVIIIe siècle*, Paris, Hachette, 1912.

———— *Le Sentiment de la nature en France*, Paris, Hachette, 1907.

Naves, Raymond, *Le Goût de Voltaire*, Paris, Garnier, 1938.

Pellisson, M., "La Question du bonheur au XVIIIe siècle," *Grande Revue*, 15 mars, 1906.

Petit de Julleville, *Histoire de la langue et de la littérature française des origines à 1900,* Paris, Armand Colin, 1924-27, 8 vols.

────── *Le Théâtre en France, depuis ses origines jusqu'à nos jours,* Paris, A. Colin, 1927.

Peyre, Henri, *Qu'est-ce que le classicisme?* Paris, E. Droz, 1933.

Piron, Alexis, *Oeuvres complètes,* publiées par Rigolet de Juvigny, Amsterdam, 1776, 9 vols.

Prévost, l'Abbé, *Oeuvres choisies,* Amsterdam, 1783-85, 39 vols.

Quérard, Joseph Marie, *La France littéraire,* Paris, Firmin Didot père et fils, 1827-64.

Rand, Benjamin, *The Classical Moralists,* New York, Houghton Mifflin, 1909.

Regnier, G., *Le Roman sentimental avant l'Astrée,* Paris, Armand Colin, 1908.

Riccoboni, Mme M. J., *Oeuvres, Paris, Foucault,* 1818, 6 vols.

Richardson, Samuel, *Works,* London, H. Sotheral and Co., 1883, 12 vols.

Rousseau, Jean-Jacques, *Oeuvres complètes,* Paris, Furne, 1835, 4 vols.

Roustan, Marius, *The Pioneers of the French Revolution,* London, Benn, Ltd., 1926. *(Les Philosophes et la société française au XVIIIe siècle,* Lyon, A. Rey, 1906).

Sainte-Beuve, Charles Augustin, *Causeries du lundi,* 6me édition, Paris, Garnier s.d., 16 vols.

────── *Portraits littéraires,* Paris, Garnier, 1864, 5 vols.

Saint-Pierre, Bernardin de, *Oeuvres complètes,* publiées par Aimé-Martin, Paris, P. Dupont, 1826, 12 vols.

Saintsbury, George, *Essays on French Novelists,* London, Percival and Company, 1891.

Saint-Victor, Paul de, *Les Deux Masques,* Paris, Calmann-Lévy, 1884.

Sarcey, Francisque, *Quarante Ans de théâtre,* Paris, Bibliothèque des Annales, 1900-1902, 8 vols. Vol. 2, *La Comédie classique, Molière. Regnard, Marivaux, Beaumarchais.*

Scudéry, Madeleine de, *Artamène, ou le Grand Cyrus,* 1649-1653, 10 vols. *Artamène ou le Grande Cyrus.* Par Mr de Scudéry. Imprimé à Rouen et se vend à Paris, A. Courbé, 1654. 10 vols.

Shaftesbury, Anthony, Earl of, *Characteristicks of Men, Manners, Opinions, Times,* 5th edition, London, J. Darby, 1732, 3 vols.

Staal, Marguerite Jeanne, (Cordier de Launay), *Mémoires,* London, 1755, 2 vols.

Staël, Mme de, *Oeuvres complètes,* Paris, Treuttel, de l'imprimerie de Crapelet, 1820, 17 vols.

Stendhal (Henri Beyle), *De l'amour,* Edition Daniel Muller et Pierre Jourda, Paris, Champion, 1926, 2 vols.

Stephen, Sir Leslie, *History of English Thought in the Eighteenth Century,* New York, G. P. Putnam's Sons, 1927, 3rd edition, 2 vols.

Sterne, Laurence, *Works,* Edited by G. Saintsbury, London, J. M. Dent and Co., 1894, 6 vols.

Suard, J. B. A., *Mélanges littéraires,* Paris, Dentu, 1804.

Taine, H., *Les Origines de la France contemporaine,* Paris, Hachette, 1896, 11 vols.

Tchemerzine, Avenir, *Bibliothèque d'éditions originales et rares des XVe, XVIe, XVIIe et XVIIIe siècles,* Paris, M. Plée, 1927, 10 vols.

Tencin, Mme de, *Mémoires du comte de Comminges,* Paris, A. Quantin, 1885.

Texte, J., *Rousseau et les origines du cosmopolitisme littéraire,* Paris, Hachette, 1895.

Thieriot, "Lettre à Voltaire," *Revue d'Histoire Littéraire de la France,* XV (1908), 717.

Tilley, Arthur, "Marivaudage," *Modern Language Review,* XXV (1930), 60-77.

———— *Three French Dramatists,* Cambridge University Press, 1933.

Torrey, Norman L., *Voltaire and the English Deists,* New Haven, Yale University Press, 1930.

Trahard, Pierre, *Les Maîtres de la sensibilité française au XVIIIe siècle,* Paris, Boivin et Cie., 1931, 4 vols.

Trublet, l'Abbé, *Mémoires pour servir à l'histoire de la vie et des ouvrages de M. de Fontenelle.* Tirés du *Mercure de France,* 1756, 1757, 1758. 2me édition, Amsterdam chez Marc Michel Rey, 1759.

Valéry, Paul, *Variété II,* Paris, Edition de la *Nouvelle Revue Française,* Gallimard, 1930.

Van Tieghem, Paul, *Le Préromantisme,* Paris, Alcan, 1931.

Venturi, Franco, *La Jeunesse de Diderot,* Paris, Skira, 1939.

Vial, Fernand, *Luc de Clapiers, Marquis de Vauvenargues,* Paris, Librairie E. Droz, 1938.

Villemain, *Cours de littérature française. Tableau de la littérature au XVIIIe siècle,* Paris, Didier, 1859, 4 vols.

Voisenon, l'Abbé, *Oeuvres complettes,* Paris, Moutard, 1781, 5 vols.

Voltaire, *Oeuvres complètes,* Moland edition, Paris, Garnier, 1880, 50 vols.

Voltaire, *Traité de métaphysique* (1734), edited by H. Temple Patterson, Manchester Univ. Press, 1937.

Waldberg, Max, Freiherr von, *Der Empfindsame Roman in Frankreich,* Strasbourg, Karl J. Truber, 1906.

Wells, B. W., "The Novels of Marivaux," *Sewanee Review,* VII (1899), 287-302.

Wells, H. G., *An Experiment in Autobiography,* New York, Macmillan, 1934.

Wilson, A. M., "Sensibility in France in the Eighteenth Century: A Study in Word History," *The French Quarterly,* XIII (1931), 35-45.

Wright, E. H., *The Meaning of Rousseau,* London, Oxford University Press, 1929.

Zimmermann, J. P., "La Morale laïque au commencement du XVIIIe siècle: Madame de Lambert," *Revue d'Histoire Littéraire de la France,* 1917, pp. 42-63 and 440-465.

NOTES

*, Parts VI, VII, VIII of *Le Paysan parvenu*
D, Duchesne edition of Marivaux
G, Garnier edition of Marivaux

INTRODUCTION

1. André Gide, "Les Dix Romans français que . . . ," *Oeuvres*, VII, 458.
2. Grimm, *Correspondance littéraire*, V, 236.
    Villemain, *Tableau de la littérature française*, I, 329.
    Helen Sard Hughes, "Translations of *La Vie de Marianne*," *Modern Philology*, XV, Dec., 1917, 491-512.
    C. Grimm, "Encore une fois La Question Marivaux-Richardson," *Revue de la Littérature Comparée*, IV, August, 1924, 590-600.
    Edith Birkhead, "Sentiment and Sensibility in the Eighteenth Century Novel," in *Essays and Studies by Members of the English Association*, Oxford, Clarendon Press, 1925, p. 99: "Gray once affirmed lightly that it was his idea of paradise to read eternal new romances by these authors [Marivaux and Crébillon *fils*]. (Letters, April, 1742)."
3. *Nouvelle Revue Française*, XLVI, 1 April, 1936, 533.
4. D'Alembert, *Oeuvres*, X, 210, Note.
5. *Revue d' Histoire Littéraire de la France*, XV, (1908), 717.
6. Sainte-Beuve, *Causeries du lundi*, IX, 345, 16 January, 1854.
7. Ibid., IX, 356.
8. J. Janin, Th. Gautier, P. de Saint-Victor, F. Sarcey, Jules Lemaître.
9. Brunetière, *Etudes critiques*, 3me série, pp. 121-187.
10. E. C. Baldwin, "Marivaux's Place in the Development of Character Portrayal," P.M.L.A., XXVII, 1912, 168-187.
    Edmund Gosse, *History of Eighteenth Century Literature*, p. 243.
11. E. A. Baker, *History of the English Novel*, IV, 30-31; 79-80; 269.
    Brunetière, op. cit., p. 187: "Dans la littérature moderne, en France comme en Angleterre, il n'y a pas de roman de moeurs où l'on ne trouve au fond quelque chose de Marivaux."
12. Gustave Lanson, *Histoire de la littérature française*, 1912 edition, p. 659.
13. Pierre Trahard, *Les Maîtres de la sensibilité française au dix-huitième siècle*, I, 15, 21.
14. Lanson, *Nivelle de La Chaussée et la comédie larmoyante*, pp. 236-37.
15. Ibid., p. 225.
16. Ibid., p. 238.
17. Lanson says, however, in his *Histoire de la littérature française*, p. 676: "Marivaux a été chez nous un des fondateurs de la sensibilité littéraire."
18. Saintsbury, *Essays on French Novelists*, p. 145.
19. Ibid., p. 115.
20. Ibid., p. 135.

21. Pierre Trahard, *Les Maîtres de la sensibilité*, I, 20.

22. Ibid., I, 18-19.

23. Ibid., I, 19-20.

24. Legouis and Cazamian, *A History of English Literature*, p. 869.

25. D'Alembert, "Eloge de Marivaux," *Oeuvres*, X, 229.

26. Tchemerzine (*Bibliothèque d'éditions originales et rares d'auteurs français des XVe, XVIe, XVIIe et XVIIIe siècles*, VII, 427) lists "*Le Paysan parvenu ou les Mémoires de M. ****, par M. de Marivaux, chez Prault père, Paris, 1735, 4 vol. en 12." S. P. Jones (*A List of French Prose Fiction from 1700 to 1750*, p. 53) mentions a copy in the Library of Congress, 1734-36, in five volumes, Prault père, and adds: "Gay lists an edition, La Haye, 1734-36." He concludes from the title pages and approbations of the 1734-36 edition and of the 1735 edition (Prault) that "the first four parts were published in 1734 and that the fifth part was published in 1735." He considers the Library of Congress copy to be unique and gives a detailed description of it. The Bibliothèque Nationale lists editions as of 1738, 1748, and 1764.

27. Lesbros de la Versane, *Eloge historique de Marivaux*, p. 17: "Il n'est pas nécessaire de prévenir les lecteurs que M. de Marivaux n'a point fait la 12me partie de *Marianne* et qu'il n'a composé que les cinq lres parties du *Paysan parvenu*. La différence du style est trop marquée pour ne pas être généralement sentie."

28. Gustave Larroumet, *Marivaux, sa vie et son oeuvre*, p. 616-17.

29. *Le Paysan parvenu*, G. 377, D. VIII, 430.

30. *Le Paysan parvenu*, Parts 1-4, Paris, Prault père, 1736; Part 5, Paris, Prault, 1736; Parts 6, 7, 8, La Haye, H. Scheuleer, 1756.

31. Fleury says (p. 225): "Dans les premières éditions, ces Suites [of *Marianne* and *Le Paysan parvenu*] étaient imprimées en caractères plus petits, pour qu'on ne les confondît pas avec le texte authentique."

32. J. Fleury, *Marivaux et le marivaudage*, Paris, Plon, 1881.

     G. Larroumet, *Marivaux, sa vie et son oeuvre*, Paris, Hachette, 1882.

33. Fleury, op. cit., pp. 222-227.

34. Ibid., p. 225; Larroumet, op. cit., pp. 616-17.

35. Ibid., p. 226.

36. Gossot, *Marivaux moraliste*, p. 129.

37. Marivaux, *Oeuvres*, XII, 46.

38. Fleury, op. cit., p. 224. Crébillon *fils*, *Oeuvres*, V, 157-203.

39. Mme Riccoboni, *Oeuvres*, I, 511-12, Avertissement: Mme Riccoboni accepted a wager from M. de Saint-Foix that Marivaux's work was inimitable. Her imitation surprised him so greatly that at first he believed the manuscript stolen from Marivaux. "Il vouloit le faire imprimer; Madame Riccoboni s'y opposa, dans la crainte de désobliger M. de Marivaux. Dix ans après, cette suite parut dans un journal dont le rédacteur eut la permission de M. de Marivaux pour l'y insérer."

40. *Discours* de Languet de Gergy, février, 1743. In Marivaux, *Oeuvres complettes*, Duchesne edition, V, 273.

41. Lesbros, op. cit., quoted in Fleury, p. 224.

42. *Le Paysan parvenu,* Preface by Duviquet, Garnier edition, p. 103.
43. F. C. Green, *Minuet,* p. 392.
44. Ibid., p. 370.
45. Trahard, op. cit., I, 63-64.

CHAPTER I

1. Details of Marivaux's life are few and inexact. There are three contemporary biographies: a sketch by the Abbé de la Porte, published in *L'Observateur littéraire* in 1759 and reprinted as a preface to *Oeuvres diverses* of Marivaux, Duchesne, 1765, and to *Oeuvres complettes* of Marivaux, Veuve Duchesne, 1781; an *Eloge historique* by Lesbros de la Versane, introducing *l'Esprit de Marivaux,* Paris, Veuve Pierres, 1769; and the *Eloge de Marivaux* by d'Alembert. The work of Gustave Larroumet, *Marivaux, sa vie et ses oeuvres,* Paris, Hachette, 1882, is the definitive modern biography. Recently a series of articles by Mme Marie-Jeanne Durry, "Quelques Nouveautés sur Marivaux," in *Revue des Cours et Conférences* (30 déc., 1938; 15 jan., 15 fév., 15 mai, 1939) have contributed a number of interesting details as to Marivaux's personal affairs.

E. Meyer, Marivaux's most recent biographer, states that Marivaux came to Paris between 1712, the date of the printing of his first comedy at Limoges, and 1716, the date of the appearance of *L'Iliade travesti,* printed in Paris (*Marivaux,* Boivin, 1929, p. 17). Larroumet (p. 23) says: "Marivaux ne songea pendant six ans qu'à goûter le charme de vivre dans la société journalière de ceux dont il aimait la tournure d'esprit et de sentiment." The six years appear to end in 1720, when the presentation of his first successful comedy at the Théâtre des Italiens launches Marivaux's literary career.

2. Pierre-Maurice Masson, *Mme de Tencin,* pp. 182-3: Masson describes Mme de Tencin's early career as that of an adventuress. After the La Fresnais affair in 1726 "la femme galante est morte, la femme de salon commence." He quotes the Abbé Trublet: "Après la mort de Mme de Lambert, le mardi fut chez Mme de Tencin." From the Lambert salon came Fontenelle, Marivaux, and Mairan, "le trio lambertiste."

3. Marmontel, *Mémoires,* II, 222.
4. Grimm, *Corréspondance littéraire,* V, 236, février 1763.
5. Taine, *L'Ancien Régime,* II, 186: "Si vous voulez retrouver ce monde évanoui, cherchez-le dans les oeuvres qui ont conservé les dehors ou l'accent, d'abord dans les tableaux et dans les estampes, chez Watteau, Fragonard et les Saint-Aubin, puis dans les romans et dans les comédies, chez Voltaire et Marivaux, même chez Collé et chez Crébillon *fils.*"
6. Larroumet, op. cit., 170; Lanson, *Histoire de la littérature française,* p. 655.
7. Lytton Strachey, *Main Currents of French Literature,* p. 145.
8. F. C. Green, *Minuet,* p. 156.
9. A. Feugère, "Rousseau et son temps: la littérature du sentiment au XVIIIe siècle," *Revue des Cours et Conférences,* 15 janvier, 1935, p. 344.
10. Fontenelle, "Eloge de Mme de Lambert," *Oeuvres,* IX, 266; D'Argenson, *Mémoires,* I, 284; D'Alembert, "Eloge de Saint-Aulaire," *Oeuvres,* X, 333.
11. Mme de Lambert, *Oeuvres,* p. 194.

12. Abbé Trublet, *Mémoires,* p. 69.
13. Fontenelle, *Oeuvres,* IX, 266.
14. A. LeCouvreur, *Lettres,* pp. 152-53.
15. D'Alembert, "Eloge de Sacy," *Oeuvres,* VII, 368-69.
16. Zanetta-Rosa Benozzi, dite Silvia, c.1700-1759.
17. Anne Boutet, dite Mlle Mars, 1779-1847.
18. Jules Janin, *Histoire de la littérature dramatique,* II, 101.
19. Ibid., II, 420 (From *Le Journal des Débats,* avril, 1841).
20. Jacques Debu-Bridel, "La Préciosité—conception héroïque de la vie," *Revue de France,* 15 sept., 1938, p. 207: "La préciosité est essentiellement un acte de volonté, un choix, elle s'oppose au laisser-faire de l'instinct en matière de langage, mais aussi, mais d'abord, dans les moeurs. Elle est morale."
21. Mme de Lambert, *Oeuvres,* p. 176. This is not equally true of Marivaux. He depicts both aristocratic and bourgeois society, and finds virtues to admire in both.
22. Mme de Lambert, *Oeuvres,* p. 33.
23. Ibid., p. 204.
24. Ibid., p. 195.
25. Mathieu Marais, *Journal et Mémoires,* III, 144.
26. Le Sage, *Le Bachelier de Salamanque, Oeuvres,* Amsterdam, 1783, I, 400. Also *Gil Blas,* IV, 8.
27. F. Gohin, *Les Transformations de la langue française pendant la deuxième moitié du XVIIIe siècle,* p. 16: "Les circonstances secondèrent les efforts des puristes et hâtèrent leur victoire; en 1733 Mme de Lambert mourait, tous les écrivains qui s'étaient rassemblés autour d'elle se dispersèrent. Fontenelle vieilli songea à se démettre de ses fonctions de secrétaire perpétuel; c'en était fait de la préciosité."
28. Victor DuBled, *La Société française au XVIIIe siècle,* V, 166-7.
29. D'Alembert, "Eloge de Saint-Aulaire," *Oeuvres,* X, 333.
30. D'Argenson, *Mémoires,* I, 284.
31. It is difficult to determine the exact dates of the writings of Mme de Lambert. The two *Avis* were written in 1701 or 1702, the other works probably during the Regency. See Sainte-Beuve, *Causeries du lundi,* IV, 226, and Zimmermann, "La Morale Laïque," in *Revue d'Histoire Littéraire de la France,* 1917.
32. Daniel Mornet, *Origines intellectuelles de la révolution française,* pp. 41-42.
33. Pierre Bayle (Edition Cazes), pp. 116, 119, 124.
     Norman L. Torrey, *Voltaire and the English Deists,* pp. 100-101: "It was Pierre Bayle who launched vigorously into eighteenth century deism the idea of the complete separation of religion and morality."
34. Montesquieu, *Les Lettres persanes,* Edition Barckhausen I, 163.
35. Le Père Buffier, *Traité de la société civile.* Quoted in *La Vie et l'oeuvre du père Buffier,* F. K. Montgomery, p. 171.
36. Studies of lay morality on which this paragraph is based are: Paul Hazard, *La Crise de la conscience européenne,* I, 1re partie, "Hétérodoxie," pp. 105-130; I, 2me partie, *Contre les croyances traditionnelles,* pp. 158-317; II, 3me

partie, Chapitre 4, "La Morale sociale," and V, "Le Bonheur sur la terre," pp. 71-98.

Pierre Hermand, *Les Idées morales de Diderot*, Introduction historique, "Etat de la conscience française vers 1740," pp. 1-46.

Lanson, "Origines et premières manifestations de l'esprit philosophique," *Revue des Cours et Conférences*, 1909-10.

Daniel Mornet, *La Pensée française au XVIIIe siècle*.

J. P. Zimmermann, "La morale laïque au commencement du XVIIIe siècle," *Revue d'Histoire Littéraire de la France*, 1917.

37. Descartes, *Traité des passions*, Art. 212, XI, 488.

Fontenelle, *Dialogue entre Erostrate et Démétrius*, I, 67-70: "Les passions sont chez les hommes des vents qui sont nécessaires pour mettre tout en mouvement, quoiqu'ils causent souvent des orages."

38. Mme de Lambert, *Oeuvres*, p. 93.

39. Ibid., p. 29.

40. Ibid., p. 196.

41. Ibid., p. 97.

42. Ibid., p. 155.

43. Ibid., p. 84.

44. Ibid., p. 49: "ce sentiment intérieur d'un honneur délicat, qui vous assure que vous n'avez rien à vous reprocher."

45. Voltaire, *Oeuvres*, Moland edition, IX, 450.

46. Marivaux, *Spectateur français*, IX, 251.

47. Mme de Lambert, op. cit., p. 58.

48. Grimm, *Correspondance littéraire*, I, 147.

49. Mornet., op. cit., p. 41.

50. Mme de Lambert, op. cit., p. 186.

51. Ibid., p. 186.

52. Ibid., pp. 47-48.

53. Ibid., pp. 204-05.

54. Scudéry, *Le Grand Cyrus*, II, livre 1, p. 269: "[Mandane] Mais enfin, Artamène, il faut que la raison soit plus forte que toutes choses; et il ne faut pas tant considérer ce qui nous plaît que ce qui nous doit plaire."

55. Ibid., VI, livre 1, p. 113.

De Goncourt, *La Femme au XVIIIe siècle*, I, 157: "Il [l'amour sous le règne de Louis XIV] exige toutes les épreuves et toutes les décences de la galanterie, l'application à plaire, les soins, la longue volonté, le patient effort, les respects, les serments, la reconnaissance, la discrétion. Il veut des prières qui implorent et des agenouillements qui remercient, et il entoure ses faiblesses de tant de convenances, ses plus grands scandales d'un tel air de majesté, que ses fautes, ses hontes même, gardent une politesse et une excuse, presque une pudeur. Un idéal, dans ces siècles, élève à lui l'amour, idéal transmis par la chevalerie au bel esprit de la France, idéal d'héroïsme devenu un idéal de noblesse."

56. Lanson, op. cit., *R.C.C.*, 1909-10, p. 28: "Ce qu'on voit dans l'amour, ce n'est plus la gloire et le plaisir de triompher d'un coeur; mais on se retourne vers soi-même, on regarde les troubles de son propre coeur. . . . Il arrive un moment où, dans les représentations dramatiques, ce n'est plus

l'amant, mais l'amante, qui a le rôle principal. Tant que l'homme est le principal héros, l'amour est un siège, une campagne, un effort pour prendre possession d'un bien. Mettez la femme au premier plan, l'amour devient essentiellement l'émotion intérieure de la personne qui aime.

57. *Le Grand Cyrus,* VI, livre 1, p. 113: "Il y a presque une égale nécessité d'être amant et malheureux."
58. Mme de Lambert, *Oeuvres,* pp. 207-08.
59. Ibid., p. 209.
60. Ibid., pp. 212-213.
61. Ibid., p. 122.
62. Ibid., p. 132.
63. Ibid., pp. 245-46.
64. Ibid., p. 240.
65. Ibid., p. 20.
66. Ibid., p. 20.
67. Ibid., p. 87.
68. Ibid., p. 43.
69. Ibid., p. 20.
70. Ibid., p. 40.
71. G. Desnoiresterres, *Les Cours galantes,* IV, 337.
72. Taine, *Origines de la France contemporaine,* II, 208: "[La galanterie] Les femmes qui l'ont érigée en obligation sont les premières à en sentir le mensonge, et à regretter, parmi tant de froids hommages, la chaleur communicative d'un sentiment fort. Le caractère du siècle reçoit alors son trait final, et *l'homme sensible* apparaît."
73. Paul Valéry, *Variété II,* "Les Lettres persanes," p. 61.

CHAPTER II

1. A. Tchemerzine, *Bibliographie d'éditions originales et rares d'auteurs français des XVe, XVIe, XVIIe et XVIIIe siècles,* VII, 414: "Les Effets Surprenants de la Sympathie," Tome I, II . . . V, A Paris, chez Pierre Prault, MDCCXIII.
2. A work written earlier, *Pharsamon, ou les Folies romanesques* (1712, published in 1737), a feeble imitation of Cervantes, satirizes a modern Don Quixote. Trahard (*Maîtres de la sensibilité,* I, 57, Note 2) has pointed out a few traces of sensibility in this work. *La Voiture embourbée* (1714) is considered by some critics a parody of the heroic novel, by others the thing itself. If accepted in good faith, the book shows evidences of sensibility, particularly in the characters of the Lady and the Daughter (Marivaux, *Oeuvres,* XII, 147-48). Paul Morillot (*Le Roman en France,* p. 211) says of this book: "On y distingue à travers le fatras romanesque, quelques traces d'observation minutieuse et fine. C'est le vrai Marivaux qui point." The parodies of the *Iliad* and of *Télémaque* contribute nothing to a study of Marivaux's sensibility. In all these early works Marivaux was evidently feeling his way. Perhaps he believed that the heroic novel, in spite of its

improbability, gave the novelist a wider opportunity to display his inventive skill. Brunetière points out (*Etudes critiques,* III, 134) that his taste for parody, which involves an expression of the sublime in terms of the familiar, grows into the realism of the later Marivaux.

3. Dorothy F. Dallas, *Le Roman français de 1660 à 1680,* p. 27: "The *roman d'aventure,* which reached its apogee in 1650, was read to the end of the 18th century by Crébillon, Montesquieu, Marivaux, Voltaire, Rousseau, the Abbé Prévost."

4. Magendie (*Le Roman français au XVIIe siècle de l'Astrée au grand Cyrus,* p. 301) comments on the sudden and irrevocable passions so frequent among the superb heroes of the adventure novels: "Le désaccord entre le coeur et la raison n'existant jamais, le riche domaine des conflits de sentiments est fermé à l'analyse."

5. Marivaux, *Les Effets,* in *Oeuvres complettes,* V, 282.

6. Max Freiherr von Waldberg, *Der Empfindsame Roman in Frankreich,* p. 423: "Belle âme! Seit Platos ψυχὴ καλή ist dieser Begriff nicht mehr aus der Weltliteratur verschwanden. Unter seinem Einflusse haben die Autoren der italienischen Renaissance, Castiglione in seinem *Cortegiano,* Palavicini in einem besonderen Traktat und viele andere von der *bellezza dell'anima* gehandelt, Baltasar Gracian, der sich auf Virgil stützt, spricht von der "hermosura del alma," er fehlt nicht in Sidneys *Arcadia,* erscheint öfter bei den deutschen Lyrikern des siebsehnten Jahrhunderts, taucht im Sprachschatze der Preziosen ebenso auf wie in der Porträtgalerie der Montpensier, Tristan l'Hermite, l'abbé Cotin verwenden ihn, aber die ästhetisch-ethische Ausgestaltung seiner Bedeutung erfolgt erst unter den Einwerkungen der Empfindsamkeit, und er erhält erst in den Romanen des ausgehenden Jahrhunderts den Inhalt der in weiterer Ausbildung durch Shaftesbury, durch Hinzutreten religiöser Elemente zur "Schönen Seele" Rousseaus, Goethes und Schillers fuhrt."

7. *Les Effets,* V, 455. Magendie, op. cit., p. 421: "Etre un amant soumis, respectueux, fidèle, voilà quelle sera la première et la plus forte obligation d'une belle âme."

8. *Les Effets,* V, 469.

9. Ibid., V, 386.

10. Ibid., V, 300.

11. Ibid., V, 284.

12. Ibid., V, 322.

13. F. C. Green, *French Novelists of Manners and Ideas from the Renaissance to the Revolution,* pp. 153-55: "The seventeenth century is not concerned with sensibility, but with passion. . . . That is why Marivaux's role in the evolution of the novel is so important, since by his minute analytic procedure, he showed that love is not always a torturing passion."

14. *Les Effets,* V, 354.

15. Ibid., V, 360-64.

16. Ibid., V, 361.

17. Ibid., V, 406.

18. Ibid., V, 431.

19. *Les Effets*, V, 396.
20. La Fontaine, *Psyché*, in *Oeuvres*, VIII, 233.
21. Waldberg, op. cit., pp. 29, 32-33.
    Lanson, *R.C.C.*, op. cit., 18 novembre, 1909, pp. 22-29.
22. *Lettres d'une religieuse portugaise* (Edition Asse), p. 8.
23. Ibid., p. 55.
24. Green, op. cit., p. 152: "There are few tender heroines in the French novel of the 17th century. . . . The studied *galanterie* of the lovers in these heroic novels is without a vestige of true sensibility. The celebrated Carte du Tendre itself, despite its misleading name, is a striking testimonial to the lack of sentiment in the novel of that period."
25. *Les Effets*, V, 443.
26. Ibid., V, 435.
27. Rousseau, *La Nouvelle Héloïse*, in *Oeuvres complètes*, Edition Furne, II, 37.
    The novel *Péristandre* of Martin Fumée describes a young girl of noble blood who is forced to disguise herself as a shepherdess and find refuge in a peasant family. This change in her way of life reduces her to despair. She tells her story to a friend, who shares "le sensible regret que vous pouvez avoir d'estre soumise à une si honteuse vie, vue votre illustre naissance." Magendie comments, "Cette dernière phrase est caractéristique du mépris où les gens du XVIIe siècle tenaient la campagne quand elle n'était pas peuplée de bergers polis comme ceux de l'Astree." Magendie, op. cit., p. 30.
28. *Les Effets*, V, 428.

CHAPTER III

1. Mme de Lambert, *Oeuvres*, p. 209.
2. *La Vie de Marianne*, novel in eleven parts, 1731-41.
   Le Paysan parvenu, novel in five parts, 1734-36, with three additional parts, 1755.
3. Magendie, op. cit., p. 425: "Dans les romans, tous les personnages ont les larmes faciles. . . . Ce n'est pas une faiblesse honteuse, c'est une distinction. . . . Dans les ouvrages de La Calprenède, cette propension naturelle aux larmes atteint son paroxysme. 'Les larmes de Démétrius font un ruisseau qui mêle presque à l'Euphrate.' *Cassandre*, II, 271."
4. Waldberg, op. cit., p. 255. Marivaux, *L'Ile des Esclaves*, V, 62: "Il est vrai que je pleure; ce n'est pas le bon coeur qui me manque."
5. Foster Guyer, *The Influence of Ovid on Chrétien de Troyes*, p. 120.
6. *La Vie de Marianne*, G. 117; D. VI, 450.
7. Ibid., G. 39; D. VI, 319: "J'épuisai mes forces; il ne me resta plus que des pleurs, jamais on n'en a tant versé; et la bonne femme, voyant cela, se mit à pleurer aussi du meilleur de son coeur."
8. Ibid., G. 308; D. VII, 198: "Un torrent de larmes termina mon discours. Valville, pâle et abattu, paraissait prêt à se trouver mal."
9. Ibid., G. 129; D. VI, 472.

10. *La Vie de Marianne*, G. 67; D. VI, 365-66.

11. Ibid., G. 174; D. VI, 549: "Ses pleurs coulèrent après ce peu de mots; il ne les retint plus: elles attendrirent Mme de Miran, qui pleura comme lui et qui ne sut que dire; nous nous taisions tous trois, on n'entendait que des soupirs."

12. E. Legouis, *The Youth of Wordsworth*, p. 153: "Mr. Henry Morley finds fifty instances of an outburst of tears in Mackenzie's short novel, *The Man of Feeling* (1771), and he does not include the sobs. Weeping was the infallible sign of virtue and the favorite source of voluptuous feeling." Cf. "Index to Tears," in *The Man of Feeling*, Intr. V, VI.

13. De Goncourt, *La Femme au XVIIIe siècle*, II, 164-65.

14. *La Vie de Marianne*, G. 25; D. VI, 295; also G. 533; D. VII, 580: "J'étais faible, pâle et comme dans un état de stupidité"; and G. 349; D. VII, 268-69: "Je restai bien encore une demi-heure dans une si grande confusion de pensées et de mouvements que j'en étais comme stupide."

15. *La Vie de Marianne*, G. 174-75; D. VI, 550: "Eh, seigneur, m'écriai-je avec amour, avec douleur, avec mille mouvements confus que je ne saurais expliquer. . . ." Also G. 76; D. VI, 382: "Un mélange de plaisir et de confusion, voilà mon état."

16. Ibid., G. 182; D. VI, 562: "J'éclatai ici par un transport subit: Ah, ma mère, m'écriai-je, je me meurs; je ne me possède pas de tendresse et de reconnaissance. . . . Et Valville, éperdu de joie et comme hors de lui, se jeta sur nos deux mains, qu'il baisait alternativement."

17. Ibid., G. 257; D. VII, 113.

18. Rousseau, *La Nouvelle Héloïse*, II, 368.

19. *La Vie de Marianne*, G. 10; D. VI, 270.

20. Ibid., G. 235; D. VII, 76.

21. Marivaux, *Pièces détachées*, IX, 319.

22. Ninon de Lenclos, *Correspondance authentique*, p. 57.

23. Mme de Lambert, *Oeuvres*, p. 151: "Les caractères sensibles ont plus à souffrir: le coeur ne s'use pas comme les sens."

24. *La Vie de Marianne*, G. 418; D. VII, 385: "Nous qui sommes bornées en tout, comment le sommes-nous si peu quand il s'agit de souffrir?"

25. Ibid., G. 14; D. VI, 277.

26. *Le Spectateur français*, IX, 309: "Je n'avais été jusque-là que triste et attendri sur moi-même; je n'avais songé à rien qu'à nourrir ma tristesse de tout ce qui pouvait me la rendre plus sensible." Cf. *La Nouvelle Héloïse*, II, 368: "On ne sait pas . . . quelle douceur c'est de s'attendrir sur ses propres maux et sur ceux des autres."

27. *La Deuxième Surprise de l'amour*, I, 385.

28. Ibid., I, 405.

29. Ibid., I, 405.

30. Ibid., I, 407.

31. *La Vie de Marianne*, G. 342; D. VII, 256.

32. Lanson, *Nivelle de La Chaussée*, p. 233: "Torrents de larmes . . . signes universels de toutes les émotions et qui, au fond, n'en représentent qu'une

seule, le plaisir égoïste de la sensibilité qui joue avec le monde extérieur."
33. *La Deuxième Surprise de l'amour*, I, 501.
34. *La Vie de Marianne*, G. 340; D. VII, 254: "Je ne survivrai point à ce tourment-là." Ibid., G. 347; D. VII, 264: "Je ne vivrai pas longtemps. . . ." Ibid., G. 341; D. VII, 254: "Il me regrettera, mais je n'y serai plus. . . . Il pleurera ma mort."
35. *La Vie de Marianne*, G. 307; D. VII, 197.
36. Ibid., G. 356; D. VII, 280.
37. Ibid., G. 356; D. VII, 279.
38. Ibid., G. 505; D. VII, 532: "A la vérité, je crois jusqu'ici que mes malheurs surpassent les vôtres; mais quand vous aurez tout dit, je changerai peut-être de sentiment."
39. Trahard, *Les Maîtres de la sensibilité*, II, 64, Note 2.
40. *La Mère confidente*, III, 109 and III, 136. Also *La Femme fidèle*, in Fleury, *Marivaux et le Marivaudage*, pp. 368-71. These are Marivaux's only sentimental comedies.
41. John Hughes, *Amanda*, or *Virtue in Distress*, *Spectator* No. 375, May 10, 1712.
42. Marivaux was himself extremely responsive to human suffering. He tells in this essay of *Le Spectateur* (IX, 33): "Je viens de rencontrer, ce soir, dans le détour d'une rue, une jeune fille qui m'a demandé l'aumône; elle pleurait à chaudes larmes; son affliction m'a touché. Je l'ai regardée avec attention: je lui ai trouvé de la douceur et des grâces dans la physionomie; beaucoup d'abattement, avec un air confus et embarrassé. . . . J'ai été tenté de la laisser, sans lui en demander davantage, pour me sauver de l'intérêt douloureux qu'elle commençait à m'inspirer pour elle."
43. *La Vie de Marianne*, G. 112-13; D. VI, 443.
44. Ibid., G. 266; D. VII, 128.
45. Ibid., G. 384-85; D. VII, 329.
46. Ibid., G. 327-28; D. VII, 231.
47. Ibid., G. 309-10; D. VII, 200.
48. *Le Paysan parvenu*, G. 321; D. VIII, 340.
49. Mme de Lambert, *Oeuvres*, p. 183.
50. Ibid., p. 185.
51. *La Vie de Marianne*, G. 25; D. VI, 296: "Je me disais déjà que dans le monde il fallait qu'il y eût quelque chose qui valait mieux que cela; je soupirais après, j'étais triste d'être privée de ce mieux que je ne connaissais pas. Dites-moi d'où cela venait? Où est-ce que j'avais pris mes délicatesses? Etaient-elles dans mon sang? Cela se pourrait bien. Venaient-elles du séjour que j'avais fait à Paris? Cela se pourrait encore. Il y a des âmes perçantes à qui il n'en faut pas beaucoup montrer pour les instruire, et qui sur le peu qu'elles voient soupçonnent tout d'un coup tout ce qu'elles pourraient voir."
52. Ibid., G. 187; D. VI, 571.
53. Ibid., G. 26; D. VI, 296-97.
54. In the preface of an early work, *L'Iliade travesti* (1716), X, 124-25, Marivaux says of La Motte: "La composition de M. de La Motte tient de l'esprit

pur; c'est un travail du bon sens et de la droite raison. . . . Elle frappe
bien plus ceux qui pensent d'après l'esprit pur que ceux qui, pour ainsi
dire, sentent d'après l'imagination." Naves comments on Marivaux's
remark (R. Naves, *Le Goût de Voltaire*, p. 24): "Et c'est là un éloge,
l'imagination étant le propre de la foule." In later years Marivaux revised his opinion of La Motte, pointing out a certain coldness in his works
(Le Miroir, XII, 46): "Ne nous donner que des lumières, ce n'est encore
embrasser que la moitié de ce que nous sommes, et même la moitié qui nous
est la plus indifférente: nous nous soucions bien moins de connaître que de
jouir."

55. A. Monglond, *L'Histoire intérieure du pré-romantisme,* p. 48: (Note 1)
"Sans doute le XVIIe siècle, et Pascal, et l'Académie avaient disserté sur le
je ne sais quoi. Mais, qui ne le voit, chez Marivaux l'expression se charge
d'un sens, d'une vertu locale. C'est l'heure où les grâces chiffonnées succèdent à la beauté olympienne de Louis XIV, où les ordonnances géométri-
ques de Le Nôtre vont céder la place à la fantaisie du jardin anglais. Déjà,
au sommet de l'âge classique, comme une discrète nostalgie de la poésie
perdue, comme un pressentiment, paraît le *je ne sais quoi* de Bouhours.
Après avoir tenté de le définir, l'auteur des *Entretiens d'Ariste* renonçait. Si
l'on pouvait en pénétrer le mystère, il cesserait d'être. . . . Il retrouvait le
je ne sais quoi dans les grâces fines et cachées des oeuvres d'art."

56. *Le Cabinet du philosophe,* IX, 556.

57. Ibid., IX, 556.

58. Ibid., IX, 565.

59. Quoted in Folkierski, *Entre le classicisme et le romantisme,* p. 40.

60. *Le Spectateur français,* IX, 192.

61. **Le Paysan parvenu,* G. 379; D. VIII, 434.

62. *Ibid., G. 381; D. VIII, 436.

63. Cf. Fernand Baldensperger, *Sensibilité musicale et romantisme,* p. 30.
M. Baldensperger comments on the rareness, in French literature before
the nineteenth century, of pleasure in pure music, without words to supply
the stimulus.

64. A. Feugère, "Rousseau et son temps: la littérature de sentiment au XVIIIe
siècle," *R.C.C.,* 15 jan., 1935, p. 333: "En quoi diffère-t-il [Marivaux] de
Fontenelle? C'est qu'il ne partage pas ses préventions contre la sensibilité.
Tandis que Fontenelle et son groupe dédaignent les preuves de sentiment,
Marivaux tient le sentiment pour une lumière plus certaine que l'esprit.
. . . Telle est la philosophie de Marivaux, qui, par cette préférence ac-
cordée au sentiment, s'oppose à la philosophie tout intellectualiste, chère à
l'Encyclopédie."

65. Duclos, *Considérations sur les moeurs,* I, 69. Also I, 69: "Qu'il y a d'idées in-
accessibles à ceux qui ont le sentiment froid!"

66. *La Vie de Marianne,* G. 145; D. VI, 497.

67. Ibid., G. 15; D. VI, 278.

68. *La Nouvelle Héloïse* II, 128.

69. M. de Climal, the Mlles Habert, Jacob's sister-in-law.

70. Mme de Lambert, *Oeuvres*, p. 399 (Lettre de Fénelon); p. 402, (Lettre de Mme de Lambert à Fénelon).
71. *Le Cabinet du philosophe*, IX, 568.
72. Ibid., IX, 569.
73. Ibid., IX, 570.

Chapter IV

1. Rousseau, *Confessions*, I, 1: "Je ne suis fait comme aucun de ceux que j'ai vus; j'ose croire n'être fait comme aucun de ceux qui existent. Si je ne vaux pas mieux, au moins je suis autre."
2. Mme de Lambert, *Oeuvres*, p. 69.
3. *La Vie de Marianne*, G. 190; D. VI, 576.
4. Mme de Lambert, *Oeuvres*, p. 152.
5. *La Deuxième Surprise de l'amour*, I, 389.
6. *La Vie de Marianne*, G. 74; D. VI, 378.
7. Marivaux, *Oeuvres*, IX, 12.
8. Ibid., IX, 211.
9. *La Surprise de l'amour*, IV, 154.
10. *La Surprise de l'amour*, IV, 156.
11. Ibid., IV, 157.
12. Ibid., IV, 189.
13. Ibid., IV, 189.
14. Ibid., IV, 208.
15. *Le Cabinet du philosophe*, IX, 626.
16. *Pièces détachées*, IX, 360.
17. *La Vie de Marianne*, G. 48; D. VI, 333.
18. *La Vie de Marianne*, G. 286; D. VII, 161.
19. *La Deuxième Surprise de l'amour*, I, 445.
20. *Pièces détachées*, IX, 360.
21. *La Vie de Marianne*, G. 43; D. VI, 325.
22. Ibid., G. 43; D. VI, 325.
23. *Pièces détachées*, IX, 324. The Countess, in *L'Heureux Stratagème*, sees no reason why love should limit her sphere of conquest. "Dorante est en vérité plaisant! n'oserais-je, à cause qu'il m'aime, distraire un regard de mes yeux? N'appartiendra-t-il qu'à lui de me trouver jeune et aimable? Faut-il que j'aie cent ans pour tous les autres; que j'enterre tout ce que je vaux; que je me dévoue à la plus triste stérilité de plaisir qu'il soit possible?" III, 284.
24. *La Vie de Marianne*, G. 49; D. VI, 335.
25. Ibid., G. 168-69; D. VI, 539.
26. Ibid., G. 184; D. VI, 566.
27. Ibid., G. 44; D. VI, 327.
28. Fénelon, *L'Education des filles*.
29. De Goncourt, *La Femme au dix-huitième siècle*, II, 163.
30. Supra, p. 41.

31. *La Vie de Marianne*, G. 328; D. VII, 232: "En un mot, je ne mentis en rien, je n'en étais pas capable; mais je peignis dans le grand: mon sentiment me menait ainsi sans que j'y pensasse."
32. D'Alembert, "Eloge de Marivaux," in *Oeuvres*, X, 244.
33. Marmontel, *Mémoires*, I, 233; also II, 90.
34. Ibid., II, 222-24.
35. D'Alembert, "Eloge de Marivaux," X, 245. Also the Abbé Trublet, *Mémoires*, p. 210.
36. Collé, *Mémoires*, II, 288: "Il était rempli d'amour-propre lui-même; et je n'ai vu de mes jours à cet égard personne d'aussi chatouilleux que lui. Il fallait le louer et le caresser comme une jolie femme."

    Grimm, *Corr., litt.*, V., 236: "Marivaux était honnête homme, mais d'un caractère ombrageux et d'un commerce difficile; il entendait finesse à tout; les mots les plus innocents le blessaient, et il supposait volontiers qu'on cherchait à le mortifier: ce qui l'a rendu malheureux et son caractère épineux et insupportable."
37. D'Alembert, op. cit., X, 253. La Porte, *Essai sur la vie et les ouvrages de M. de Marivaux*, in *Oeuvres complettes de Marivaux*, I, 7.
38. *Le Spectateur français*, IX, 64.
39. Ibid., IX, 279.
40. *La Vie de Marianne*, G. 58; D. VI, 350.
41. Ibid., G. 58; D. VI, 350.
42. Ibid., G. 78; D. VI, 385.
43. Ibid., G. 78; D. VI, 386.
44. Ibid., G. 78-79; D. VI, 386.
45. Ibid., G. 22-23; D. VI, 290-291.
46. Ibid., G. 206; D. VII, 28.
47. Ibid., G. 38; D. VI, 317.
48. Ibid., G. 135; D. VI, 482.
49. Ibid., G. 194; D. VII, 8.
50. Ibid., G. 422; D. VII, 392.
51. Ibid., G. 136; D. VI, 484.
52. *Pièces détachées*, IX, 330.
53. *La Vie de Marianne*, G. 353; D. VII, 275.
54. Ibid., G. 355; D. VII, 278.
55. Ibid., G. 390; D. VII, 338.
56. Ibid., G. 346; D. VII, 263.
57. Matthew Arnold, *Poems*, Collier edition, p. 19.
58. Jacob too has a consciousness of personal dignity, but he is far less fastidious about it than Marianne. Often it seems little more than conceit. It accompanies all his actions, and his comments on it are delightfully candid. Everything, from the acquisition of a new dressing gown to the conquest of a noble lady, nourishes his *amour-propre*. But his can hardly be called a "sensitive ego" in the same way that Marianne's is. Although he is responsive to flattery even to the point of swaggering, he is not easily hurt, and his spirits quickly rebound after he has been put in a ridiculous light. His peasant saneness and sturdy self-confidence render his pride less finical,

and the triumphs of his masculine ego, though highly amusing, are the obvious ones of the *parvenu* making his way in society.

59. *La Vie de Marianne,* G. 240; D. VII, 83.
60. Ibid., G. 342-43; D. VII, 258.
61. Mme Riccoboni, *Oeuvres,* I, 523.
62. La Rochefoucauld, *Maximes,* 200.
63. Marivaux, *Le Spectateur français,* IX, 287.
64. *Le Spectateur français,* IX, 201.
65. *Le Paysan parvenu,* G. 295-96; D. VIII, 299.
66. Ibid., G. 317; D. VIII, 335.
67. Mme de Lambert, *Oeuvres,* p. 47.
68. Lanson, *Nivelle de La Chaussée,* pp. 228-29; p. 232. A. M. Wilson, "Sensibility in France in the Eighteenth Century: A Study in Word History," *French Quarterly,* XIII, 1931, pp. 40-41.
69. *La Vie de Marianne,* G. 325; D. VII, 227.
70. C. G. Jung, *Psychological Types,* pp. 588-91.
71. H. G. Wells, *An Experiment in Autobiography,* pp. 9-10.
72. *La Vie de Marianne,* G. 25; D. VI, 295.
73. Ibid., G. 44; D. VI, 328.
74. Ibid., G. 45; D. VI, 329.
75. Ibid., G. 167; D. VI, 537.
76. *Le Paysan parvenu,* G. 242; D. VIII, 212.
77. Ibid., G. 188 and 192; D. VIII, 128 and 134.
78. Ibid., G. 132; D. VIII, 43.
79. Ibid., G. 133; D. VIII, 43.
80. Ibid., G. 181; D. VIII, 117.
81. Ibid., G. 199-200; D. VIII, 145.
82. Ibid., G. 203; D. VIII, 151.
83. Ibid., G. 318; D. VIII, 336.
84. Ibid., G. 247-48; D. VIII, 222.
85. Ibid., G. 295; D. VIII, 299.
86. Ibid., G. 357; D. VIII, 399.
87. Ibid., G. 359-60; D. VIII, 403-04.
88. *Ibid., G. 418; D. VIII, 497.

CHAPTER V

1. Voltaire, *Oeuvres,* XXXI, 21.
2. D'Alembert, "Eloge de Marivaux," in *Oeuvres,* X, 223.
3. *La Vie de Marianne,* G. 11; D. VI, 272.
4. *Le Paysan parvenu,* G. 245; D. VIII, 218.
5. Treated in fanciful form, this is the theme of Marivaux's first comedy, *Arlequin poli par l'amour* (1720), in which the rustic Arlequin is softened and made human through his love for the shepherdess Silvia.
6. *Le Spectateur français,* IX, 97.
7. *Pièces détachées,* IX, 346.

8. Cf. Paul Hazard, *Etudes critiques sur Manon Lescaut,* pp. 20-21.

9. Supra, p. 32 and Note 24, p. 177.

10. *Le Paysan parvenu,* G. 463-64; D. VIII, 571-72.

11. *Le Paysan parvenu,* G. 463-64; D. VIII, 584.

12. Samuel Richardson, *Pamela,* II, 66.

13. Marivaux, *Pièces détachées,* IX, 348.

14. Mme de Lambert, *Oeuvres,* p. 419 (Lettre à l'abbé de Choisy).

15. Stendhal, *De l'amour,* Edition Flammarion, p. 21.

16. Ibid., p. 21. For an excellent description of *amour-goût,* see Crébillon, *La Nuit et le Moment,* in *Oeuvres,* I, pp. 17-19.

17. Saintsbury, "A Study in Sensibility," in *Essays on French Novelists,* p. 112.

18. Egon Friedell, *A Cultural History of Europe,* II, 142: "There was but one desire, to make life an uninterrupted round of pleasure. 'For safety,' as Madame de la Verrue said, 'we get in our paradise on earth.' Moreover, one insisted on having one's fun without paying for it. . . . Therefore the grand passion was avoided, and even branded as not *chic,* and only the sweet, frothy cream of love was tasted: one was always amorous, never seriously in love. . . . Love was to be enjoyed without much fuss, like a tasty bonbon which soon melts on the tongue and is only there to be followed by a second of a different flavor."

19. *Pièces détachées,* IX, 400.

20. Ibid., IX, 398.

21. Ibid., IX, 328.

22. Ibid., IX, 323.

23. Ibid., IX, 398.

24. Ibid., IX, 340.

25. *La Vie de Marianne,* G. 178; D. VI, 556.

26. *Le Cabinet du philosophe,* IX, 548.

27. Ibid., IX, 550.

28. De Goncourt, *La Femme au XVIIIe siècle,* I, 158.

29. Mme de Lambert, *Oeuvres,* p. 194.

30. In the seventeenth paper of *Le Spectateur* he describes a chance meeting with a lady toward whom he had formerly been "piqué de belle tendresse." He comments on the rareness of such attachments in those times: "Les sentiments n'étaient plus à la mode: il n'y avait plus d'amants, ce n'était plus que libertins qui tâchaient de faire des libertines. On disait bien encore à une femme, je vous aime: mais c'était une manière polie de lui dire, je vous désire." IX, 193.

31. *Le Paysan parvenu,* G. 314; D. VIII, 329.
    *Ibid., G. 396; D. VIII, 462.

32. Ibid., G. 289; D. VIII, 288.

33. Ibid., G. 337; D. VIII, 366.

34. Ibid., G. 337; D. VIII, 366-67.

35. Ibid., G. 342; D. VIII, 375.

36. Trahard, op. cit., I, 71. "L'on croit entendre déjà Vauvenargues."

37. *Le Paysan parvenu,* G. 342; D. VIII, 375.

38. *Le Paysan parvenu,* G. 309; D. VIII, 322.

39. Crébillon *fils, La Nuit et le Moment,* in *Oeuvres,* I, 8.
40. Crébillon *fils, Le Hasard au coin du feu, Oeuvres,* I, 237.
41. *La Réunion des Amours,* I, 559.
42. Taine, op. cit., II, 208: "Ce n'est pas que le fond des moeurs devienne différent; elles restent aussi mondaines, aussi dissipées jusqu'au bout. Mais la mode autorise une affectation nouvelle, des effusions, des rêveries, des attendrissements qu'on n'avait point encore connus."
   De Goncourt, op. cit., I, 158: "L'idéal de l'amour au temps de Louis XV n'est plus rien que le désir, et l'amour est la volupté."
   Michelet, *Histoire de France,* Vol. XV.
43. *Le Paysan parvenu,* G. 295; D. VIII, 299.
44. *La Vie de Marianne,* G. 51; D. VI, 338.
45. Ibid., G. 54; D. VI, 345.
46. Ibid., G. 34; D. VI, 310.
47. Mme de Lambert, *Oeuvres,* pp. 201-202.
48. *La Vie de Marianne,* Duchesne edition, VI, 339-383.
49. *La Vie de Marianne,* G. 50; D. VI, 337.
50. Ibid., G. 51; D. VI, 339.
51. Ibid., G. 51; D. VI, 339.
52. Ibid., G. 53-54; D. VI, 343.
53. Ibid., G. 51; D. VI, 340.
54. Ibid., G. 52; D. VI, 340.
55. Cf. *Les Fausses Confidences,* III, 449: "Il a un respect, une adoration, une humilité pour vous, qui n'est pas concevable." Also *Le Préjugé vaincu,* II, 251: "Souffrirez-vous que je parle, Madame? . . ."
56. *La Vie de Marianne,* G. 53; D. VI, 342.
57. *La Vie de Marianne,* G. 57; D. VI, 340.
58. *Le Paysan parvenu,* G. 389-90; D. VIII, 451-52: "J'étais comme immobile. . . ."
59. *La Vie de Marianne,* G. 53; D. VI, 349-50.
60. *La Vie de Marianne,* G. 76; D. VI, 382.
61. *Le Paysan parvenu,* G. 390; D. VIII, 453.
62. Mme de Lambert, *Oeuvres,* p. 210.
63. *La Vie de Marianne,* G. 53; D. VI, 343.
64. Ibid., G. 61; D. VI, 356.
65. Ibid., G. 346; D. VII, 263.
66. Ibid., G. 347; D. VII, 265.
67. *Le Cabinet du philosophe,* IX, 550.
68. *La Vie de Marianne,* G. 56; D. VI, 347.
69. Ibid., G. 58; D. VI, 351.
70. Ibid., G. 58; D. VI, 352.
71. *Le Prince travesti,* IV, 433: "Sans lui dire précisément . . . ne pouvez-vous lui glisser la valeur de cela dans quelques regards? Avec deux yeux, ne dit-on pas ce que l'on veut?"
72. *La Vie de Marianne,* G. 54; D. VI, 344.
73. Ibid., G. 60; D. VI, 354.
74. Ibid., G. 61; D. VI, 354.

75. *La Vie de Marianne*, G. 61; D. VI, 355.
76. Ibid., G. 61; D. VI, 356.
77. Ibid., G. 61-62; D. VI, 357.
78. *La Vie de Marianne*, G. 59; D. VI, 353: "Tout ce qui me vint alors dans l'esprit là-dessus, quoique long à dire, n'est qu'un instant à être pensé."
79. Ibid., G. 61; D. VI, 356.
80. Ibid., G. 67; D. VI, 367.
81. Stendhal, *De l'amour*, p. 25.
82. *La Vie de Marianne*, G. 68; D. VI, 367.
83. *La Vie de Marianne*, G. 62; D. VI, 358.
84. Ibid., G. 63; D. VI, 359.
85. Ibid., G. 63; D. VI, 360.
86. Ibid., G. 65; D. VI, 363.
87. Ibid., G. 66-67; D. VI, 364-66: "Que n'avais-je souffert depuis une heure? . . . ."
88. Ibid., G. 68; D. VI, 368. In the course of Jacob's courtship with Mlle Habert, we find the following expression of the value of a lover's doubts and reassurances: "Rien n'attendrit tant de part et d'autre que ces scènes-là, surtout dans un commencement de passion; cela fait faire à l'amour un progrès infini." *Le Paysan parvenu*, G. 200; D. VIII, 146.
89. Saintsbury's phrase.
90. *La Vie de Marianne*, G. 68; D. VI, 367.
91. Ibid., G. 211; D. VII, 36.
92. Ibid., G. 346; D. VII, 263.
93. *La Dispute* (1744), II, 294.
94. *La Double Inconstance* (1723), IV, 417.
95. *Les Serments indiscrets* (1732), I, 566: *Lucile.* "Je remarque que les hommes ne sont bons qu'en qualité d'amants. C'est la plus jolie chose du monde que leur coeur, quand l'espérance les tient en haleine; soumis, respectueux et galants, pour le peu que vous soyez aimable avec eux, votre amour-propre est enchanté; il est servi délicieusement; on le rassasie de plaisirs: folie, fierté, dédain, caprices, impertinences, tout nous réussit, tout est raison, tout est loi: on règne, on tyrannise, et nos idolâtres sont toujours à genoux. Mais les épousez-vous; la Déesse s'humanise-t-elle: leur idolâtrie finit où nos bontés commencent. Dès qu'ils sont heureux, les ingrats ne méritent plus de l'être."
96. *Le Paysan parvenu*, G. 379; D. VIII, 434.
97. *Ibid.*, G. 379; D. VIII, 435: "On sait que, dans cette ville, le nombre des conquêtes ne fait point déroger aux sentiments."
98. *Le Paysan parvenu*, G. 455-56; D. VIII, 559-60.
99. *La Vie de Marianne*, G. 370; D. VII, 304.
100. Ibid., G. 375; D. VII, 313.
101. Ibid., G. 377; D. VII, 316.
102. Ibid., G. 377; D. VII, 317.
103. *Le Spectateur français*, IX, 57.
104. *La Vie de Marianne*, G. 57; D. VI, 349.

CHAPTER VI

1. D'Alembert, *Oeuvres*, IX, 221.
2. *La Mère confidente* (1735), III, 87.
3. *Les Fausses Confidences* (1737), III, 446.
4. *La Méprise* (1734), III, 24.
5. *Le Jeu de l'amour et du hasard* (1730), V, 165 and 167.
6. *L'Ecole des mères* (1732), III, 202.
7. *La Méprise*, III, 39.
8. *La Double Inconstance* (1723), IV, 306.
9. *Le Jeu de l'amour et du hasard*, V, 234.
10. Sainte-Beuve, *Portraits littéraires*, I, 82: "Une passion qu'on n'a pas vue naître, dont le flot arrive déjà gonflé, mollement écumeux, et qui vous entraine comme le courant blanchi d'une belle eau: voilà le drame de Racine."
11. Cf. Brunetière, *Histoire de la littérature française classique*, II, 417-18. M. Alfred Fouillée says of French comedy (*La Psychologie du peuple français*, p. 218): "Elle exclue par essence le long travail d'une âme en germination. En outre, elle est la peinture de la société, où viennent se heurter mutuellement les défauts des hommes."
12. *Le Jeu de l'amour et du hasard*, V, 216. F. C. Green points out that Marivaux first among eighteenth-century writers of comedy recognized the finality of the genius of Molière, in whose plays the individual struggles against society, and created instead the psychological comedy of love, in which the sole antagonist lies in the character's inner nature. *Minuet*, p. 154.
13. Edmond Jaloux, "Marivaux," *Nouvelle Revue Française*, XLVI, 533, 1 avril, 1936. The article is general in nature, mentioning no specific plays or characters.
14. Ibid., 534: "La pudeur est on ne sait quelle peur attachée à notre sensibilité, qui fait que l'âme, comme la fleur qui est son image, se replie et se recèle en elle-même, tant qu'elle est délicate et tendre, aux moindres apparences de ce qui pourrait la blesser par des impressions trop vives ou des clartés prématurées." Quoted from Joubert.
15. Ibid., p. 536.
16. Ibid., p. 537.
17. Ibid., p. 538.
18. Ibid., p. 536.
19. M. Jaloux disclaims ability to make such an analysis.
20. Arthur Tilley, "Marivaudage," *Modern Language Review*, XXV: 60-77, January, 1930, p. 61, Note 1: "Voltaire is said to have invented the term *marivaudage*, but I cannot find any evidence of this."
21. *Les Serments indiscrets* (1732), I, 566.
22. *Les Serments indiscrets*, I, 566.
23. Ibid., I, 566.
24. *Le Jeu de l'amour et du hasard*, V, 144.
25. *Le Petit Maître corrigé*, II, 81.
26. *Les Serments indiscrets*, I, 694.
27. *Les Serments indiscrets*, I, 696.

28. *Le Jeu de l'amour et du hasard*, V, 198.
29. Ibid., V, 218; "Allons, j'avais grand besoin que ce fût-là Dorante."
30. Ibid., V, 216.
31. Ibid., V, 234.
32. Ibid., V, 259.
33. *Le Petit Maître corrigé*, II, 133.
34. Dancourt, Florent Carton, 1661-1725.
35. Dancourt, *Oeuvres*, II, 9.
36. Ibid., II, 9.
37. Ibid., II, 70.
38. For a contemporary opinion of Marivaux as compared with Dancourt, see La Harpe, *Oeuvres*, III, 352: "Quelqu'un lui aurait dit que comme auteur comique il était au-dessous de Dancourt, l'aurait bien étonné, et pourtant lui aurait dit vrai. Marivaux avait peu de talent pour le théâtre."
39. *Le Prince travesti* (1723), IV, 438.
40. Supra, pp. 50-51.
41. *La Surprise de l'amour* (1722), IV, 174.
42. Ibid., IV, 175.
43. Ibid., IV, 248.
44. Ibid., IV, 231.
45. Ibid., IV, 243.
46. Ibid., IV, 263.
47. Trahard, op. cit., I, 42-43; I, 45; I, 49.
48. *La Deuxième Surprise de l'amour* (1727), I, 386.
49. Ibid., I, 452.
50. Ibid., I, 455-56.
51. Ibid., I, 456.
52. *Le Legs* (1733), II, 148.
53. *Le Legs*, II, 173.
54. Ibid., II, 159.
55. Ibid., II, 206.
56. Trahard, I, 42-43 (speaking of *La Fausse Suivante*).
57. Sainte-Beuve, *Causeries du lundi*, IX, 372; Petit de Julleville, *Le Théâtre en France*, p. 275: "pièce à grand tort oubliée . . ."; Jules Lemaître, *Impressions de théâtre*, II, 23.
58. *Les Sincères*, III, 669.
59. *Les Sincères*, III, 678.
60. Ibid., III, 705-06.
61. *L'Ile des Esclaves*, V, 23; *L'Ile de la Raison*, I, 319.
62. *Le Préjugé vaincu*, II, 243.
63. *Les Fausses Confidences* (1737), III, 412.
64. Ibid., III, 493.
65. A curious point of view in regard to this comedy appeared recently in the *Mercure de France* (275:588-91, May, 1737), in a review by Pierre Lièvre of a performance of the play at the Vieux Colombier. Dorante, it will be remembered, engaged himself with the help of Dubois as a steward in the house of Araminte, in order to be near her, though he felt his love to be

hopeless. M. Lièvre objects particularly to the implications of the plot. He says in part: "Il y a dans Marivaux quelque chose d'affreux où je ne peux pas m'habituer. . . . *Les Fausses Confidences,* c'est peut-être celui des ouvrages de l'auteur où la laideur morale s'étale le plus largement et, semble-t-il, avec le plus d'inconscience. . . . Je ne sais si l'on traita jamais une femme avec une semblable cruauté." He finds most objectionable the final speech of Araminte: "Puisque vous m'aimiez véritablement, ce que vous avez fait pour gagner mon coeur n'est point blâmable." Her "forced" capitulation reveals in Marivaux "une sorte de dureté de coeur, ou tout au moins . . . un manque de délicatesse, qui sont d'autant plus surprenants que la douceur du coeur et la délicatesse sont précisément les traits où l'on prétend qu'il se reconnaît le mieux." M. Lièvre then proceeds to attack Marivaux as "un homme un peu bête, un peu épais, qui ne se rendait pas exactement compte de la nature réelle de ce qu'il inventait (à moins qu'il ne l'eût observé?). Et lorsqu'il avait fait grimper des roses autour d'une fenêtre, il ne se souciait point que la fenêtre fût celle d'une maison où mieux valait ne point jeter les yeux." His estimate reveals a complete misunderstanding of Marivaux's intention in the play, a false interpretation of the characters of Araminte and Dorante, and a blindness to the delicacy of feeling and the sensitive handling of situations throughout the play. This twentieth-century detractor of Marivaux is more bitter than the most sharptongued contemporaries, who never alleged immorality in the theatre.

66. *L'Heureux Stratagème* (1733), III, 318.
67. Ibid., III, 284.
68. Ibid., III, 284.
69. Ibid., III, 331.
70. Ibid., III, 382.
71. *Arlequin poli par l'amour* (1720), IV, 112.
72. Ibid., IV, 114.
73. *La Double Inconstance* (1723), IV, 383.
74. *La Mère confidente* (1735), III, 89.
75. *La Mère confidente,* III, 140.
76. *L'Ecole des mères* (1732), III, 229.
77. Fleury, *Marivaux et le marivaudage,* p. 144. Sarcey finds it better than Musset.
78. *L'Epreuve* (1740), IV, 8.
79. *l'Epreuve,* IV, 77.

CHAPTER VII

1. Henri Peyre, *Qu'est-ce que le classicisme?* p. 41: "Un moment fortuné d'équilibre forcément instable. . . ."
2. Henri Peyre, Ibid., Introduction, and p. 43. Also Paul Hazard, *La Crise de la conscience européenne,* I, 3-37; and II, 287-289.
3. M. Pellisson, "La Question du bonheur au XVIII siècle," *La Grande Revue,* 15 mars, 1906, p. 476.

4. Lanson, *Histoire de la littérature française*, p. 626: "C'est de l'affaiblissement de la foi, et d'une observation de la manière dont vivent les honnêtes gens, des maximes sur lesquelles se guide leur conscience, c'est d'un désir de rétablir l'accord entre la théorie morale et l'expérience morale, que naissent les morales rationnelles et laïques. . . ."

5. *Le Paysan parvenu*, G. 283; D. VIII, 279.

6. *Ibid., G. 474; D. VIII, 589.

7. *Ibid., G. 450; D. VIII, 551. (Duchesne—"préjugé de soumission.")

8. *Ibid., G. 450; D. VIII, 551: "J'étais trop simple pour aller plus en avant. Je le serais moins aujourd'hui." (Duchesne—"Je le ferais aujourd'hui.")

9. *Le paysan parvenu*, G. 449-500; D. VIII, 550. It is interesting to observe how closely the four passages quoted from the doubtful parts of *Le Paysan* correspond in tone with the passages on religion quoted from *Le Spectateur* in Chapter III, and with the discussion of *dévots* and "enthusiasts" in the subsequent paragraphs of this chapter.

10. Ibid., G. 303 and 448-450; D. VIII, 312 and 549-551.

11. Ibid., G. 162; D. VIII, 87.

12. Ibid., G. 171-172; D. VIII, 101-102.

13. Ibid., G. 222; D. VIII, 181-182.

14. A. Feugère, "Rousseau et son temps," *R.C.C.*, 15 jan., 1935 p. 343: "Il y a, chez Marivaux, comme un parti pris d'optimisme. Par là surtout, il est bien de son temps et contredit la sévère doctrine et l'attitude morale du XVIIe siècle."

15. *Le Paysan parvenu*, G. 337; D. VIII, 366: "Il y a bien des amours où le coeur n'a point de part. . . ."

16, 17. Ibid., G. 125; D. VIII, 32.

18. Brunetière (*Etudes critiques*, III, 160) denies Marivaux's right to be called a moralist. He quotes Diderot in support of his assertion, using as illustration Diderot's description of the library of the libertines, in the *Promenade du Sceptique* (I, 237), which contained all writings on the mysteries of love, from Anacreon to Marivaux. In meditating on *Marianne*, young people learned the mysteries of amorous adventure. Licence cloaked in decency describes for Brunetière *Marianne* and *Le Paysan parvenu*. "Je ne comprends donc pas que le dernier biographe de Marivaux ait pu laisser échapper cette phrase: 'qu'il y avait plus d'élévation en dix pages du *Paysan parvenu* que dans tout *Gil Blas*, et que Jacob est une âme d'élite en comparaison de son émule.'—Ame d'élite? M. Larroumet veut rire." (p. 165) Brunetière blames the spirit of the times, fundamental vulgarity under a veneer of preciosity. He overlooks the fact that Marivaux has a double claim to the title of moralist, both as a student and advocate of a certain type of human conduct and as a recorder of the manners of his day.

19. *La Vie de Marianne*, G. 220-21; D. VII, 51.

20. Ibid., G. 223; D. VII, 56.

21. Leslie Stephen, *English Thought in the Eighteenth Century*, II, 442.

22. Babbitt, *Rousseau and Romanticism*, p. 131.

23. Shaftesbury's *Enquiry concerning Virtue and Merit* (1699) was later republished along with various other treatises written from 1699 to 1710, in

Characteristics of Men, Manners, Opinions, Times (1711). His disciple Francis Hutcheson, who expanded the theory of the moral sense, dwelling more on its reasonable side than Shaftesbury, did not begin publishing till 1725, and his most systematic work, *System of Moral Philosophy*, did not appear until 1755.

24. Legouis and Cazamian, *A History of English Literature*, p. 816.

25. Cf. Ennemond Casati, "Quelques Correspondants français de Shaftesbury," *Revue de la Littérature Comparée*, 1931, p. 614.

26. Franco Venturi, *La Jeunesse de Diderot*, p. 49.

27. Voltaire, in his *Traité de Métaphysique* (1734), borrows freely from Shaftesbury, particularly in his discussion of the innate moral sense universal among men. The 1711 edition of Shaftesbury's works is listed by Voltaire himself in the manuscript catalogue of his library. Cf. the critical edition of the *Traité de Métaphysique* by H. Temple Patterson, p. 58 and p. 64, Notes 12 and 13.

28. Sainte-Beuve, *Causeries du lundi*, IV, 231: (Mme de Lambert) "Elle est aussi l'un des premiers moralistes qui, au sortir du XVIIe siècle, soient revenus à l'idée très-peu janséniste que le coeur humain est naturellement droit, et que la conscience, si on sait la consulter, est le meilleur témoin et le meilleur juge: 'Par le mot conscience, j'entends ce sentiment intérieur d'un honneur délicat, qui vous assure que vous n'avez rien à vous reprocher.' Elle donne, à sa manière, le signal que Vauvenargues, à son tour, reprendra, et qui, aux mains de Jean-Jacques, deviendra un instrument de révolution universelle."

29. Supra, p. 116.

30. Pierre Bayle, *Pensées diverses sur la comète*, CLXXII (Cazes, p. 119).

31. Ibid., CXXXVI (Cazes, p. 99). Also CXXXVIII: "Ce ne sont pas les opinions générales de l'esprit qui nous déterminent à agir, mais les passions présentes au coeur."

32. Norman L. Torrey, *Voltaire and the English Deists*, p. 203.

33. Shaftesbury, *Enquiry*, in *Characteristicks*, Edition 1727, II, 30.

34. Ibid., II, 172.

35. Ibid., II, 99-101.

36. Ibid., II, 162.

37. Ibid., II, 176.

38. *La Vie de Marianne*, G. 398; D. VII, 350: "Il n'y a point de condition qui mette à l'abri du malheur. . . ." And G. 530; D. VII, 575: "Qu'est-ce que c'est que la vie! et que le monde est misérable!"

39. Ibid., G. 346; D. VII, 262.

40. Ibid., G. 346; D. VII, 262.

41. Ibid., G. 345-46; D. VII, 261-62.

42. *Le Spectateur français*, IX, 251.

43. *L'Ile des Esclaves*, V, 59-63. Sainte-Beuve, *Causeries du lundi*, IX, 374: "Dans une petite pièce intitulée *l'Ile des Esclaves*, il est allé jusqu'à la théorie philanthropique; il a supposé une révolution entre les classes, les maîtres devenus serviteurs et *vice versa*. Après quelques représailles d'insolence et de vexations, bientôt le bon naturel l'emporte; maîtres et valets

se réconcilient et l'on s'embrasse. Ce sont les saturnales de l'âge d'or. Cette petite pièce de Marivaux est presque à l'avance une bergerie révolutionnaire de 1792."

44. Diderot, *Le Rêve de d'Alembert*, II, 121.

45. *Le Cabinet du philosophe*, IX, 593. Also IX, 592: "La plus étonnante chose du monde, c'est qu'il y ait toujours sur la terre une masse de vertu qui résiste aux affronts qu'elle y souffre, et à l'encouragement qu'on y donne à l'iniquité même: car tous les honneurs sont pour l'iniquité, quand elle peut échapper aux lois qui la condamnent."

46. *Le Spectateur français*, IX, 251.

47. *Le Spectateur français*, IX, 294.

48. Rousseau, *La Nouvelle Héloïse*, II, 27: "J'ai toujours cru que le bon n'était que le beau mis en action, que l'un tenait intimement à l'autre, et qu'ils avaient tous deux une source commune dans la nature bien ordonnée. Il suit de cette idée que le goût se perfectionne par les mêmes moyens que la sagesse, et qu'une âme bien touchée des charmes de la vertu doit à proportion être aussi sensible à tous les autres genres de beautés."

49. *La Vie de Marianne*, G. 300; D. VII, 184.

50. For instance, when Marianne's pride is deeply offended by the infidelity of her lover, she is obliged for once to plan a course of action and to execute it through an effort of will. *La Vie de Marianne*, G. 355; D. VII, 279.

51. *Le Paysan parvenu*, G. 432; D. VIII, 521.

52. *Le Paysan parvenu*, G. 413; D. VIII, 489.

53. Shaftesbury, op. cit., II, 175: "To yield or consent to anything ill or immoral is a breach of interest and leads to the greatest ills; and . . . on the other side, everything which is an improvement of virtue, or an establishment of right affection or integrity, is an advancement of interest, and leads to the greatest and most solid happiness and enjoyment."

54. *La Vie de Marianne*, G. 262; D. VII, 120.

55. *Le Paysan parvenu*, G. 413; D. VIII, 490.

56. *La Vie de Marianne*, G. 134; D. VI, 481.

57. *Le Paysan parvenu*, G. 315; D. VIII, 331.

58. *Le Spectateur français*, IX, 10.

59. *La Vie de Marianne*, G. 13; D. VI, 275.

60. Ibid., G. 233; D. VII, 72.

61. Ibid., G. 308; D. VII, 198.

62. Babbitt's translation, in *Rousseau and Romanticism*, p. 135. Cf. Rousseau, *Confessions*, in *Oeuvres*, I, 185: "Cet attendrissement, cette vive et douce émotion que je sens à l'aspect de tout ce qui est vertueux, généreux, aimable. . . ."

63. *La Vie de Marianne*, G. 309; D. VII, 199.

64. *Le Paysan parvenu*, G. 147; D. VIII, 66.

65. *La Vie de Marianne*, G. 418; D. VII, 386.

66. *La Vie de Marianne*, G. 13; D. VI, 275.

67. Ibid., G. 541; D. VII, 595. Shaftesbury considers the moral sense strong enough to operate "even in the dark." "Why even then, though I had neither nose nor eyes, my sense of the matter would still be the same; my

nature would rise at the thought of what was sordid; or if it did not, I should have a wretched nature indeed, and hate myself for a beast." (*Wit and Humor*, I, 125) For Marivaux's characters this inner satisfaction provides a sufficient motive for being good, regardless of more substantial rewards.

68. *Le Paysan parvenu*, G. 318; D. VIII, 335.
69. *Ibid., G. 407; D. VIII, 480. This is one of the finest passages in the apocryphal parts, in close accord with Jacob's conduct in earlier pages. Compare also *Le Spectateur*, IX, 192, and *La Vie de Marianne*, G. 145; D. VI, 497.
70. Rousseau, *Les Confessions*, I, 136.
71. *Le Paysan parvenu*, G. 474; D. VIII, 589.
72. Ibid., G. 147; D. VIII, 66.
73. Ibid., G. 125; D. VIII, 32.
74. Ibid., G. 318; D. VIII, 336.
75. *La Vie de Marianne*, G. 155; D. VI, 516.

CHAPTER VIII

1. Her *Traité de l'amitié* was much admired, particularly by Voltaire (XIV, 86). See also La Dixmerie, *Les Deux Ages du goût et du génie français*, Amsterdam, 1770, p. 256.
2. Mme de Lambert, *Oeuvres*, p. 119.
3. Ibid., p. 122.
4. Ibid., p. 143: "Il n'y a qu'elles qui savent tirer d'un sentiment tout ce qu'elles en tirent. Les hommes parlent à l'esprit, les femmes au coeur."
5. *Les Effets*, V, 470.
6. Ibid., VI, 236.
7. *La Vie de Marianne*, G. 237; D. VII, 78.
8. *La Vie de Marianne* G. 327; D. VII, 230.
9. *Le Paysan parvenu*, G. 361; D. VIII, 406.
10. Ibid., G. 372; D. VIII, 424; also *G. 400; D. VIII, 468.
11. *Le Paysan parvenu*, G. 396; D. VIII, 463: "M. de Dorsan . . . voulut m'épargner la honte de déclarer que je ne connaissais point les cartes. L'amitié a toujours ses ressources prêtes pour obliger l'objet de son affection."
12. *Ibid., G. 398; D. VIII, 465: "La naissance n'y fait rien, je n'y puis toucher; ce que vous m'en avez déclaré me suffit."
13. *Les Lettres persanes*, No. 55: "Les Français ne parlent jamais de leurs femmes; c'est qu'ils ont peur d'en parler devant des gens qui les connaissent mieux qu'eux."
14. De Goncourt, *La Femme au XVIIIe siècle*, I, 236-244. Cf. p. 239: "L'amour conjugal est regardé par le temps comme un ridicule et une sorte de faiblesse indigne des personnes bien nées."
15. *La Provinciale*, p. 31.
16. Ibid., p. 35. Mme Thibaudière, a rich widow newly arrived in Paris, says: "Je crains toujours ma vertu de Province."

17. *Le Petit Maitre corrigé,* I, 13.
18. *L'Héritier du village,* V, 83. See also *La Colonie,* in Fournier edition of *Théâtre complet* of Marivaux, p. 621: Mme Sorbin, to Arthénice: "Dame, je parle en femme de petit état. Voyez-vous, nous autres petites femmes, nous ne changeons ni d'amant ni de mari, au lieu que des dames il n'en est pas de même, elles se moquent de l'ordre et font comme les hommes."
19. Nivelle de La Chaussée, *Oeuvres,* I, 63.
20. Sainte-Beuve, *Causeries du lundi,* III, 83.
21. *La Vie de Marianne,* G. 46; D. VI, 330.
22. Sainte-Beuve, op. cit., III, 83.
23. *La Vie de Marianne,* G. 406; D. VII, 467.
24. Ibid., G. 496; D. VII, 515.
25. Ibid., G. 402-03; D. VII, 358.
26. Ibid., G. 533; D. VII, 581.
27. *Le Paysan parvenu,* G. 427; D. VIII, 512. From the possibly apocryphal sixth part, this scene is acknowledged even by Fleury to be worthy of Marivaux. Fleury, op. cit., p. 226.
28. An early expression of Marivaux's interest in education appears in *Les Effets,* V, 516: "Ce fut une éducation simple, plus conforme à la vertu qu'à la politesse, qui accoutumait mon coeur à des sentiments généreux et naturels."
29. *Le Spectateur français,* IX, 190: "Voulez-vous faire d'honnêtes gens de vos enfants? ne soyez que leur père et non pas leur juge et leur tyran. Et qu'est-ce que c'est qu'être leur père? c'est les persuader que vous les aimez. Cette persuasion-là commence par vous gagner leur coeur. Nous aimons toujours ceux dont nous sommes sûrs d'être aimés . . . vous verrez alors avec quelle félicité la raison passera dans leur âme, à la faveur de ce sentiment tendre que vous leur aurez inspiré pour vous."
30. *Le Spectateur français,* IX, 293: "Quand elle me disait quelque chose, je connaissais sensiblement que c'était pour mon bien; je voyais que c'était son coeur qui me parlait; elle savait pénétrer le mien de cette vérité-là, et elle s'y prenait pour cela d'une manière qui était proportionnée à mon intelligence, et que son amour pour moi lui enseignait sans doute; car je la comprenais parfaitement tout jeune que j'étais, et je recevais la leçon avec le trait de tendresse qui me la donnait, de sorte que mon coeur était reconnaissant aussitôt qu'instruit, et que le plaisir que j'avais en lui obéissant m'affectionnait bientôt à ses leçons mêmes."
31. *Le Jeu de l'amour et du hasard,* V, 148.
32. *La Mère confidente,* III, 109.
33. Mme Argante of *Les Fausses Confidences,* and of *L'Epreuve.*
34. *La Vie de Marianne,* G. 182; D. VI, 561.
35. *Le Paysan parvenu,* G. 455-56; D. VIII, 559: "Le coeur, me disais-je, parle bien ici; et c'est le seul dont on doive prendre conseil pour former une union de cette importance. Calculer les revenus ou éplucher la naissance, ce sont là les soins d'une âme trop tranquille pour que l'amour soit de la partie. . . . C'est par cette voie, lui dis-je, qu'à la campagne, où je suis né, les mariages sont ordinairement heureux."

36. *Le Paysan parvenu*, G. 110; D. VIII, 8.

37. See Cayrou, *Le Français classique*, 1923, and A. M. Wilson, Jr., "Sensibility in France in the Eighteenth Century: A Study in Word History," *French Quarterly*, XIII, 1931.

38. *La Vie de Marianne*, G. 13; D. VI, 274.

39. Ibid., G. 162; D. VI, 528. Also G. 157; D. VI, 518. And G. 159; D. VI, 521. And G. 294-95; D. VII, 174-75.

40. Ibid., G. 174; D. VI, 548. Also G. 156; D. VI, 517. And G. 307; D. VII, 195. And G. 355; D. VII, 279.

41. Ibid., G. 315; D. VII, 209.

42. *La Vie de Marianne*, G. 182; D. VI, 561. And G. 301; D. VII, 185. Conversely, Marivaux denounces the ungrateful child in an essay of *Le Spectateur français* (IX, 153), described by d'Alembert as possibly Marivaux's best work, "full of the most touching sensibility." (D'Alembert, X, 234) It is a letter from a father who has sacrificed his fortune for his son's advancement, only to be cast off and obliged to spend the rest of his days in neglect and solitude. The father finds this ingratitude harder to bear than would be a childless old age. D'Alembert finds the letter "simple and eloquent," quite out of the vein of the subtle Marivaux. To the modern reader its contrasting blacks and whites, with few nuances, seem exaggerated and form one of the few instances when Marivaux's heart seems to have got the better of his head. For once, his picture of virtue in distress borders closely on the sentimental.

43. *La Vie de Marianne*, G. 194; D. VII, 8.

44. *Le Dénouement imprévu*, I, 172.

45. *La Double Inconstance*, IV, 401.

46. Ibid., IV, 407.

47. *Les Fausses Confidences*, III, 433.

48. *Les Fausses Confidences*, III, 424.

49. *L'Ile de la Raison*, I, 319.

50. Supra, p. 120.

51. *L'Ile des Esclaves*, V, 15-16.

52. *La Vie de Marianne*, G. 524; D. VII, 565.

53. *Le Paysan parvenu*, G. 143; D. VIII, 60.

54. Ibid., G. 318; D. VIII, 335: "Je m'applaudissais. . . ."

55. Ibid., G. 315; D. VIII, 331: "Je ne doutai pas un instant que M. de Fécour ne se rendît; je trouvais impossible qu'il résistât. Hélas! que j'étais neuf! Il n'en fut pas seulement ému."

56. *La Vie de Marianne*, G. 476; D. VII, 484.

57. *La Vie de Marianne*, G. 22-23; D. VI, 291.

58. Ibid., G. 31; D. VI, 305.

59. Ibid., G. 136; D. VI, 484.

60. Ibid., G. 162; D. VI, 528: "Songez-vous que sans ma mère j'aurais actuellement la confusion de demander ma vie à tout le monde; et malgré cela, vous avez peur de m'humilier: y a-t-il un coeur comme le vôtre?"

61. *La Vie de Marianne*, G. 295; D. VII, 175: "[Mme de Miran] Vous savez qu'elle ne possède rien, et vous ne sauriez croire combien je l'ai trouvée

noble, généreuse et désintéressée. . . . Je crois qu'elle mourrait plutôt que de me déplaire; elle pousse cela jusqu'au scrupule; et si je cessais de l'aimer, elle n'aurait plus le courage de rien recevoir de moi."

62. **Le Paysan parvenu*, G. 452; D. VIII, 554. This reflection of Jacob's bears an interesting resemblance to Marianne's speech on true charity (Supra, p. 136-137) and to the passage on Mme Dorsin (*Infra*, Note 63). It is similar in tone to several essays in *Le Spectateur*, notably *Feuilles* I and IX. Its style is that of the best passages of Marivaux dealing with humanitarian sentiments.

63. *La Vie de Marianne*, G. 196-97; D. VII, 11: "[Mme Dorsin] Je l'ai servi plusieurs fois, je l'ai donc accoutumé à croire que je dois le servir toujours . . . il ne faut donc pas tromper cette opinion qu'il a, et qui m'est chère; il faut donc que je continue de la mériter."

64. Ibid., G. 299; D. VII, 182.

65. Ibid., G. 301; D. VII, 185.

66. Supra, p. 124.

67. *Le Paysan parvenu*, G. 320; D. VIII, 339.

68. *Le Paysan parvenu*, G. 324; D. VIII, 346.

69. Ibid., G. 325; D. VIII, 347.

70. The small number of anecdotes about Marivaux concern in large part his active sympathy and generosity. See the early biographies of La Porte, Lesbros, and d'Alembert.

71. Larroumet, *Marivaux*, p. 306.

72. *Le Spectateur français*, IX, 7.

73. *L'Indigent Philosophe*, IX, 5me feuille.

74. *Le Spectateur français*, IX, 315.

75. Ibid., IX, 315.

76. *Le Spectateur français*, IX, 39. Marivaux then goes farther than Bossuet, who, holding a like belief in the divine disposition of things, urges the poor to rejoice in their poverty and to await patiently their recompense in another world. The rich, however, should observe charitable practices both as a duty and as a precaution against future reversal of their lot in a day when "the rich shall be poor and the poor rich." Marivaux is more practical—he shows the eighteenth-century concern for the here and now. (See Bossuet, *De l'eminente dignité des pauvres dans l'église*, 2me point.)

77. Deschamps, *Marivaux*, p. 73: "L'ami de la marquise de Lambert eût été fort étonné si l'on eût aperçu, dans ses oeuvres morales ou dramatiques, des utopies de révolution violente. Il n'est pas nécessaire, Dieu merci! d'être socialiste professionnel, pour avoir pitié de la souffrance humaine. L'auteur de l'*Indigent Philosophe* était simplement un moraliste charitable, un honnête homme, nullement idéologue, mais volontiers attendri."

78. *Le Spectateur français*, IX, 42.

79. Wilson, op. cit., p. 77. Also Lanson, *Nivelle de La Chaussée*, pp. 228-29: "Voilà le secret de cette sensibilité, qui emploie la sympathie à rassasier l'égoïsme et qui au fond ne voudrait point supprimer le mal, condition de la pitié, exercice de la vertu."

80. Mandeville, *An Enquiry into the Origin of Moral Virtue*, first printed

in the second edition of *The Fable of the Bees*, London, 1723. Reference is from Rand's *Classical Moralists*, p. 352.

81. Ibid., p. 353.

82. Ibid., p. 353.

83. Ibid., p. 354.

84. *The Encyclopedia of Social Sciences*, "Humanitarianism," by Crane Brinton, VII, 545: "An emotional experience of direct, intense love for mankind in the mass is probably rare."

85. Leslie Stephen, op. cit., II, 437: "We may say, in a general way, that the growth of sentimentalism was symptomatic of a social condition daily becoming more unhealthy. In France an intelligent noblesse, having no particular duties to discharge, was beginning to play at philanthropy. In England, though the dissociation of the upper classes from active life was not so wide, there was a daily increasing number of rich and idle persons, who found the cultivation of their finer feelings a very amusing luxury."

86. D'Argenson, Taine, Michelet, Sainte-Beuve, and many others.

87. De Goncourt, *La Femme au XVIIIe siècle*, II, 165: "Il semble que ce coeur de la femme, gros de larmes, dilaté par la sensibilité, ne puisse plus vivre en lui-même: il est pris de je ne sais quel irrésistible besoin, quel immense désir de se répandre, de participer à la solidarité humaine, de battre avec tout ce qui respire. . . . Des individus qu'elle touche par les sens, la sympathie de la femme ira aux peuples, aux nations les plus lointaines, à tous les hommes, à l'humanité tout entière, dont elle conçoit pour la première fois la notion."

88. A. Lichtenberger, *Le Socialisme au XVIIIe siècle*, p. 17: "Nous avons dit tout à l'heure, combien le XVIIIe siècle a été épris de justice et de sensibilité. L'amour de l'humanité, traduit parfois sous des formes fausses ou grotesques, mais réel néanmoins, a été une de ses grandes vertus et sa passion dominante. Le droit de chacun au bonheur a été la maxime qu'il a prônée entre toutes. L'idée religieuse a été s'affaiblissant, et l'esprit de résignation et de foi a fait place à celui de raison et de stricte justice. Cette disposition générale apparaît à peu près chez tous les écrivains du XVIIIe siècle. . . . Tout ce grand mouvement philanthropique et sensible qui se marque dans la littérature, surtout depuis le milieu du XVIIIe siècle, et qui ne s'arrête pas, est une des formes les plus bienfaisantes alors de l'esprit humanitaire."

89. Taine, *Origines*, II, 208.

90. Wilson, op. cit., p. 38: "Emotionalism runs counter to the eighteenth-century rationalistic spirit. But the charitable impulses of sensibility were powerfully seconded by that spirit."

91. Grimm, *Correspondance littéraire*, V, 236.

CHAPTER IX

1. Molière, *Le Malade imaginaire*.

2. *Le Dénouement imprévu*, I, 186.

3. *Le Dénouement imprévu*, I, 220-21.
4. Except when, as in *Les Effets*, he is imitating the adventure novel, or when, as in *L'Ile des Esclaves*, he is writing a fantasy.
5. *Les Effets*, VI, 199-208.
6. *La Mére confidente*, III, 192.
7. Mme de Lambert, *Oeuvres*, p. 93.
8. Marivaux, *Oeuvres*, XII, 66.
9. *La Vie de Marianne*, G. 10; D. VI, 270.
10. In *Le Miroir* (XII, 64) Marivaux attempts a philosophy of history, based on the idea of progress. "L'augmentation des idées est une suite infaillible de la durée du monde: la suite de cette augmentation ne tarit point, tant qu'il y a des hommes qui se succèdent, et des aventures qui leur arrivent."
11. Diderot, *Oeuvres*, VIII, 387.
12. Venturi, *La Jeunesse de Diderot*, p. 51.
13. Ibid., p. 52.
14. Ibid., p. 55: "l'apologie et l'exaltation de la valeur morale d'une ex-périence vivante et concrète par opposition aux schèmes abstraits, l'apolo-gie et l'exaltation de la valeur morale de l'abandon à la partie la plus in-time et la plus profonde de nous-mêmes."
15. *Le Paysan parvenu*, G. 379-81; D. VIII, 434-36. This passage, highly char-acteristic of Marivaux's attitude toward the emotional life, has been dis-cussed in connection with sensibility in matters of taste. (Chapter III, p. 45.)
16. Henri Peyre (*"Qu'est-ce que le classicisme?* p. 59) cites this curious comment of Jacques Rivière in appreciation of the classical character of Marivaux: "Mes maîtres sont Descartes, Racine, Marivaux, Ingres, c'est-à-dire, ceux qui refusent l'ombre."
17. *La Vie de Marianne*, G. 44; D. VI, 326-27.
18. Ibid., G. 31; D. VI, 305.
19. Ibid., G. 55; D. VI, 345.
20. *Le Paysan parvenu*, G. 130; D. VIII, 40.
21. *La Vie de Marianne*, G. 346; D. VII, 262.
22. Ibid., G. 398; D. VII, 350.
23. Ibid., G. 235; D. VII, 55.
24. Ibid., G. 346; D. VII, 262.
25. Ibid., G. 3; D. VI, 257.
26. Ibid., G. 345; D. VII, 261.
27. *Le Paysan parvenu*, G. 108; D. VIII, 5.
28. Ibid., G. 112; D. VIII, 11.
29. *Le Paysan parvenu*, G. 150; D. VIII, 70: "Je crois que ce détail n'ennuyera point, il entre dans le portrait de la personne dont je parle."
30. *La Vie de Marianne*, G. 79-84; D. VI, 386-395.
31. D'Alembert, *Oeuvres*, X, 230.
32. Brunetière, *Etudes critiques*, III, 171.
33. Fleury, op. cit., p. 178.
34. *Le Paysan parvenu*, G. 108; D. VIII, 4.
35. *Ibid., G. 378-79; D. VIII, 433. Also G. 396; D. VIII, 462.

36. *La Vie de Marianne*, G. 187-188; D. 571-73. Note the similarity in point of view between this passage and the passage quoted above from Part VI of *Le Paysan parvenu*.
37. D'Alembert, X, 269.
38. *Le Spectateur français*, 8me feuille, IX, 86-88.
39. *Le Paysan parvenu*, G. 156-60; D. VIII, 79-84.
40. *Le Paysan parvenu*, G. 271-72; D. VIII, 260.
41. Ibid., G. 205-06; D. VIII, 154.
42. Ibid., G. 352; D. VIII, 391.
43. *Le Paysan parvenu*, G. 162-75; 303-04; *G. 423-427; D. VIII, 506-513.
44. *La Vie de Marianne*, G. 22; D. VI, 290.
45. Ibid., G. 221; D. VII, 52.
46. Ibid., G. 36 and 86, and 237; D. VI, 313 and 400; VII, 77.
47. *Le Paysan parvenu*, G. 222; D. VIII, 181.
48. *Le Paysan parvenu*, G. 208; D. VIII, 157-58.
49. *La Vie de Marianne*, G. 196; D. VII, 10.
50. Ibid., G. 196; D. VII, 10.
51. Ibid., G. 178; D. VI, 556.
52. Ibid., G. 262; D. VII, 121.
53. Ibid., G. 385; D. VII, 329.
54. Clarice in *Les Effets* is an exception.
55. *La Vie de Marianne*, G. 349; D. VII, 267.
56. Ibid., G. 528; D. VII, 572. Cf. also *Le Petit Maître corrigé*, II, 126, and many similar references in Marivaux's theatre.
57. *Le Paysan parvenu*, G. 132; D. VIII, 43.
58. Jacob's affair with Madame de Vambures constitutes an important part of the subject matter of Parts VI, VII, and VIII of *Le Paysan parvenu*.
59. *La Vie de Marianne*, G. 11; D. VI, 276.
60. Jung, *Psychological Types*, p. 236.
61. Jung, op. cit., p. 237.
62. D'Alembert, X, 245.
63. Ibid., X, 245. And the Abbé Trublet, *Mémoires*, p. 210.
64. *Le Paysan parvenu*, G. 108; D. VIII, 5.
65. Voltaire, *Oeuvres*, XXXIII, 260 (à M. de Formont, 29 avril, 1732).
66. Ibid., XXXIII, 407, à M. de Mairan, 1 fév., 1734.
67. Voisenon, *Oeuvres complettes*, Anecdotes littéraires, IV, 89.
68. Collé, *Mémoires*, II, 289.
69. Grimm, *Corr. litt.*, V, 236, fév., 1763. This remark of Grimm's seems to be the basis for the general attribution to Voltaire of the term *marivaudage*.
70. D'Alembert, X, 213.
71. Quoted in d'Alembert, X, 230.
72. Fontenelle, *Réflexions sur la Poétique*, III, 84, Par. XI.
73. Marivaux, *Le Spectateur français*, 7me feuille, IX, 71.
74. *Le Cabinet du philosophe*, 6me feuille, X, 12.
75. *Le Paysan parvenu*, G. 370; D. VIII, 421.
76. Sainte-Beuve, *Causeries du lundi*, IX, 355: "Ce n'est point par le style qu'il pèche . . . c'est donc par sa nature même et par son tour d'esprit, par la

conformation ingénieuse, mais minutieuse aussi et méticuleuse, de son talent."

77. Richard Aldington, "Marivaux and Marivaudage," *North American*, 216, 8 Aug., 1922, 254-58.

A. Tilley, "Marivaudage," *Modern Language Review*, XXV, Jan., 1930, 60-77.

E. Jaloux, "Marivaux," *Nouvelle Revue Française*, XLVI, 1 avril, 1936, 533.

F. C. Green, *Minuet* (1935), p. 180: "the charming people whose conversation reveals, so naturally and so wittily, the ultimate recesses of their mind and soul. . . ."

78. Prévost, *Le pour et le contre*, No. 132, IX, 273.

79. *La Vie de Marianne*, G. 15; D. VI, 278.

80. *Le Miroir*, XII, 62.

INDEX